Mai Pa'a I Ka Leo

HISTORICAL VOICE IN HAWAIIAN PRIMARY MATERIALS,
LOOKING FORWARD AND LISTENING BACK

Mai Pa'a I Ka Leo

Historical Voice in Hawaiian Primary Materials,
Looking Forward and Listening Back

M. Puakea Nogelmeier

Bishop Museum Press | Awaiaulu
Honolulu, Hawai'i

Native Hawaiian Culture and Arts Program

Ua lehulehu a manomano ka ʻikena a ka Hawaiʻi.
Great and numerous is the knowledge of the Hawaiians.
ʻŌlelo Noʻeau 2814

This project is funded under the Native Hawaiian Culture and Arts Program in celebration of the Legacy of Excellence of Native Hawaiian culture. The Legacy of Excellence volumes are devoted to generating an appreciation of Native Hawaiian traditions, art, and language through education, awareness, and recognition of excellence in Native Hawaiian achievement.

The views and conclusions contained in this document are those of the authors and should not be interpreted as representing the opinions or policies of the U.S. Government. Mention of trade names or commercial products does not constitute their endorsement by the U.S. Government.

Bishop Museum Press
1525 Bernice Street
Honolulu, Hawaiʻi 96817
www.bishopmuseum.org/press

Awaiaulu Press
2667 ʻAnuʻu Place
Honolulu, Hawaiʻi 96819
www.awaiaulu.org

Copyright © 2010 by M. Puakea Nogelmeier

All rights reserved. No part of this book may be reproduced or transmitted in any form or by any means, electronic, mechanical, or digital including photocopying, recording, or by any information storage and retrieval system, without prior written permission from the publisher.

Hardcover ISBN: 978-1-58178-086-4
Softcover ISBN: 978-1-58178-087-1

Cover images by David Franzen

Design by Nancy Watanabe

Printed in Korea

Library of Congress Cataloging-in-Publication Data

Nogelmeier, Puakea.
Mai paʻa i ka leo : historical voice in Hawaiian primary materials : looking forward and listening back / M. Puakea Nogelmeier.
     p. cm.
"Native Hawaiian Culture and Arts Program"--T.p. verso.
Includes bibliographical references.
ISBN 978-1-58178-086-4 (hardcover) -- ISBN 978-1-58178-087-1 (softcover) 1. Hawaii--History--Sources. 2. Hawaii--Historiography. 3. Hawaiian literature--History and criticism. 4. Canon (Literature) 5. Point of view (Literature) 6. Hawaiian language--Political aspects. 7. Hawaiian language--Social aspects. 8. Hawaiians--Ethnic identity. 9. Hawaiians--Public opinion. 10. Public opinion--English-speaking countries. I. Native Hawaiian Culture and Arts Program. II. Title.
DU625.N64 2009
996.90072--dc22

2009032380

Dedication

This is for Kamuela and Ululani Kumukahi and to all of the elders who have considered knowledge and knowing to be a legacy, and have patiently worked to perpetuate, transmit, and foster that legacy through teaching, writing, or example.

Contents

VIII		**PREFACE**
X		**ACKNOWLEDGMENTS**
XI		**INTRODUCTION**
1	1	**A DISCOURSE OF SUFFICIENCY**
		The Power of Discursive Practice
		Discourse in Hawai'i and the Pacific
		Power and Voice
		Power and Silence
		The Fruits of Compliance
		Discourse Shapes A Hawaiian Canon
31	2	**SHAPING POWER: CREATION OF THE HAWAIIAN CANON**
		A Vacuum of Hawaiian Resources
		Davida Malo
		A Changing Audience
		Abraham Fornander
		Martha Beckwith
		Kepelino
		John Papa 'Ī'ī
		Samuel Mānaiakalani Kamakau
		Articulation of Texts
		Cultural Authority
		Normalization of the Canon
		Institutional Validation
58	3	**BEYOND THE CANON**
		The Historical Hawaiian-Language Repository
		Books
		Manuscripts
		Newspapers
		Hawaiian Production of A Written Discourse
		Literacy
		Print in Hawai'i
		Newspapers as Locus of Discourse
		A Shifting Paradigm of Representation
		Public Press
		1861 — The Independent Hawaiian Press
		Orality and Newspapers
		Growth of Participation

NO NA KUMUKULA.

    Content and Form as Reflection of Orality
    Orality and World View
    Dialogue in the Press
    Ancient Religion
    Perpetuation

105   4 | MISREPRESENTATIONAL TEXTS
    Samuel Mānaiakalani Kamakau
        Shaping the Hawaiian Text: Criticism and Debate
        Intertextual Writing
        Editorial Constraints
        Shaping the English Text: Extraction and
         Decontextualization
        Translation
        Reordering
        Editing
        Elision
    John Papa ʻĪʻī
        The Hawaiian Text
        Criticism
        Editorial Constraints
        The English Text
        Extraction
        Translation
        Editing
        Reordering Text
        Elision
    Editorial Additions
    Intertextuality: Kamakau and ʻĪʻī

158   5 | NEW HORIZONS
    Hoʻolaupaʻi
    Awaiaulu
    The Hawaiian Language Newspaper Index
    Other Internet Resources
    Contemporary Scholarship

173   APPENDIX

224   REFERENCES

Preface

This publication and the research that led to it are a few of the many outcomes of the Hawaiian language revitalization that has flourished for more than three decades in Hawaiʻi and beyond. In the often-fractured and ongoing search for educational materials to support Hawaiian-language classrooms, the archives have been explored, and some gems have been extracted for new, mostly young, audiences, yet up through the early 1990s, university classes relied completely on mimeographs, typescripts, photocopies, and microfilm printouts, some of it historical and most of it newly-generated. It was 1990 when cultural proponent and language student Nakila Steele encouraged me and others to take on the development of books for adult readers, pointing out that one could fulfill a Bachelor of Arts degree in Hawaiian without ever seeing a real published book in the language. Change is happening, but it is a slow process.

With Nakila's encouragement, financial support, and participation, we chose to develop S. M. Kamakau's many years of newspaper writings for reprinting in Hawaiian.[1] From the beginning of this process, it became apparent that the original columns did not correspond to the published translations of his works.[2] The research that grew from that realization, such as the charting of historical writings and modern translations, led me to complete a Ph.D. in Anthropology in 2003.[3] The dissertation that fulfilled the degree is the basis of this publication, and was also the stimulus for several other projects, some of which are detailed in this book's conclusion.

This and other current work in the field has brought about enough change that the entire text had to be updated to reflect the developments of the last seven years. The setting that was described in 2003 has already been altered, with the availability of new resources, an emerging awareness about the importance of the historical cache, and exploration of new directions in research. Those who are directly involved with Hawaiian-language research will see familiar terrain

---

[1] S. M. Kamakau, *Ke Kumu Aupuni* (1996) and *Ke Aupuni Mōʻī* (2001). See Appendix for complete listings of his original publications.

[2] S. M. Kamakau, *Ruling Chiefs of Hawaii* (1961), *Ka Poʻe Kahiko: The People of Old* (1964), *The Works of the People of Old* (1976), and *Tales and Traditions of the People of Old* (1991).

[3] *Mai Paʻa i ka Leo: Historical Voice in Hawaiian Primary Materials, Looking Forward and Listening Back*. A dissertation submitted to the Graduate Division of the University of Hawaiʻi in partial fulfillment of the requirements for the degree of Doctor of Philosophy in Anthropology, December 2003.

here, while others will find an unexpected and challenging landscape, one being explored and charted anew by people and projects. As current endeavors continue to flourish, this book will help to mark where the field stands today.

The dissertation was originally composed for a small academic audience, but eventually seemed appropriate for a much broader readership, so it has been reworked for those with a general interest in the fields of history, language, and culture. The writing style had to be rescued from the doctoral dialect, but some of that language, of course, remains. There are still references to philosophers and theorists who might be unfamiliar to some readers, but such citations are useful in linking these findings about Hawaiian language to larger issues and circles of discussion. Reference to the work of leading scholars distills large arguments into the small spaces appropriate for this presentation.

For instance, French philosopher Michel Foucault is quoted several times, because his writings grapple with how power controls knowledge in a society. Foucault seeks his points for exploration in the breaks and fractures that exist in what may otherwise appear as a seamless historical flow of action and understanding. Cultural theorist Edward Said brings a similar perspective about power to the international and intercultural level, showing how a dominant nation or culture defines not only the past and present of others, but the very identity of those with less sway. Historian Greg Dening is cited because of his Hawaiian and Polynesian research, and regarding his view that all of history, both fact and artifact, becomes "cargo" to the present, always from elsewhere in time or place, and always needing to be "unpacked" by successive generations in order to be recognized or understood anew. These and other theorists' works apply to the topics presented in this book, and hopefully the pieces drawn from their discussions fit comfortably here.

Hawaiian-language excerpts and references in this study are presented in both Hawaiian and English. Hawaiian text, in various marked and unmarked forms, reflects the periods in which the quotes were printed. Text quoted from Hawaiian-language newspapers have few, if any, markings, while language from more recent texts and Hawaiian words used in the narrative appear with modern conventional spellings, including the *'okina*, or glottal stop, and the *kahakō*, or macron. Hawaiian terms in the narration are italicized and glossed in English upon first usage, and Hawaiian-language excerpts are followed by a translation in brackets. Unless otherwise noted, translations are by the author.

Acknowledgments

This book, like the dissertation from which it was drawn, was only possible through the help of many active hands and generous hearts, including those of Sahoa Fukushima, Nahua Patrinos, Kauʻi Sai-Dudoit, Isabella Abbott, Kamuela, Ululani and Kuʻuipo Kumukahi, Lolena Nicholas, Nakila and Marti Steele, Patience Nāmaka Bacon, Edith McKinzie, Noenoe Barney-Campbell, Bill Char, Lalepa Koga, Kaʻananā Akima, Dorothy Barrère, Kaʻanoʻilani and June Fuller, Kamaoli Kuwada, the remarkable staffs of the Bishop Museum Library and Archives, Hawaiian Historical Society, Hawaiʻi Mission Children's Society Library, Hawaiʻi State Archives, the University of Hawaiʻi Hamilton Library Hawaiian and Pacific Collection, and the professors of my doctoral committee whose earnest support made this research possible: Emily ʻIoliʻi Hawkins, Geoff White, Bion Griffin, Pauline Nāwāhine King, and especially the committee chair, Ben Finney. Powerful influences now long-departed, but still guiding, include Theodore Kelsey, June Gutmanis, Sarah Nākoa, Mililani Allen, Maiki Aiu Lake, ʻEhulani Lum, Mary Kawena Pukui, the many elders who shared and encouraged, and the Hawaiian scholars of the past. They are gratefully reflected in the best of this work, but all errors and omissions are my own.

No ʻoukou pākahi koʻu mahalo palena ʻole, mau a mau.

Introduction

Mai paʻa i ka leo—he ʻole ka hea mai ē.[4]
Do not hold back the voice—to deny the welcoming call.

Some stories have no voice now. A century of Hawaiian "stories," ranging from social commentaries to ancient epics, have remained silent in archives for generations. Knowledge about Hawaiʻi's past has been drawn from every language ever linked to these islands, assembling pieces from two centuries of observation and written history. Ironically though, most of the Hawaiian-language material, the core of that collective knowledge, has been neglected. Modern audiences have not heard the "stories," retold them, or made them part of what we know and believe today.

The impact of leaving most of the Hawaiian writings out of the mix of modern knowledge is that every form of history written, every cultural study undertaken, and every assumption made over most of the last century should be revisited in light of those neglected sources. Lacking the core insight of these sources affects the entire system—how people today understand Hawaiʻi, past and present; the nature of education available to residents and millions of annual visitors alike; the way Hawaiians are perceived here and abroad; and how Hawaiians view themselves, those around them, and the rest of the world. Misconceptions that have been generated and perpetuated without this foundation of reference vary from benign to destructive. The need to restore the missing pieces, to give new voice to the silent "stories," should be obvious.

For nearly a hundred years, researchers and scholars have excerpted bits and pieces from Hawaiian primary resources, while overlooking or disregarding other important materials. Those extracted fragments have been inadequately re-presented. A handful of Hawaiian writings were translated and published in English, and those heavily-edited translations have become the Hawaiian *canon*, the reference standard. Used as though they were originals, they have overshadowed the actual writings from which they were drawn and blocked other available sources from view.

---

[4] This is an interpretation of the closing line of a *mele komo*, a chant for requesting entrance, drawn from the legend of Pele and Hiʻiaka and used today by students asking to enter the *hālau hula*, the school of the dance.

The canon is self-replicating, being constantly repeated through other texts, curricula, and reference. Its power drowns out all other historical voices, and if unchallenged, would effectively eclipse the knowledge those silenced voices contain, while calcifying the fixed body of information that the canon perpetuates.

This book focuses on how Hawaiian knowledge from the past has been handled in a basically English-speaking world. It highlights the need to recognize and reincorporate the full array of historical Hawaiian resources into the foundations of current knowledge. The extent of those resources, the process in which they were generated, and their eventual displacement from mainstream awareness are parts of a story that should be familiar today.

As soon as the native language was rendered into written form, Hawaiians enthusiastically took up reading and writing as a national endeavor. In two generations, nearly the entire Hawaiian population was literate in their own language, surpassing America, England, and most of the world for the percentage of people able to read and write. For the remainder of the 1800s and beyond, general literacy among Hawaiians was the norm.

In just over a century, from 1834 to 1948, Hawaiian writers filled 125,000 pages in nearly 100 different newspapers with their writings. While literacy was at its highest, Hawaiians embraced the Hawaiian-language newspapers as the main venue for news, opinion, and national dialogue, but also as an acknowledged public repository for history, cultural description, literature, and lore. Though national independence yielded to what became territorial status, and English usurped Hawaiian as the common language of the islands, Hawaiian newspapers continued to be published nearly halfway through the 20th century.

The contents of those papers span a period when noted historians, expert genealogists, skilled storytellers, and cultural specialists were numerous, and their knowledge was intentionally recorded in writing. Editorials pleaded for those with expertise to submit material for publication so that it would be available for those of the future. Their writings were published in weekly or daily columns, along with responses or additions from their peers and contemporaries. Accompanying such writing was the routine reporting of local and global issues as well as the many reactions or analyses that such coverage generated. The ongoing dialogue documented a century of change, the continual negotiation of the Hawaiians' perspectives with the transitioning world around them.

Hawaiian-language materials as a whole are a time capsule of important historical and cultural writings, and the newspapers are the most dense, most interconnecting portion of that historical cache. Though scholars have generated entire books of history and legend with what they have extracted from these papers, only a tiny fraction, less than one percent of the whole, has been translated and published. The rest, equal to well over a million letter-size pages of text, remains untranslated, difficult to access in the original form, unused, and largely unknown.

The most familiar English translations have developed into a canon of chosen texts, meaning that collectively, they have become the authoritative basis for reference. The books that make up this powerful canon are problematic at best, and yet flawed as they are, they have been the foundation of Hawaiian knowledge for most readers, teachers, and researchers for generations. Not only do these translations inadequately represent even the originals from which they were taken, but they further compound the problem by eclipsing the larger body of original writings that remain unrecognized.

The canon referred to here is made up of seven books translated from the works of 19th-century Hawaiian authors. Four of the books were drawn from the serial columns on history by Samuel Mānaiakalani Kamakau, one from the articles containing John Papa ʻĪʻī's memoirs, and two were translated from the unpublished manuscripts of Davida Malo and Kepelino Keauokalani. While other Hawaiian texts have been published in English, the translated works of these four authors have become an articulated bastion of Hawaiian reference, and have been granted an overwhelming and far-reaching authority about Hawaiian culture and history.

The existence and perpetuation of such a canon raises a number of issues, perhaps the most critical being that these translations are accepted as being the best of what Hawaiians wrote about themselves. These few works have been deemed *sufficient* to represent what is known of historical Hawaiian writings, and an entire framework of knowledge, a *discourse*, has been built around that acceptance. The term "discourse of sufficiency" is used here to describe how the system of understanding Hawaiian history has been based on a widespread acceptance of very little as being enough.

Beyond quantifying representation to show that a slight fraction is replacing the whole, this study also examines the re-ordered translations of Kamakau and ʻĪʻī. It shows that the content, sequence, and form of the two authors' original columns have been completely reworked into books that bear little resemblance to what was presented to reading audiences in the 1860s and 1870s. These men are considered stellar examples of Hawaiian writers, as they were in their own time, yet the integrity of their work has been lost in translation and through the heavy editing and reorganizing of their writings.

The other 99 percent of the Hawaiian published material, the part left behind, is still largely uncharted, but research already shows that it will prove to be a treasury of intellectual, historical, and cultural insights. It not only includes a host of writers spanning generations, but it also makes up the setting from which the canon writings were extracted. Every single item in those weekly or daily papers, from editorials to advertisements, adds clarity to the historical contexts that make the published writings of Kamakau and ʻĪʻī, as well as the manuscripts of Malo and Kepelino, understandable. The newspapers provide a chronological network of information that illuminates other archival holdings as well—letters, manuscripts, government records, and such, extending the import and impact far beyond these few translated writers.

Research highlighted a need for change and has set many forces in motion. The findings have encouraged people to build on earlier efforts and have become a catalyst for new projects that can change how knowledge from the past is connected, or reconnected, to today. Archival files, especially newspapers, are being made into searchable text to improve the way the materials can be accessed and used. Translations are again being generated to allow a broader range of students, scholars, and practitioners to understand and utilize the historical writings. New forms of reference tools, published as texts or available online, are in demand and are actively being developed. While these new directions are in process, the most important change is the dismantling of the long-standing mindset that the little fraction that has been available is *sufficient*.

New directions and changing mindsets have been common in my own pursuit of Hawaiian scholarship, but it is particularly exciting to witness this current paradigm shift. Coming to Waiʻanae in 1972 as an eighteen-year-old, I stepped into the frenetic opening of what would come to be called the Hawaiian Renaissance. It flourished in every direction, and I was one of many who got swept up in it.

All of my initiation to "Hawaiiana" took place in the community through various forms of oral tradition: hula, chant, language, and stories.[5]

Training came through teachers who identified with a cultural lineage, a personal transmission of knowledge and the mastery of skills. Each physical routine of the hula came with vignettes about a hero, a place, or an event. Each *oli*, or chant, was a story encapsulated in poetry. Language was as much about why and when to say something as to how the grammar worked. Knowledge taught through hula, chant, and language was regularly connected to the present, regardless of the antiquity of the subject:[6]

> ... and that's why you don't pick lehua when entering the forest.

> ... and the hole is still there, showing the power of his thrust.

> ... a hiki mai kāna mau pua i ke ao mālamalama.
> [many of her descendants are still prominent today.]

When I eventually entered the university, there was a sensitivity to the importance of "native voice," but the approach relied on written knowledge over oral transmission. Classes that touched on Hawaiian culture included Hawaiian authors, but with so few available in translation, the same ones were used repeatedly, sometimes exclusively. Davida Malo's *Hawaiian Antiquities* was called "the bible," and whole courses were devoted to his single translated work. Other courses focused on the books of Kamakau or Fornander, with the translations of Kepelino and ʻĪʻī filling gaps.

---

[5] I trained in hula under Mililani Allen, George Holokai, and Kamāmalu Klein, learned Hawaiian chant from Edith Kanakaʻole and Edith McKinzie, and my mentors in language and culture included Theodore Kelsey, Sarah Nākoa, Noelani Losch, Lolena Nicholas, and Kamuela Kumukahi.

[6] The quoted excerpts are from Edith Kanakaʻole, Patience Nāmaka Bacon, and Theodore Kelsey, respectively, although they are parts of an oral tradition recited and repeated from many sources.

University was an immersion into the carefully organized dates and details of the Hawaiian canon and its by-products, presenting a culture and history more consistent than what I had learned. This new perspective was well articulated, single-layered, seldom contradictory, and chronologically documented. Sometimes differing with or dismissing what I had learned from my earlier mentors, this body of knowledge was powerful. It was also self-replicating, being continually reproduced in new texts, students, and teachers. Disempowering the canon by opening up the archives of Hawaiian writings has the potential of aligning academic scholarship with community wisdom, while bridging both to a legacy of knowledge that has grown ever more distant for nearly a century.

Beyond the canon is a historical written legacy of Hawaiian self-expression: Hawaiians writing their own stories, in their own language, for themselves, their peers, their descendants, and all who would come after them. Cultural practice and intergenerational exchange have perpetuated parts of that legacy, and translation has preserved a small portion. Much, though, has been allowed to slip into obscurity.

The changing nature of Hawaiian scholarship calls for a more extensive and methodical incorporation of the historical Hawaiian writings that do exist. The fact that the materials are in Hawaiian presents challenges, but there are exciting new efforts under way to meet those challenges. Historian S. M. Kamakau encouraged his own contemporaries to strive for knowledge about the past with these words, still applicable today:

> Ua noa i na kanaka apau loa ka moolelo, hookahi mea nana i keakea, o ka naaupo o kanaka. (1868c)
>
> [History is freely accessible to all; the only obstruction is ignorance.]

1 | A Discourse of Sufficiency

For generations, knowledge about Hawai'i has been limited at every level by scholarship that accepts a fraction of the available sources as being sufficient to represent the huge collection of material that actually exists. Over a century of documentation by Hawaiian writers[7] has been ignored or dismissed through this mindset of acceptance, and perceptions about Hawai'i, past and present, are seriously affected. The few Hawaiian primary sources that have been incorporated into modern scholarship are problematic themselves, but additionally, their presence has helped to keep the remaining resources obscure. This setting, this *discourse*, limits and obstructs all related fields of study.

I use the term *discourse of sufficiency* to describe this long-standing recognition and acceptance of a small selection of Hawaiian writings from the 19th century as being sufficient to embody nearly a hundred years of extensive Hawaiian

---

[7] The word *Hawaiian* is used here in reference to those fluent in the language, most of whom were Native Hawaiian, writing in Hawaiian for a mostly native audience. The body of Hawaiian-language material discussed in this study may include instances of material written by non-Hawaiians or by anonymous writers who could have been Hawaiians, non-Hawaiian residents, or even foreigners. As those writings are in Hawaiian and make up part of the dialogue within the mostly Native Hawaiian audience, the inclusion of non-native writers is acknowledged, but no active distinction is made here.

auto-representation—Hawaiians writing for and about themselves.[8] Hawai'i stands out among all Pacific island groups for the massive extent of literature written in their native language, a pastiche of historical native production which if measured in letter-sized, typed pages would easily exceed one million pages of printed text.[9] The very existence of such a broad range of Hawaiian published works left untapped during the last century of research, analysis, publication, and practice is evidence of a discourse of sufficiency, the force of which has obscured the majority of Hawaiian writings and shunned critique of modern texts which disregard them.

In this study, I address the Hawaiian auto-representational works of the first century of Hawaiian literacy, which effectively began in 1820,[10] investigating the writings of the period, especially the Hawaiian-language newspapers. This analysis compares the actual range of published Hawaiian writings with the tiny subset of those writings utilized today in studying the history and culture of Hawai'i, as well as the broader fields that include study of Polynesian and Pacific societies.

The subset of writings referred to here, which has become the canon of references for nearly all Hawaiian-related publications for decades, is drawn and translated from works by four Hawaiian authors: Davida Malo, K. Z. Kepelino Keauokalani,[11] Samuel Mānaiakalani Kamakau, and John Papa 'Ī'ī. The sum of these works makes up only a fraction of one percent of the available primary material, and yet for decades these few extracted and translated texts from a handful of authors have been accepted as being enough to represent the bulk of Hawaiian cultural and historical knowledge. Such a setting disregards nearly all of Hawaiian public exchange of the 19th and early 20th centuries, a body of writings generated by and widely disseminated among the Hawaiian population of the period.

---

[8] This text focuses on the public written record, while acknowledging that history, culture, or representation cannot be distilled within the written record to the exclusion of other forms of knowing and of transmitting knowledge. This discussion does not privilege the public record over the private and inherited histories that inform personal and collective identities or claim to illuminate knowledge that is more "real" than what is already in use, but rather shows how one important assembly of knowledge within the larger sphere has been handled historically and is addressed today.

[9] The most comparable archive would be New Zealand Māori published writings, equaling approximately 30,000 pages of letter-sized text, 17,000 pages of which are contained in the Māori Newspaper section of the *New Zealand Digital Library*, http://www.nzdl.org/cgi-bin/library. See Chapter 3 for more details about the extent of the Hawaiian language archival sources.

[10] Although contact and interaction by Hawaiians with literacy and writing occurred prior to the arrival of the American missionaries in 1820, it was the formal reduction of the language to a consistent written form upon their arrival that made literacy generally accessible to Hawaiians. The first printed material became available in 1822.

[11] Kahoali'ikūmai'eiwakamoku Keauokalani was named Zepherin by his Catholic teachers, a name Hawaiianized as Kepelino, which was then used in the publication of his manuscript writings (1932, 1978, and 2007). Because it is the name by which he is best recogized today, Kepelino will be used in this work.

Although these four men provided a wealth of information, their writings are only a fragment of what hundreds of Hawaiian writers generated in the span of more than a century. Compounding the problem of representation is the fact that in the translated versions, the content of the original works was reduced, re-ordered, and decontextualized. The small number of extracted texts and the problematic qualities of the English forms of those texts stress the importance of primary sources and the need for exploring the fuller extent of the original Hawaiian-language record.

Consideration of the actual scope of historical Hawaiian-language resources starkly illuminates major gaps in most modern scholarship. It also brings to light analytical possibilities that can only be made feasible by stepping beyond the limited resources used today. This narrative gives focus to published Hawaiian-language writings of the past, but the implications of this study apply to other fields in Hawai'i and beyond.

The Power of Discursive Practice

Discourse can be simple dialogue, but the word also includes whole formations of practices, systems, prevailing mindsets, and the institutional and financial support for the perspectives that gain credibility and acceptance. It becomes the "way of knowing" in a given time and place, and this study addresses current discourse, our way of knowing today, about 19th- and 20th-century Hawai'i.

In the 21st century, the way in which knowledge about Hawai'i is framed differs greatly from what historian S. M. Kamakau proposed to his fellow citizens of the Hawaiian Kingdom in the 1860s:

> He makemake ko'u e pololei ka moolelo o ko'u one hanau, aole na ka malihini e ao ia'u i ka mooolelo o ko'u lahui, na'u e ao aku i ka moolelo i ka malihini. (1865b)
>
> [I want the history of my homeland to be correct. The foreigner shall not teach me the history of my people, I shall teach the foreigner.]

Thirty years later, Kamakau's proposal was apparently already being undermined when publisher Thomas Spencer criticized English history books, the presence of which reflect the already-shifting power over knowledge:

O na Buke Moolelo Hawaii namu haole i hoopuka mua ia e pili ana ia kakou, he hapa uuku wale no ia mau hoakaka, a he ono ole kona waiu ke moni aku. (1895)

[The English-language Hawaiian history books that have been published about us provide only fragmentary insights, and there is no flavor to taste in the milk of that breast.]

The kind of power shift that changed the framing of knowledge in Hawai'i is analyzed on a grander scale in regard to other settings. In *Orientalism,* Edward Said (1979) documents an array of the social and government forces involved in creating and maintaining the European and American discourses of knowledge regarding the people of the "Orient." These multiple discourses, which Said shows to be interconnected and mutually empowering, have for centuries defined and authorized, for the powerful nations of Europe and America, "knowledge" about the people of the Middle East and Asia—their histories, cultures, languages, politics, and their characters. The perceptions that such power controls guide everything from diplomatic relations to what is taught, understood, and reinforced on both sides of the boundaries of power.

This kind of power over knowledge is able to essentialize the people and place, define the field in which they exist, and completely frame the understanding about the entire subject. Left unchecked, the power-generated "knowledge" is internalized by the disempowered subjects of the discourse, the people themselves. In Hawai'i, this insidious process has affected the place, the people, and their own perceptions of the past and present, as generations have internalized a modern presentation about culture and history that has been skewed by the dynamics of power over knowledge. It is often expressed that whoever controls the present controls the past, and whoever controls the past shapes the future.

Drawing from French philosopher Michel Foucault's treatises on power and knowledge, Said points to the economic and military forces of the West that have enabled such an elaborate network of knowledge to be created, institutionalized, interlaced, embellished, and maintained for centuries. Said also explores how the power relations of Europe that are different from those of the U.S. result in different networks of knowledge—different orientalisms—and how those systems of knowledge influence and foster the national and international institutions that come to be in place. Power, then, is both the agent of knowledge and its beneficiary, as Foucault asserts:

> ... there is no power relation without the correlative constitution of a field of knowledge, nor any knowledge that does not presuppose and constitute at the same time power relations. (1977:27)

Europe and the United States were the focus for Foucault in his writings analyzing the institutional links between power and knowledge. In *Orientalism*, Said (1979) extended that investigation to the Middle East and Asia to address the powers of Europe and the U.S. in those areas. In *Culture and Imperialism* (Said 1993), he expanded the purview to describe a more global operation of those processes, detailing the silencing effects of Western control over knowledge upon the peoples and cultures wherever such power is imposed:

> Without significant exception the universalizing discourses of modern Europe and the United States assume the silence, willing or otherwise, of the non-European world. There is incorporation; there is inclusion; there is direct rule; there is coercion. But there is only infrequently an acknowledgement that the colonized people should be heard from, their ideas known. (1993:50)

Said connects the power of Western universalizing discourse to the silencing and shaping of contemporary voices. Historical voices that once wielded power, locally, if not globally, can be affected in the same way, especially in the manner in which they are included or excluded from contemporary fields of knowledge. His point about contemporary silencing accentuates the need to delve into the historical creation and framing of knowledge in those areas where the power of the West has been dominant, in some cases for centuries. Knowledge, the "facts" that support knowledge, and the institutions that generate, maintain, and foster that knowledge today have certainly been shaped, at least in part, by the agency of U.S. and European powers that touched every part of the globe during centuries of Western expansion. In *Culture and Imperialism*, Said notes how control of knowledge is a foundation for the related realms of cultural and imperialist dominance:

> The power to narrate, or to block other narratives from forming and emerging, is very important to culture and imperialism, and constitutes one of the main connections between them. (1993:xiii)

Discourse in Hawai'i and the Pacific

Like every island group throughout the Pacific Ocean, Hawai'i interacted on what became an ongoing basis with the agents of Western, mainly Euro-American, expansion. After just over a century of continuous intercourse, Western eyes saw the area to be the domain of the West, as in this exuberant 1884 report:

> The white race is conquering and civilising all the earth. It has peopled the New World, it has penetrated Asia and Africa. Oceania, as her elders, is not but a vast European domain in the hands of five nations. (Aldrich 1990:243)

The history of foreign nations exercising control over the peoples of the Pacific is one of military might, technological advantage, economic power, and cultural assertion. While each cultural and political sphere in Oceania experienced a unique history of contact and interaction with Western influences, each of those spheres succumbed to the eventual domination by Western power, Hawai'i being no exception.[12] Unlike most other Pacific societies, Hawai'i was never a colony of a foreign power, being internationally recognized as an independent and sovereign nation until falling to U.S. domination at the close of the 19th century. Current studies dealing with colonialism and decolonization are, however, pertinent to Hawai'i, whereas the inequities of power inherent in colonialism have many parallels in regard to Western influence and occupation in Hawai'i, past and present.

Outside influences have been continuous in Hawai'i from the beginning of sustained contact with the islanders in 1778 until today. There have been dramatic and sometimes disastrous impacts, both immediate and eventual. Many of those impacts are readily recognizable, such as depopulation, and upheaval of social, cultural, and governmental systems. Other effects have been less apparent, but no less important. Anthropologist Elizabeth Buck in *Paradise Remade* (1993) points to the long-term connections between language and change. Though she mistakenly overlays the historical development of literacy with the switch to English primacy, she does show how interaction and adoption of Western languages and literacy altered thinking processes and shifted the loci of power over the production of knowledge:

> Along with the radical shift from orality to literacy came the displacement of Hawaiian by English as the dominant language

---

[12] Tonga, united as a kingdom in 1845, avoided complete domination by European powers, becoming a British protectorate in 1900, and gaining full independence in 1970.

> of discourse. The first altered basic cognitive processes and the second shaped social consciousness. The repositioning of Hawaiians and their culture by Western discourses about Hawai'i further reconstituted social relationships and shifted sites of power. Any one of these linguistic events would have had far-reaching consequences for Hawaiians and their position vis-a-vis Western society; coming together as they did, the effects were compounded. (1993:121)

Change and repositioning continued in the kingdom of Hawai'i throughout the 19th century, ending with complete and direct control of the Islands by the U.S. in 1898. After that point, certain forces holding sway over the networks of knowledge became readily apparent while others have remained less obvious. Legislative action, military presence, government policies, judicial decisions, and education systems clearly shaped the formal discourse, while changing cultural and social practices continued to be less overt.

Anthropologists White and Tengan (2001) summarize how one field in Hawai'i, anthropology, has been guided by outside forces since its inception, meaning American and non-native agency has dictated its theories, research paradigms, personnel, methodologies, and benefits. Part of that setting has been the division of intellectual territory of Hawaiian anthropology that began in the 1930s between the Bishop Museum, which was dedicated to the study of traditional native culture, and the University of Hawai'i, whose focus was to be modern native adaptation.

The division they describe matches anthropology's customary project of temporal, social, or geographical "othering"—taking a role of an exterior observer, a positioning critiqued by many.[13] This "othering" relies on setting apart Hawaiians of the past as a separate social entity from modern Hawaiians, a polarized view that contrasts those who lived the culture against those simply espousing it today. This kind of distancing has only been made possible by the erasure of a century of Hawaiian commentary that threaded through the continuum of adaptation and change in the 19th and early 20th centuries. Dismissing Hawaiian self-expression from that period of change helps maintain a clear, and inaccurate, opposition between Hawaiians of old who were *culturally intact* and modern-day, *acculturated* Hawaiians. Recognition of the continuity, renewal, and invention that marked the interim can be clarified by the voices of those who initiated, guided, experienced, or resisted the processes of change, but power over knowledge has worked to silence those historical voices.

---

[13] For examples, see Linnekin (1983), Michaelson (1999), White and Tengan (2001).

Sociologist Skutnabb-Kangas Tove, addressing global language shifts, spoke to the power held in the reins of government, regarding control and influence over education and economy:

> Those who have a monopoly of preferred access to official discourses can also make their own ideas into Foucauldian "regimes of truth" which regulate the kinds of ideas which can be legitimately presented and debated (Bourdieu's "doxa"). It is also within these broad regimes of truth that the criteria of validation and invalidation of non-material resources are accomplished. What falls outside the discourses permitted by prevalent regimes of truth is not only *labelled* deficient—it simply *is* invisible and invalid. This makes it easier to manufacture the hegemonic consent. (2000:413 [emphasis in original])

Both Foucault and Said discussed hegemony as a basis of how discursive power strengthens the framework that defines the boundaries of authoritative knowledge. They are referring to the openly coercive force of political society, seen in laws, rulings and funding priorities, and also to the less-visible but more penetrating hegemony of those same forces once they are brought to bear through the cultural practices of civil society, what anthropologist Bruce Knauft identifies as: "the cultural dispositions and social institutions that predispose consent to (if not compliance with) politically repressive regimes" (Knauft 1996:187). In regard to Hawaiian language, this kind of penetrating hegemony of support for English is more apparent than coercive laws or practices, but the effect is as powerful as direct coercion. English being perceived as a necessary and desirable tool, rather than overtly imposed, becomes a nuanced and dynamic historical force.

Openly coercive forces took control of Hawai'i at the close of the 19th century, including hostile seizure of the constitutional monarchy, reformation of the government, purported annexation, and military occupation of the islands. The imposition of martial law, control of all government functions, and restraint of any popular resistance were clear and well documented.[14] Secondary support for compliance with policies of the new regime was guaranteed by the removal from their positions of any persons who did not sign an oath of allegiance to the usurping

---

[14] For more coverage on this topic, see Coffman (1998), Lili'uokalani (1964), and Spencer (1895).

government.[15] Such allegiance to the direct agencies of power, whether willing or forced, fostered an illusion of cultural consent, or at least compliance, as acceptance of imposed practices eventually became normalized.

The move from Hawaiian to English as the language of the island population was one aspect of that more general network of implied consents and compliances. This language shift framed and enabled English discursive power in Hawai'i throughout the 20th century. An overview of that historical language shift shows that the process of change from Hawaiian to English paralleled social changes in the development of the current discourse.

The indigenous language of Hawai'i developed over the course of nearly two millennia of Polynesian migration and societal settlement, developing as a unique branch of the Polynesian language family.[16] Although earlier exposure to non-Polynesian languages undoubtedly occurred prior to Captain Cook's arrival in the islands in 1778, that event marked the beginning of documented, prolonged interaction with foreign cultures.[17] From 1778 on, many foreign languages, especially English, held an expanding position in the lives of natives and foreigners alike in Hawai'i.

The English language steadily gained importance in economic and political spheres during the century following Cook's arrival. The Chiefs' Children's School, begun in 1839, used English as the language of instruction to prepare the young chiefs for their future responsibilities, locally and internationally (Schütz 1994:342). At the same time, in the late 1830s and early 1840s, English periodicals couldn't yet survive because of a paucity of foreign residents, but by 1844 the government saw it worthwhile to subsidize an English newspaper, *The Polynesian*, to communicate with the growing foreign population. English newspapers thrived from that time to the present.

---

[15] See Burns, Eugene (1939); an interview of Oliver Kawailahaole Stilman, referring to oaths of allegiance, and also *Hawaiian Gazette* (1900): "In 1893 the white people controlled the Government. What did they do? They fired every Hawaiian from office who did not hold the same political opinions as they did themselves."

[16] For more coverage on the development of the Hawaiian language, see Schütz (1994).

[17] There is ample evidence of foreign contact with Hawai'i prior to the arrival of Capt. Cook and the ongoing interactions with foreigners that followed Cook's arrival. For Hawaiian discussion about that topic see Dibble (1838:4–6), and Kamakau (1866b, Dec. 22 and Dec. 29), Kamakau (1867, Jan. 5, Jan. 12, and Jan. 19). Currently, however, there is insufficient oral and written evidence to clarify the extent to which these preceding contacts were prolonged, or to illuminate the social or linguistic changes that may have resulted from them.

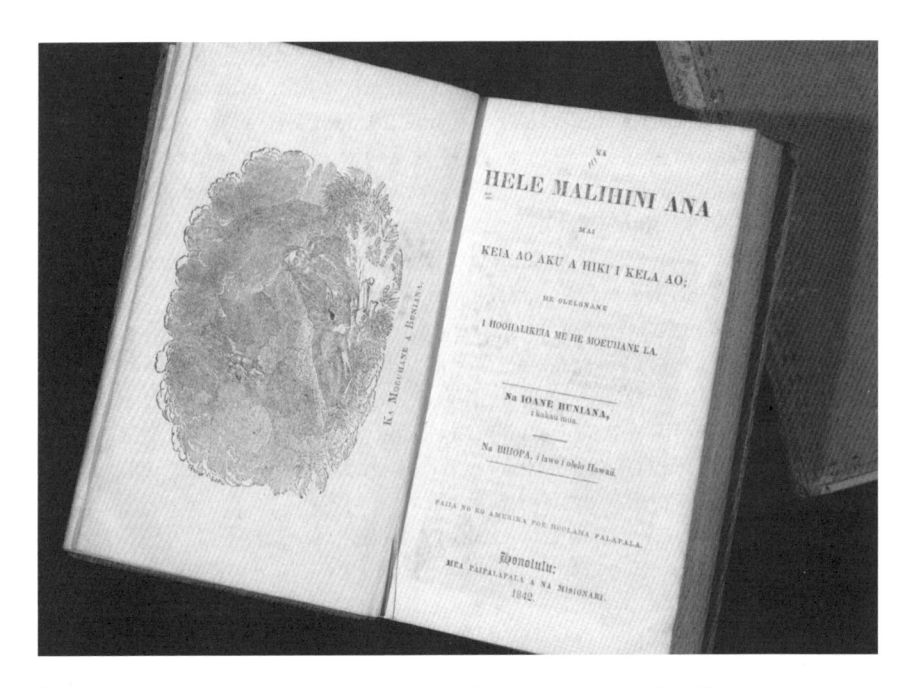

Ka Hele Malihini Ana, *a Hawaiian version of* The Pilgrim's Progress, *translated by Reverend Artemas Bishop and published by the American Tract Society in 1842. For a listing of 654 Hawaiian language texts produced during the ascendancy of Hawaiian language, see Judd, Bell, and Murdoch,* Hawaiian Language Imprints, 1822–1899: A Bibliography *(1978). Photo by David Franzen, Bishop Museum.*

English became a second official language of the Hawaiian kingdom, and by 1859 was granted a degree of primacy in legal interpretation of the law.[18] English was the first language of a growing foreign resident population that included, but was not limited to, missionaries, merchants, and traders. The Calvinist mission established the first press in the islands in 1822, producing educational and religious material, mostly in Hawaiian. Hawaiian-language newspapers were initiated in 1834, flourishing for over a century. English-language newspapers began in 1836, with locally printed books in English appearing by 1838,[19] showing a growing English language presence in the Islands.

---

[18] Hawaiian Civil Code Section 1493, May 17, 1859 (amended and broadened, 1864): "If at any time a radical and irreconcilable difference shall be found to exist between the English and Hawaiian versions of any part of this Code, the English version shall be held binding." Also see Lucas (2000) for an overview of legal sanctions regarding Hawaiian language.

[19] *The Sandwich Island Gazette* and *Journal of Commerce* ran from 1836–1839, and was followed by a growing number of other periodicals. *The Hawaiian Spectator*, a quarterly journal appearing in 1838 and 1839, was published in book form, and was the first of its kind in the islands.

For the next 60 years, language necessities of regional and foreign trade, government processes, and international relations were constantly shifting, and the social and political roles of Hawaiian and English were the subject of heated dialogue throughout the years of the constitutional monarchy, continuing into the Territorial era.[20] In the Hawaiian press, natives, local-born *haole*, or non-native residents, as well as foreign-born residents argued about the value of each language, some advocating teaching all schools in English and others supporting the perpetuation of the native language.[21] An array of positions appears in editorials and commentaries throughout the period.

In 1893, a faction of pro-American businessmen seized the Hawaiian government, establishing first a Provisional Government, then the Republic of Hawai'i. The intent was to annex the islands to the United States, a move that was carried out by American legislative resolution, rather than by treaty, in 1898.[22] In 1896, the revised laws of the Republic of Hawai'i, Act 57, Section 30, mandated that all schools use English as the medium of instruction.[23] The few Hawaiian-language schools remaining at the time were closed, and English was made the language of instruction in all public schools. When the United States took formal control of the islands as a territory in 1898, full primacy was granted to English, the language of the governing power, even though a large part of the native population, literate in their own language, had limited fluency in English at the time.[24] The Organic Act of 1900 dictated that all legislative proceedings be held in English, and that

---

[20] While other languages, particularly French, Spanish, and Russian, were also important in many fields of trade and government during the period, English was the most widely used foreign language.

[21] Hawaiian and non-Hawaiian opinion regarding the role of Hawaiian and English languages was published regularly in the newspapers throughout the latter half of the 19th century. Such public commentary was especially frequent following actions by the government, for example, after the adoption of English for instruction at Lahainaluna in 1877 (see *Ka Nupepa Kuokoa me Ke Au Okoa i Huipuia* 1877). Such public input also impacted the actions of government, as in the non-adoption of recommendations by the 1882 Committee for Public Instruction to begin English as the language at all government schools. (Hawai'i Legislature, Report of the Committee on Public Education 1882:4–5)

[22] The historical legality and validity of both the overthrow and the annexation of Hawai'i are hotly contested today. For more information, see http://www.alohaquest.com and http://www.Hawaiian Kingdom.org.

[23] Act 57, sec. 30 of the 1896 Laws of the Republic of Hawai'i states:
"The English Language shall be the medium and basis of instruction in all public and private schools, provided that where it is desired that another language shall be taught in addition to the English language, such instruction may be authorized by the Department, either by its rules, the curriculum of the school, or by direct order in any particular instance. Any schools that shall not conform to the provisions of this section shall not be recognized by the Department." This act affected all non-English schools, including a number of Chinese language schools founded, in part, by the government.

[24] Michelson (1897) quotes many native sources who address their limited ability in English.

while voters could be fluent in English *or* Hawaiian, jurors in the courts must be able to speak English.[25]

Following purported annexation, military occupation, along with changing governmental and economic control, had a range of impacts on Hawaiian society, but the new policy formalizing the use of English as the language of instruction directly facilitated the development of the discourse of sufficiency discussed here. This interplay between government policy and language status clearly exemplifies Foucault's descriptions of discursive practice as an aspect of power, which transforms and reconstructs society, and his examples of how such processes both follow and enable the transformations that occur (Wilkin 1999). During the first decade and a half after the 1893 seizure of the kingdom, there was actually a surge in Hawaiian-language publications attempting to counteract the decline of the language. The closure of any instructional use of Hawaiian was eventually followed, not surprisingly, by a dwindling Hawaiian-language press and a few book publications in Hawaiian. Thus, by the second decade of the 20th century English became the language of nearly all published materials.[26]

Editorials in the remaining Hawaiian papers continued a dialogue on language, but the focus was no longer on which language would gain ascendancy, but rather on recovery or the foreseeable loss of Hawaiian language. Some writers lamented that opportunities for regenerating the language through government schools had been denied by the legislature, even in the first decades of the Territorial legislature where a Hawaiian majority was at the helm.[27] Others addressed that language loss would lead to the loss of Hawaiians as a people.[28]

---

[25] Organic Act: An Act to Provide a Government for the Territory of Hawaii (Act of April 30, 1900, C 339, 31 Stat 141). Article 2, Sec. 44, Enacting clause—English language. "… All legislative proceedings shall be conducted in the English language."; Article 4, Sec. 83, "no person…who cannot understandingly speak, read, and write the English language shall be a qualified juror or grand juror in the Territory of Hawaii."; and, Article 2, Sec. 60, "That in order to be qualified to vote for the representatives a person shall…Be able to speak, read and write the English or Hawaiian language."

[26] An exception to this trend was the Bishop Museum's early attempts at bilingual publications of translated works of Fornander (1916–1920) and Kepelino (1932), but the effort was short-lived (see Beckwith 1939), and monolingual English publications prevailed for the rest of the 20th century. The creation of Hawaiian-language immersion schools in 1983 initiated a new movement toward monolingual Hawaiian-language publications, which has continued since that time. Many of these recent publications are translations from English texts or contemporary writings in Hawaiian, but a number of resources from the 19th century have been incorporated into these immersion school texts as well. Hawaiian-language newspapers, in diminished numbers and circulation, continued until 1948.

[27] *Ka Puuhonua o na Hawaii* (1917).

[28] Ibid., **and** Poepoe, J. M., editor, *Ka Na'i Aupuni*, 4 January 1906, pg. 2. "Mai Haalele i Kau Olelo Makuahine" (Don't Abandon Your Mother Tongue); *Hawaii Holomua*, 10 April 1912, pg. 23–24. "Ka Olelo Makuahine a ka Lahui Hawaii" (The Mother Tongue of the Hawaiian People); Kalihiwai o Lanihome "Ka Kakou Olelo Makua" (Our Ancestral Language), in *Ke Alakai o Hawaii*, 14 June 1828, pg. 2.

In the 1920s, English language became a mark of patriotism to the United States, and there was a clamor to close the Japanese language schools, the most numerous foreign-language institutions functioning in Hawaiʻi at the time. Pressure to close the Japanese schools came from many sectors, including the Hawaiian language community that had lost its own schools.[29] The public demand for all in Hawaiʻi to assimilate into a monolingual society was widespread.

English flourished as the language of the government and education in the islands, and in the community, Hawaiian-speaking parents were encouraged to have their children learn English as their only language. Students who used Hawaiian on the school grounds were ofttimes scolded or punished for the offense. In the course of a few generations, monolingualism in English became normalized in the islands.[30] As the 20th century opened, the number of English publications produced for local readers soared while the Hawaiian publications diminished and eventually disappeared. Because of the continued pervasiveness of English during most of the 20th century, Hawaiian-language materials effectively stopped being produced. Fluent speakers of the language who could directly utilize existing materials diminished greatly in number, and within a few generations, those seeking Hawaiian historical materials depended completely upon what was available in the English language.[31]

English spread even while there still existed a large adult Hawaiian-speaking population. The common use of English, even by those fluent in Hawaiian, quickly changed the next generation's grasp of the language.[32] Although statistics are unclear for the period, Hawaiian speakers of the time continued to recognize and write about the impact of the change on their own community. By the first decades of the 20th century, Hawaiian papers carried numerous articles lamenting the loss of the language among the younger generations, the following quote being an example:

> I keia la, ke hepa mai nei ka oleloia ana o ka kakou olelo makuahine. Aole keiki o 15 makahiki e hiki ke kamailio polo-lei i ka olelo makuahine o keia aina. A no keaha ke kumu i hiki ole ai? No ka mea, aole aʻo ia i ka olelo pololei. A i ka hala ana

---

[29] See Chapin (1996:140–147), and editorials, such as *Ka Nupepa Kuokoa* (1919, Nov. 14).

[30] Excluding Niʻihau and a few isolated rural areas where Hawaiian remained the primary language, and with the exception, of course, of immigrant communities, where language dynamics were, and are, somewhat unique to each group. See Wilson, C. (2002).

[31] The first report of the Historical Commission of the Territory of Hawaii (1925:14) made reference to important historical writings which were "buried in the files of the native newspapers," indicating the difficulty of access to such materials already at that time.

[32] See coverage in Michelson (1897). Reinecke (1969) gives statistics of speakers in the opening decades of the 20th century, but those are revisited and contested by Bickerton and Wilson (1987).

Many variations of this poster were displayed in public places and businesses in Hawaiʻi during the WWII years. Most had catchy, patriotic messages, like "Say it with flowers; say it with bonds; say it with music; but WHATEVER you say—SPEAK AMERICAN." Some, like this one, used photos of local kids, declaring "Loyal Americans speak American, the one language for all of us," while others read "Pidgin is better than nothing—the American language is best—but nobody wants to hear foreign tongues, especially the enemy's—use and encourage others to speak American." Any "foreign" language, including Hawaiian, was spurned. Speak American Campaign (RSCN1607), Hawaii War Records Depository, University of Hawaiʻi at Mānoa.

> o na la pokole wale no o ka pau no ia, a mai uwe aku kakou no ka mea, na kakou no i nanamaka. (*Ka Puuhonua o na Hawaii* 917)[33]

> [Today, the manner in which our native tongue is being spoken is sloppy. There are no children of fifteen who are able to converse correctly in the native language of this land. And for what reason are they unable? Because they have not been taught correct speech. And in the passage of a few short days it will be gone and we should not weep, because all of us have watched it happen.]

The shift to English primacy worked through most avenues dealing with the production and dissemination of knowledge, especially writing. English presided in the production of texts, the documentation of government, business and community activity, the stocking of libraries, and the collection and maintenance of archive materials. In a 1930s critique on the dates used in published histories, Bishop Museum scholar John Stokes mentioned the sheep-like manner in which people were already relying on English sources:

> Being in English, Fornander's writings were generally followed, blindly and ovinely it is true, and have been widely quoted as highly authoritative. (1932:23)

By these first decades of the Territory, the authority granted to English sources was creating the foundation that would eventually sustain the discourse of sufficiency when it developed later in the century.

The primacy of English language over Hawaiian was not the sole or initial cause for the current obscurity of Hawaiian materials, but more of an indicator of larger social forces that were encouraging one kind of knowledge over the other. Primacy and obscurity are each aspects of an ongoing process of contest, one that is never either complete or static. Literary theorist Lisa Lowe, who was critical of Said and Foucault for the monolithic nature of the discourses they describe, points out that throughout the intercourses of power, there are "tensions and contradictions within any discursive terrain" (1991:25). As long as contesting

---

[33] See also *Ka Na'i Aupuni* (1905 and 1906) and *Hawaii Holomua* (1912). Many other examples exist from the period, although the published controversy about language choice and language fluency is first generated decades earlier.

powers still exist there is no absolute victor, no obliteration of discourse within the entire sphere, only change in the balance.

While Hawaiian language diminished to near invisibility for decades, spoken mainly in remote communities such as Niʻihau, Kekaha, Keʻanae and Miloliʻi, it did not cease to exist, nor did it disappear from the intellectual landscape. Recent language revitalization has effected a renewed empowerment of the contesting forces in that balance. Archival Hawaiian materials and oral records continued to be considered, albeit intermittently, and the tension brought about by increased recognition that such sources have been dismissed will continue to work toward further empowerment of the Hawaiian-language presence.

Power and Voice

There are, however, so many facets of knowledge generation and dissemination that such a radical change in the balance of the language powers at the time multiplied the effects of those changes throughout the network of contemporary knowledge. With the official empowerment of English in Hawaiʻi, especially as the foundation of education and government, available English sources which were aligned with that locus of power have continually been incorporated as part of the developing network of knowledge. These resources, including writings, policies, curricula, textbooks and so on, have then become mutually strengthening within the fabric of knowledge being produced and circulated. They reinforce one another within the same pool of knowledge.

In reference to a similar situation in Tahiti, Robert Nicole (2001) of the University of the South Pacific describes how the accepted knowledge is solidified by these entwining validations of one source upon another, and how each validating source would be emphasized by an empowering change in the discursive terrain. Regarding a pro-francophone discourse in French Polynesia similar to the pro-anglophone setting in Hawaiʻi today, Nicole echoes both Said and Foucault in describing the relationship between language and power. He notes that texts are connected in ways that give mutual validation to one another and to the larger guiding discourse in place:

> Texts produced about Tahiti, whether these were written by poets, novelists, navigators, botanists, philosophers, or colonial administrators, signaled their allegiance to this discourse by constantly repeating each other, and often plagiarizing each other. This pattern of overlaying and repetition merged into powerful discursive formations that assumed extraordinary intertextual strength. (2001:7)

The repositioning of power over knowledge is enhanced expanding intertextual support, bringing changes to the selection of those voices that are recognized as authentic. Historian Grego how this sanctioning power is enacted on individual historical voices empowering certain sources over others and granting authority through the position of the speaker and the form of the testimony:

> The authenticity of a witness is magnified by the witness's official status and the testimony's encoded form. (1995:21)

This works retroactively on historical voices as power shifts over time. Status authorized in later years by the agency of English language and granted to documents already encoded in English forms gave new and ready power to a set of voices of explorers, missionaries, visitors, traders, and other historical observers, while excluding once-authoritative Hawaiian voices that now remain inaccessible or unrecognizable to modern English documentors. The power Dening mentions above as giving authority to individuals is then magnified through the validation occurring among "authoritative" English-language texts. Historical English voices gained new power in Hawai'i and New Zealand with the later rise of English dominance, as historical French voices did in French Polynesia. In each setting, the native voice was drowned out.

The English and French presentation of Polynesian cultural history has lent similar emphasis to the historical voices of outside observers over those of native participants. Like the missionaries and visitors mentioned above, this has been the case for the last century, with readily accessible English or French-language sources being given credence over those available in Hawaiian, Samoan, Māori, or the multiple native languages of French Polynesia.

Even in native language writings, those created by non-natives have sometimes been selected for ready reference. Second-language learners' writings are often accessible to a broader audience, usually cast in a simple style, and not being "cluttered" with seemingly obscure or opaque idiom and cultural reference that makes writings by native speakers difficult. As such, non-native speakers of the language writing in Hawaiian can mistakenly be considered more objective or more academic than those of Hawaiian participants and practitioners because of the form in which their writings are presented and the manner in which topics are handled.

Hawaiian remained the language of public and political discourse throughout the kingdom, with many foreigners learning and writing in the native language. Abraham Fornander is a good example. A judge, schoolmaster, antiquarian, author, and researcher during the latter part of the 19th century, Fornander published a detailed representation of Polynesian cultural history in his three-volume text *An Account of the Polynesian Race* (1878, 1880, 1885). The narrative is mostly in English, but his accounts relied heavily on Hawaiian published sources and oral traditions, reworked and presented by Fornander himself. Because of its form as a scholarly analysis of the subject presented in a Western academic frame, the text was, and is, given great credence. His later compilation of cultural material *Hawaiian Folklore* (1916–1920), relying on a number of native sources but largely recast by him in Hawaiian, has also been accepted as an authoritative text.

In *Decolonizing Methodologies* (1999), political scientist Linda Tuhiwai Smith points out that Percy Smith and Elsdon Best in New Zealand helped create orthodoxies that, while contested and eventually devalued in some circles, still are given great credibility and used as legitimate references by scholars and the general public. Fornander, like Smith and Best, helped to shape similar orthodoxies through his writings. Part of the credibility and legitimacy granted to such texts has to do with the formal scholarly style in which the collected material was presented, or "the testimony's encoded form," as per Dening (1995:21). The fact that Fornander's later work is largely written in the native language lends even greater authority to the translated form of those works even though much of the Hawaiian is Fornander's own rewriting and the translations are questionable, as will be discussed later in Chapter 2.

Mission accounts, which modern scholars are re-evaluating with regard to their inherent biases and for their unstated goals of generating financial and spiritual support from their missionary headquarters, frequently still hold primacy as authoritative resources over existing native documentation of the same periods. Local missionaries were urged to publish their accounts in the newspaper so all could follow the developing progress of the nation, reports of which would both encourage and come to document the movement:

> Pehea ka nui o ke kula? Ehia haumana? Pehea ka halawai Sabati? O ka halawai kakahiaka a me ka halawai ahiahi? Pehea ka halawai loa? Ehia na mea i make? Ehia ka poe i hanauia. Ehia na kanaka mihi? na kanaka molowa ole? na kanaka wahahee ole? na kanaka i malama i ko ke Akua kanawai? Pehea la e hiki ia kakou ke hoomalamalama i ka pouli o keia pae aina? Nui loa ka hana e koe a kakou e hana ai, i ike pono ko Hawaii nei i na mea e pono ai ko lakou mau kino a me ko lakou mau uhane. (*Ke Kumu Hawaii* 1837, Mar. 15)

[How many schools? How many students? How about the Sunday services? Morning and evening services? What about extended services? How many deaths? How many births? How many have repented? How many are not lazy? not lying? maintaining God's laws? How can we enlighten the darkness of these islands? Much work remains for us to do so that those here in Hawai'i will see the things their bodies and spirits need.]

In the same way, seafarers' observations or visitor travelogues have regularly been considered primary source materials. English newspapers, travel records, and other archival records from the 19th century have been relied upon as central to historical and cultural description. While these historical sources have their own essential value, reliance upon such texts to the exclusion of those created by native writers crystallizes the non-native power over discursive practice.

The power of discourse not only establishes which voices will be heard, but also in what form they will speak in order to be recorded and recognized. Anthropologist Jeffrey Tobin (1997:75) addresses another way in which this power was applied, with Hawaiians being coerced to speak, as Foucault says, "within the true" or establishing voice only when the writing or utterance is aligned with controlling powers. Tobin gives the example of Hawaiians admitting to sins that may well not have been committed, in an effort to please missionaries who gladly recorded such data in order to validate their own efforts and to raise support for the missions. Discussions that conflict with the recorder's efforts may well go undocumented, if not unheard. In this way, those voices that are not usually granted some official position do become heard, utilized, and incorporated into the fabric of validation, but only when their content or their form is tailored to that which is more widely acceptable to the intended audience.

Linda Tuhiwai Smith, in the context of New Zealand Māori, speaks to this same link between larger forces and the product of the individual. She reviews the historical processes whereby the gathering of information, institutionally empowered, changed personal views into facts. These "facts," accreting authority over time, have come to frame a discourse which today guides the manner of social interactions with and among Māori as well as the spheres in which those interactions occur (1999:78–94). Views that were recorded and which have come to be seen as official, as objective, as learned, or as validated by some other qualification of "in the true" have gained status as authoritative historical data and thereby inform and influence modern interactions.

Power and Silence

The opposite case comes into play when native voices that were once influential throughout Hawai'i are no longer recognized or identified in the available record. When no "authentic" documentation validates historical understanding of cultural practice presented as tradition, the validity and authenticity of such tradition becomes questionable, even if perpetuated through an oral lineage. If documentation is not readily available from recognized sources, especially those included in the small Hawaiian canon, it is easy to dismiss such tradition as being invented and not to be historically grounded.

In his introduction to the text, *The Invention of Tradition* (1983), historian Eric Hobsbawm describes examples of European practices that involve invention of cultural and historical depth as validating tools of authenticity:

> "Invented tradition" is taken to mean a set of practices,... which seek to inculcate certain values and norms of behaviour by repetition, which automatically implies continuity with the past. In fact, where possible, they normally attempt to establish continuity with a suitable historic past. (1983:1)

Anthropologists, including Jocelyn Linnekin and Roger Keesing, have brought this same study into a Pacific setting in their writings in order to question so-called "traditions" that appear to be modern political inventions. For instance, ceremonial activities on Kaho'olawe have been termed by Linnekin as modern inventions because of a lack of validated historical documentation about the origin of such practices (1983). With no validation or refutation available in the trusted canon texts, her analysis went uncontested. Keesing referred in a more general Pacific sense to "emerging ideologies of the past" as problematic and contradictory:

> The ancestral ways of life being evoked rhetorically may bear little relation to those documented historically, recorded ethnographically, and reconstructed archaeologically. (1989:19)

Lack of formal documentation can easily invoke questions of validity or continuity, but what qualifies as evidence? The historical documentation, ethnographic method, and archaeological reconstructions Keesing speaks of are highly contested areas of discursive power, relying on select validating sources and methods. These systems of validation reinforce existing power structures while dismissing the existence of alternatives, including native narratives, as discussed

later. Hawaiian Studies professor Haunani-Kay Trask dismisses ᵗ
by such Western academic validating forces in a critique of Ke

> ... Keesing, with many Western academics, shares a ͜͝
> assumption: Natives don't know very much, even about theiɪ
> own lifeways, thus there is no need to read them. (The only
> "real" sources are *haole* sources, hegemony recognizing and
> reinforcing hegemony.) (1991:160)

The antiquity or recent emergence of traditions is a nebulous and contested arena, and yet claims of continuity or invention are common topics in modern scholarship and public discussion.[34] One running dialogue on the topic in relation to Hawai'i began with anthropologists Handler and Linnekin (1984), which was then expanded upon in Keesing (1989), subsequently rejected by Trask (1991), then reiterated by Linnekin (1991), and eventually responded to by Keesing (1991) and others.[35]

In the course of this interchange, aside from Trask's single reference to the oral tradition through genealogies (1991:160), each writer in the series of articles listed above called upon only modern sources to investigate the existence, invention, or continuation of old practices. Contemporary scholars and the dominant discourse, which includes the available canon of Hawaiian resources, were the validating sources used to illuminate, contextualize, support, or negate claims of antiquity or charges of invention. In the process, each of the arguments made becomes another layer of substantiation.

If Malo, Kepelino, Kamakau, or 'Ī'ī did not address a certain practice, or if an early explorer, visitor, or resident foreigner did not describe it, then it can be assumed that sufficient research has been done and the practice in question is not granted historical validity. This setting highlights the need to expand the written canon to include the much broader range of Hawaiian materials that could clarify such traditions as being ancient or modern. It also illuminates a bias toward writing over all other means of transmitting knowledge, an historical trope that historian Houston Wood discussed in his 1999 study about representation in Hawai'i, "Euroamericans in the islands have generally always associated 'real' knowledge with writing" (1999:54).

---

[34] See Handler and Linnekin (1984:288) and Linnekin (1991:173).
[35] Hanlon and White (2000:12–14) give a good overview of this argument, referencing many of the pertinent issues and publications.

The Fruits of Compliance

The forces that validate knowledge are diverse: the government, the academy, the market, the church, the community, the family, and more. Coercive powers of policy and enforcement combine with more subtle social forces in changing society, shifting the balances of power within that society. Policies of English-only in island schools were eventually backed by threats of funding loss for schools, and enforced by teachers and among students through physical punishment or ostracism for non-compliance (Nākoa 1979:19). Many of the teachers placed in the role of enforcement were themselves native speakers of Hawaiian who, by their modeling of English and their compliance with the rulings, created a powerful force for acceptance among their students and their families.

Hawaiian families, churches, and other social institutions that complied with the pressure to stop using Hawaiian with their children or in public lent de facto consent and support, however unwilling by some, to a broader discourse empowering English in the territory and state. Efforts in the 1920s to close the Japanese language schools in deference to English primacy included active discussions within the Hawaiian community that indicate a growing compliance with the new mores, or at least pressure to do so. The following editorial, exhorting the Japanese to follow the Hawaiian example of compliance, is from *Ka Nupepa Kuokoa*, the longest running Hawaiian newspaper and one which often took a particularly pro-American stance:[36]

> No kekahi mau kumu lehulehu e ikeia aku nei iloko o keia mau la, ke manao nei makou, he mea pono e hoopau loa ia ke aʻoia ana o ka olelo Kepani maloko o na kula i kukuluia ae e na Kepani apuni keia Teritore, no ka mea ua kue loa ia i ke ano Amerika, elike me ia i makemakeia mai ai na makaainana apau e noho nei maanei, e ke aupuni federala.
>
> He ano kohu ole loa, i ka nana aku, i ka manawa a ke kanawai o Amerika Huipuia, i haawiia mai ai ke kuleana makaainana, i na Kepani apau i hanauia ma Hawaii nei, e aʻoia aku lakou i ka lakou olelo makuahine, aole hoi i ka olelo Beritania, ka olelo i kohu ai ka makaainana Amerika maluna o

---

[36] In the long span of *Kuokoa*, some seven decades, the editorial stance moved in many directions, from supporting the constitutional monarchy to criticizing both government and sovereign. From the outset under Whitney, the paper promoted American culture and perspective, rather than political dominance, as a role model for the kingdom and Hawaiian society, but at the end of the 19th century, the paper openly supported the overthrow of Liliʻuokalani.

lakou; a no ka mea no hoi, o ka olelo Beritania, ka olelo alakai apuni o Amerika, ame na wahi apau i kaa aku malalo o kona malu.

Ua makee kakou i ka kakou olelo makuahine, eia nae aole he mau kula e aʻo nei i na keiki a kakou i ka olelo Hawaii, no ke kumu, o ka olelo Beretania ka olelo alakai e nee nei i keia manawa. (*Ka Nupepa Kuokoa* 1919)[37]

[For many reasons seen these days, we feel that it is right for the teaching of Japanese language to be stopped in the schools built by the Japanese throughout this Territory, because it opposes the American character that is desired by the federal government of all citizens living here.

It is completely inappropriate to see, at the time when United States law has granted citizen privileges to all the Japanese born here in Hawaiʻi, that they be taught their mother tongue and not English, the language befitting the American citizenship bestowed upon them, and especially whereas English is the leading language throughout America and all places under its domain.

We all cherished our own mother tongue, however, there are no schools now teaching our children Hawaiian language, for the reason that English is the leading language progressing at this time.]

The process of coercion, eventual compliance, and at least partial emulation was not uncontested, as evidenced by editorials and letters in the few remaining Hawaiian newspapers of the time. This editorial, printed just six years earlier, is far less accepting of the appropriateness of English primacy:

Ka, ea, he nui na manawa e hiki ai e loaa ia kakou he manawa e aʻo ai i ka kakou mau keiki i ka olelo a kona makuahine, o ka pilikia, ua lilo no na ka poe makemake e make ka lahui Hawaii ame ka lakou olelo, ke alakai ana. (*Ka Puuhonua o na Hawaii* 1917)

---

[37] Solomon Hanohano was the editor of *Kuokoa* at the time, but the editorial is unsigned so authorship is uncertain.

> [Ah! There are many times that we could gain the opportunity to teach our children their mother tongue, but the problem is that the leadership has gone to those wanting the Hawaiian people and their language to die.]

Though contested, coersive forces were effective, as shown by the many personal stories of *kūpuna* telling how Hawaiian was kept as a private language among their own elders, who then encouraged their children's exclusive use of English in school and at home. Thus, the government and educational system interlocked with other social institutions leading to changes in practice and an eventual, if uneven, hegemony.[38] Coercion alone could not fully undermine a people's language, but loss of national independence, personal freedom, and economic power embodied what novelist Ngugi wa Thiong'o refers to as a *cultural bomb*:

> The effect of a cultural bomb is to annihilate a people's belief in their names, in their languages, in their environments, in their heritage of struggle, in their unity, in their capacities and ultimately in themselves. It makes them see their past as one wasteland of nonachievement and it makes them want to distance themselves from that wasteland. (1989:3)

With the distancing of cultural participants, the academy, in a blend of direct and indirect power, takes on a larger role in framing the public's perspective as well as its own in many ways. It does so through financial or academic support for research and documentation, through the selected production, printing, and utilization of texts, by way of review systems, awards, and marketing, and by incorporation of certain forms of knowledge into curricula. Academic production, including the graduates themselves, becomes an important foundation for the knowledge that is available to the general public, the government, and other public and private institutions. The model the academy provides is mirrored and echoed throughout the broader public sphere.

Robert Nicole makes note of a 1990 bibliography of Tahitian literature that won the first-place award for French and francophone scholarship in the Pacific region, while listing only a few literary works in Tahitian, or Mā'ohi, on the last page. Nicole points out that the selection of this text for academic excellence, and

---

[38] The perpetuation of Hawaiian among Ni'ihau families, in a few isolated Hawaiian communities, and in some families elsewhere worked against hegemony, but remained almost liminal to the general population until the resurgence of interest in Hawaiian language in the last decades of the 20th century.

the support that the selection exemplifies, belies the relative importance of the two spheres of literature, French and Māʻohi, within that discourse (2001:1–3).

Similar institutional validation of selected resources established the Hawaiian canon. Archaeologist Ross Cordy's text, *Exalted Sits The Chief* (2000), was cited for Excellence in General Hawaiian Culture from the Hawaiʻi Book Publishers Association in 2001. His text, a history of the Islands focusing on Hawaiʻi island, openly contradicts and dismisses numerous and extensive Hawaiian-language accounts from the 19th century regarding voyaging traditions of ancient Hawaiians, a topic that was reconsidered in the work of archaeologist Kēhau Cachola-Abad in 1993, covered again in her work of 2000 and noted in her 2001 review.

Cordy's book summarizes analyses of many archaeological studies. In weaving his data into an historical narrative and analysis, he relies on dozens of early observer accounts while referring directly to only one source from the Hawaiian-language newspaper repository. The other Hawaiian sources he included are translations contained in the canon described here and government records drawn from the formal division of land, the Māhele, in 1848. The award for "excellence" in Hawaiian culture for a text which acknowledges and then dismisses most of the Hawaiian-language resources further elevates those minimal Hawaiian references which are relied upon, while marginalizing or obscuring the bulk of other available Hawaiian sources as irrelevant.

Dismissing Hawaiian traditions that conflict with findings and then garnering awards for cultural excellence embodies the nature of empirical presentation that Houston Wood addresses in his text *Displacing Natives* (1999), where he criticizes the nebulous and nefarious power of cross-cultural discourse in and about Hawaiʻi. Wood describes different styles of rhetorical presentation that prevail in every level of discourse, with *monorhetoric* representing the foundation of a Euroamerican epistemology that is linear, empirical, and intolerant of varying explanations. This he compares to *polyrhetoric*, a way of knowing that is inherently accepting of multi-linear, multi-dimensional understandings, and which he presents as being more resonant with Polynesian cultural sense. *Polyrhetoric*, then, "Produces compelling versions, but within a context where additional, equally compelling and contradictory versions are expected, even welcomed" (Wood 1999:149). A quote by journalist L. P. Kaleilehua from 1862 embodies Wood's observation: In responding to questions about a published legend straying from another known version, he replied "*Auwe! hookahi wale no anei halau i aoia'i?*" [Goodness! do you suppose it was only ever taught in one school?]

Wood makes a case for a modern setting and interpretation of polyrhetoric as practice, creating an intentional anathema to Euroamerican empiricism and linear thought in works created today. Wood's contemporary polyrhetoric and poly-vocalism already exists as a foundation in the historical pastiche of Hawaiian writings of the 19th and early 20th centuries which should be considered in light of the arguments in *Displacing Natives*. Such polyrhetoric is both a resource and a product, one that Pacific scholar Epeli Hauʻofa celebrates as a Pacific tradition of realigning history and narrative to an end:

> One of the more positive aspects of our existence in Oceania is that truth is flexible and negotiable, despite attempts by some of us to impose political, religious, and other forms of absolutism. (2000:454)

The problem that such a cacophony of often-conflicting historical voices has presented to a modern system of knowledge informed by linear epistemology and absolutism seems to have been solved for a long time; the answer has been simply not to create or maintain space for such multiple and disparate voices.

Discourse Shapes A Hawaiian Canon

The grand matrix of powers that for centuries framed and reified the whole global area of Said's *Orient* are, perhaps on a smaller scale, the same powers that have been interlaced with knowledge production in the Pacific and Hawaiʻi. Particular historical forces shaping the production of the Hawaiian written repository are addressed in the next chapter, but the forces involved in the selection of those writings for use today are considered here. Political science professor Michael Shapiro reiterates Foucault regarding the selection and validation of historical references: "He [Foucault] looks at what the statements *are* and why *they* rather than some other statements, conveying power for other kinds of subjects, are there" (1984:220, emphasis in the original). The question then remains as to why so many English-language resources are in place, while a mass of historical Hawaiian material is not only unapparent, but also remains inaccessible through research tools or translation.

English-language primacy is a powerful force framing knowledge in Hawaiʻi, but another force has been the general dismissal of the Hawaiian-language material by researchers and the general public, something that goes beyond simple prevalence of English. The overall body of existing materials written in Hawaiian lost recognition as an important or valid source of information, aborting any concerted efforts toward access, analysis, or incorporation.[39]

---

[39] Dr. Isabella Abbott, a Hawaiian practitioner and noted academic scholar, raises the possibility that the Hawaiian written record is viewed as an extension of oral tradition and thus easily dismissed as anecdotal.

From the emergence of English primacy at the close of the 19th century and throughout the 20th century, English and foreign-language sources have been sought out, assembled, translated, or generated anew in order to supply the growing need and power of the English-speaking population. Woven by intertextual support, each text affirming and informing the others, they become an interlocking fabric of ever-increasing strength. With the ascendancy of English, the development of English language "knowledge" about Hawai'i expanded dramatically, along with the tools of access to that knowledge, an expansion that excluded the available Hawaiian writings of the previous century. Such Hawaiian-language writings, and especially those considered here, were recognized early by some, but with minimal impact on the usage of those materials. Publisher Thomas Thrum, who extracted data and narrative from those sources to include in his own annual publications, often with no reference as to original author, publication source, or context, asserted the cultural value of writings in the independent native papers:

> Persons interested in the study of the usages, customs and beliefs of Hawaiians will find much instructive material thereon from their own writings in the native papers prior to 1870, notably in the scarce volumes of the *Kuokoa*. (1903)

Nearly a century after Thrum's observations about the value of the newspaper resources of the 1860s, Hawai'i newspaper historian Helen Chapin again noted the importance of the newspaper writings of the same period, referring to them as the Hawaiian nationalist press. Describing these early independent newspapers, she writes:

> The origin of a Hawaiian nationalist press—for such it was from its first day—is a striking illustration of literacy joined to a newspaper technology conferring empowerment. (1996:59)

In the ninety or more years between Thrum's observation and Chapin's affirmation, others have noted the value of this repository and it continues to gain attention, but still today, little of the Hawaiian material has been retrieved and more importantly, in a century, no framework has been established to identify and organize access to that body of material. No research tools, such as indexes, summaries, or translations have been created to facilitate access to the whole corpus of writings for the researcher, and no network has been put in place to store the data that has been uncovered by those who delve into the primary sources.[40]

In that span between Thrum and Chapin, the works of two Hawaiian columnists from that 1860s period were extracted, translated, and edited for English publication: S. M. Kamakau and John Papa ʻĪʻī. Both their peers and those of later generations recognized the works of these writers as important, and extracts of their works are central parts of the present-day canon. But little effort has been dedicated to incorporating the remainder of that material into contemporary reference tools.

Knowledge is fractured and multi-threaded, even hegemonic knowledge that overwrites and dismisses the unchosen. Alternative knowledges do persist and help to weave the different fabrics of academic, personal, and collective knowledge in Hawaiʻi today. While whole complexes of knowledge have undoubtedly been sundered in over two hundred years of change, and some survive only tenuously, the span is only a handful of lifetimes, and more has been maintained or developed than is officially recognized.

There are oral and written lines of knowledge that have extended over time via families, through communities, social or cultural groups, and intellectual lineages of mentors and their proteges. In addition to writing and newer technologies, knowledge is transmitted through stories, poetry, dances, music, artifacts, practices and the anecdotes that contextualize or illuminate each form.

Many of these forms of discourse are socially bounded, only accessible to members of a family, a hālau, students, protégés, or particular communities. All are histories that are incorporated into individual and collective understandings of the past, and as such, work to validate or disrupt the more general discourse that may not incorporate such knowledge. Geoff White mentions the important role these personal histories assume in a geographically-bounded setting like Hawaiʻi:

> Histories told and remembered by those who inherit them are discourses of identity: just as identity is inevitably a discourse of history.... Particularly in small island communities where individual and collective identities are so tightly bound, historical discourse locates both self and community within

---

[40] A random collection of materials culled and translated or summarized by Mary Kawena Pukui during her decades of service to the Bishop Museum are contained in her files, the Hawaiian Ethnographic Notes (H.E.N.); a survey collection of writings identified and copied from the Hawaiian newspapers under the direction of Larry Kimura are housed at Hamilton Library Special Collections, and listed at http://www2.hawaii.edu/~speccoll/hawaiilaiana.html; other, similar collections do exist, although there is no interface that connects the individual assemblies.

a nexus of relations between past and present, self and other. (1991:3–4)

The power of the printed text can overpower the personal or regional histories that White addresses above, creating tension between the individual and more generally accepted knowledge. This does not, however, have to be the case. These different forms of knowledge can be sought out and used to complement each other, as anthropologist Ben Finney describes in *The Sin of Avarua* (1992:12–16), where written accounts and lineage histories were combined to clarify, validate, and reconstruct an historic event at Taputapuātea, on Raʻiātea, in French Polynesia. Such integration is, unfortunately, rare.

Printed histories, especially when drawn repeatedly from a limited range of sources, echo and reflexively empower the dominant monorhetoric. Educator Manulani Meyer's work on Hawaiian epistemology, the framing and organization of knowledge, addresses the personal disarticulation that can arise when one's inherited knowledge conflicts with the repetitive presence of the officially learned:

> It is a strange world indeed, to wake up and realize that everything I have learned in school, everything I've read in books, every vocabulary test and jumping jack, every seating arrangement and response expectation—absolutely everything—has not been shaped by a Hawaiian mind. (2001:1)

English materials and processes inherently reflect an English mental framework, but when Hawaiian materials are reshaped to reinforce such a framework there is not only a loss of content, but also an erasure of alternate arrangements of knowledge. This kind of transformation is especially detrimental when the reshaping occurs without mention. The selective reorganization of S. M. Kamakau's texts in translation, discussed in Chapter 4 of this work, is one example of an epistemological overlay, where Hawaiian writings have clearly been reworked to fit and reinforce Western intellectual paradigms. The extraction of portions of ʻĪʻī's writings, covered in the same chapter, exhibits an even more dominant overwriting, one which not only reorganizes, but evaluates and dismisses whole portions of the original material. Such intentional, and unnoticeable, reshaping of material to fit a foreign paradigm of knowledge compounds processes that are already at work in the transition between languages.

One epistemological shift from Hawaiian to English-language framework of thought involves the alphabetical arrangement of text adopted by Hawaiians along with, or possibly before, the advent of literacy.[41] A good contrast is apparent when comparing the 1865 Hawaiian dictionary by Andrews, which was edited and enlarged in 1922 as the Andrews/Parker Hawaiian dictionary. The 1865 text, published in the Hawaiian Kingdom for a largely Hawaiian-speaking audience, was alphabetized in the conventional Hawaiian alphabetical order in use at the time: A, E, I, O, U, H, K, L, M, N, P, W. Possibly drawn from Hawaiian word arrangement in the oral tradition, but definitely incorporated in early Hawaiian literacy, this alphabetical order was utilized by 19th-century Hawaiians in their published works and is also seen in their personal writings.[42] When the dictionary was republished and expanded in the Territory of Hawai'i, it was reorganized in the American alphabetical order—A, E, H, I, K, L, M, N, O, P, U, W (Andrews and Parker 1922). English speakers find the kingdom-era Andrews text baffling.[43]

The alphabetical arrangement gives a good illustration of how language change affects the way knowledge is organized. While this example is overt and tangible, other inherent changes in the way knowledge is presented or made understandable are far less distinct. The focus in Hawaiian language on action, occurance, or condition over actor, and the related importance of passive description are reversed in English, where emphasis on the actor or agent is the norm. Translation makes those changes invisible.

These more organic processes are already at work behind the intentional reorganization that has occurred in most translations, and both kinds of processes have accompanied the transition from Hawaiian to English-language dominance. While it facilitates ready comprehension for English readers and speakers, the intellectual bridges required to reach the source material must span both language and cultural ways of knowing. Already difficult to find in the largely-uncharted, Hawaiian-language archives, source materials in archaic and culturally dense forms of the language are then also framed in an unfamiliar fashion. Such compound difficulties have helped make the handful of already-translated sources into invaluable reference material for modern scholars—the canon.

---

[41] Evidence that would provide dating for such linguistic arrangement might be documented in old *mele* and other traditional recitation forms, or comments about such cognitive framing may have been reported in early foreigners' observations, but no examples have come to light.

[42] Such alphabetical arrangement is common in published examples, but it was apparently the norm in private use as well, as seen in the journal of Rev. J. Hapuku, in entries for November 1860, p. 237. Manuscript copy in the archives of Societé de Études Océaniens, Papeete, Tahiti.

[43] The recent republication of Andrews' original form of the dictionary (Andrews 1865) has generated a new wave of anecdotes about people using the text and finding words to be out of order or missing, when they actually are included, but appear in a Hawaiian ordering.

2 | Shaping Power: Creation of the Hawaiian Canon

Discursive powers and practices helped shape a recognized canon of Hawaiian historical and cultural texts. The canon referred to here is made up of translations based on the works from four Hawaiian authors from the mid-19th century: Davida Malo (1903), *Hawaiian Antiquities;* Kepelino (1932), *Kepelino's Traditions of Hawaii*; John Papa ʻĪʻī (1959), *Fragments of Hawaiian History;* and Samuel Mānaiakalani Kamakau (1961, 1964, 1976, and 1991), *Ruling Chiefs of Hawaii, Ka Poʻe Kahiko: The People of Old, The Works of the People of Old: Na Hana a ka Poʻe Kahiko,* and *Tales and Traditions of the People of Old: Na Moʻolelo o ka Poʻe Kahiko.* These translations have been touchstone resources for years in most fields of study related to Hawaiʻi; in order to exhibit adequate research, a writer, researcher, or presenter is expected to have consulted one or more of these texts. In most scholarship or research, including curriculum at every level of education, any reference to the canon apparently represents sufficient investigation into Hawaiian sources.

Within the setting of English primacy, certain contextual factors helped to generate and foster the cumulative power of the Hawaiian canon. These factors include the relative vacuum of Hawaiian resources into which the English texts emerged, the imprimatur of the presenting institution, an absence of contradiction or disagreement between the texts, and the apparent authority of the individual authors and texts themselves. Each of these four factors became and remained applicable as translations were published and the canon developed in the course of a century. These factors worked to reinforce the authority of the individual and collective English publications. At the same time, the growing presence and the manner in which each text articulated with and strengthened the other texts of the canon diminished the impetus to search beyond the published English translations to seek out the original writings or to isolate other original sources.[44]

A Vacuum of Hawaiian Resources

At the opening of the 20th century, English language texts translated from Hawaiian writers were limited. Throughout the 19th century and up through the first years of the 20th century, few secular texts had been created by Hawaiian writers outside of the newspaper venue, and only a handful had ever been translated and published in English, and yet the growing population in the new Territory and eventual State of Hawai'i[45] was increasingly made up of English speakers, and English language texts were in demand.

Reverend Sheldon Dibble's *Ka Mooolelo Hawaii* (1838), an edited collection of cultural and historical writings by Hawaiian scholars from Lahainaluna College, appeared in English translation three times, first in 1839, then again in 1843.[46] S. M. Kamakau's weekly column of historical writings for *Ka Nupepa Kuokoa* of 1866 (1866b) began to appear in translation in the *Hawaiian Gazette*

---

[44] It is important to acknowledge the extensive efforts of the Bishop Museum and their staff throughout the 20th century in developing materials for an English-speaking public and to recognize that the context in which those materials emerged has continued to change over time. This discussion is not intended to in any way diminish the value of those individual and institutional efforts.

[45] Population, which in 1890 was less than 100,000, a majority of whom were Hawaiian, doubled within the first decade of territorial status, and by the time of statehood had exceeded one-half million. Population has continued to expand to the roughly 1.2 million current residents in the Islands.

[46] Credited to Hawaiian scholars but edited by their instructor, Sheldon Dibble, *Ka Mooolelo Hawaii* was translated first by Rev. Reuben Tinker for the journal *The Hawaiian Spectator* (Tinker 1839) and later continued in *The Polynesian* (Tinker 1840). The text was translated again by Rev. Dibble for publication as a book, *The History of the Sandwich Islands* (Dibble 1843). A third translation, by D. Kahananui, was later published through the University of Hawai'i Committee for the Preservation and Study of Hawaiian Language, Art, and Culture, 1984.

in 1868, but copyright issues were quickly raised, and the English publication was curtailed.[47] Abraham Fornander's *An Account of the Polynesian Race* (1878–1885) drew on numerous Hawaiian sources, and included Hawaiian chants with translation, but the three volumes were essentially contained in English texts.

A few chant texts, notably the *Kumulipo*, an epic Hawaiian chant of creation, were translated into German and eventually English, and some periodicals, mostly *Thrum's Annual*, included translated chants and cultural or historical extracts from a variety of often unacknowledged Hawaiian sources. A book of legends by King Kalākaua (1888) was written in English and included edited and expanded forms of stories, some of which had appeared in the Hawaiian press, but they were retellings and summaries rather than translations of the originals. As the 20th century opened, no other substantial cultural or historical texts generated by Hawaiian writers had been brought to an English audience, although numerous English texts had been published, some of which, like Fornander, Thrum, and Kalākaua, drew data or excerpts from Hawaiian language sources.[48]

Davida Malo

The publication of Davida Malo's *Ka Mooolelo Hawaii* in English translation as *Hawaiian Antiquities* appears to be the first complete published translation of a scholarly text known to be the original work of a single Hawaiian writer.[49] As such, it was a breakthrough in Hawaiian resources for English-language readers (Malo 1903).[50] Publication of Malo's work by Bishop Museum, the primary institution worldwide for the study and documentation of Hawaiian history and culture, granted authority and scholarly gravity to the work, while illuminating the

---

[47] The translations, heavily edited, appeared in five consecutive columns of the *Hawaiian Gazette* (1868a). An editorial raising the copyright issue appeared in the *Pacific Commercial Advertiser* (1868), the *Hawaiian Gazette* denied the charge (*Hawaiian Gazette* 1868b), and a third editorial on the same topic appeared in *Ke Au Okoa* (A. L. 1868), after which publication of the English was terminated. According to the editorial in *Pacific Commercial Advertiser* (1868), Kamakau began his historical series in the Hawaiian newspapers at the insistence of Judge Lorrin Andrews, who intended to translate the material into English and publish it in book form, a project that was never completed.

[48] See Forbes (1999–2002) for extensive bibliographies of Hawaiian material.

[49] The publications are presented here in the order in which they were published in English.

[50] *Ka Mooolelo Hawaii* was translated and extensively annotated by Nathaniel B. Emerson; the work was then further edited by W. D. Alexander for English publication. Purchase of the manuscript and translation by Bishop Museum made those texts available to researchers at the museum and eventually through microfilm copies elsewhere. In the 1971 reprinting, Dr. Alexander Spoehr points out that in the 1903 and 1951 English publications it was difficult to tell where the work of Malo left off and that of Emerson began, and he directed readers to the microfilm or the holograph for clarification (Spoehr in Malo 1971:xxi). A recent republication of Malo in translation by Malcolm Chun (Malo 1987) is problematic and has not replaced the referential use of Emerson's earlier text.

Davida Malo was born in 1793 at Keauhou, Hawaiʻi, during Kamehameha's wars of conquest. He was almost 40 and already literate in both English and Hawaiian when he entered the first class of students at Lahainaluna in 1831. Malo was respected as a teacher and historian, and became an important advisor to the king and ruling chiefs during the reign of Kamehameha III, bridging the knowledge of the past to the events of that rapidly-changing era. His writings about Hawaiian culture were shared in manuscript form during his lifetime, but were published in translation, and eventually in Hawaiian, during the 20th century. Engraving by W. H. Dougal, after A. T. Agate, 19th century. Ray Jerome Baker Collection, Bishop Museum.

museum's collections.[51] This same museum imprimatur granted scholarly authority to each of the subsequent texts in the Hawaiian canon discussed in this study.

Davida Malo was acknowledged as one of the rare Hawaiian writers who could describe from first-hand experience the customs and practices of pre-Christian Hawai'i (Malo 1971:viii–xv). While observer accounts of early Hawai'i were widely available from explorers, missionaries, traders, or visitors, Malo offered the perspective of a Hawaiian participant, which was a new and valuable resource for those readers and researchers who did not speak Hawaiian. Unfortunately, the Hawaiian text was not included in the publication, and Malo's manuscript was available only to recognized scholars at Bishop Museum, excluding most of the Hawaiian population.[52]

A Changing Audience

The audience for which *Hawaiian Antiquities* was published was far different than those few who had access to a manuscript of *Ka Mooolelo Hawaii*.[53] By 1903 the use of English language was universal in local academic institutions and growing among the population in the Islands, and Hawaiian language, while still common among adult Hawaiians, was diminishing. Production of Hawaiian-language materials was declining along with the Hawaiian-speaking population. A small surge of Hawaiian-language publications appeared in the first decade after annexation,[54] but the Hawaiian-language presence declined rapidly soon after.

In 1910, there were 54 locally-generated periodicals in print, mostly newspapers and newsletters, but also including magazines and journals. Of these, 9 were Hawaiian-language newspapers, 3 were bilingual in English and Hawaiian, and 16 exclusively in English. The other 26 periodicals served immigrant communities of Japanese, Portuguese, Chinese, Koreans, and Filipinos, some being bilingual with English and one being trilingual in Japanese, English, and Filipino. A decade later, Hawaiian papers numbered 6 out of 56, with three others being

---

[51] The dual intention of such publication on the museum's part is discussed in Emerson (1898).

[52] For two decades now, Bishop Museum Library and Archives have been open to the public on at least a limited basis, but prior to that, access was largely restricted to professional researchers and recognized scholars.

[53] Multiple holograph copies of Malo's manuscript exist.

[54] The number of Hawaiian-language books and short-run periodicals appearing in the first few years of the 20th century are all trade publications, rather than academic productions, dealing mostly with biography, legendary material, and some cultural practice description. They present an interesting historical aspect with social and political implications about the Hawaiian-speaking population of the period. No bibliography has been completed for the decade, but these rare texts, obscure today, deserve further study as indicated here.

bilingual, English and Hawaiian. By 1930, two Hawaiian and two Hawaiian and English papers were in print along with 54 other periodicals. In 1940, 68 periodicals were in press, with two Hawaiian-language weeklies and one Hawaiian and English; English periodicals numbered 27. Of the 38 remaining periodicals, many of which were bilingual with English, 15 were Japanese, 6 were Chinese, 3 were Korean, and 13 were Filipino. English periodicals from abroad would have added substantially to the growing imbalance.

While Hawaiian language periodicals diminished, Hawaiian language books all but disappeared after the first decade of the 20th century. Following the 1898 annexation and through 1910, only a handful of Hawaiian language books were produced. John Sheldon's account of Kaluaikoʻolau (1906) and biography of Joseph Nāwahī (1908) were the lengthiest Hawaiian-language books in that decade. None of the Hawaiian-language texts were produced by the educational institutions of the time, each being private or commercial publications. In contrast, books in English on every topic about Hawaiʻi became a booming industry, produced locally and nationally in the U.S., from commercial and academic presses. The publication of Malo's *Hawaiian Antiquities* presented a unique resource in this setting.

English speakers here and abroad were interested in the new Territory and eager for information about Hawaiʻi, its history, and people. Published books on every aspect of territorial life appeared, some preceding and anticipating formal territorial status.[55] English newspapers and magazines included numerous articles about Hawaiian traditions, legends, noted places, or historical figures and events, offering nostalgia for long-term residents or those born in the Islands, while educating the growing influx of those immigrating to the new U.S. territory. *Thrum's Annual*, an almanac of business, weather, agriculture, and population data, included many such articles, searchable today through its indexes. Most were generated and submitted in English, but others were translated or recast from earlier sources, especially the Hawaiian language newspapers of the previous century. Similar content filled the pages of other English periodicals of the early Territory period, such as *Paradise of the Pacific,* a popular glossy monthly magazine focused on Island lifestyles in the changing territory.

Articles written in English and published in *Thrum's Annual* and *Paradise of the Pacific* routinely acknowledged the author and source, as was the case with some of the material extracted from the Hawaiian papers. However, many such

---

[55] See Musick (1898). See Bacchilega (2007) for detailed discussion on how this new market helped to generate a "legendary Hawaiʻi" that worked to further obscure the history, culture, people, and language, compounding the overall effect of English dominance.

translated articles, including pieces drawn from newspaper columns of the 1860s by S. M. Kamakau or John Papa ʻĪʻī, were unidentified or referenced only by original publication date.[56] Other unacknowledged sources were summarized or rewritten in English rather than being translated. Such anonymity had the effect of mystifying the original sources, and of diminishing the authority and recognition of the original authors. The regular inclusion of historical and cultural tidbits about the earlier eras of Hawaiʻi did, however, feed a growing interest among the English-speaking audience.

Abraham Fornander

In 1916, Thomas Thrum completed a task begun years earlier by W. D. Alexander of editing for publication Abraham Fornander's extensive collection of "Hawaiian mythology, traditions, meles and genealogies" (Fornander 1916–1920). Judge Abraham Fornander, the author of *An Account of the Polynesian Race* (1878–1885) who had passed away in 1887, assembled his collection of "antiquarian and traditional lore" throughout his residency in the islands and especially during the last thirty years of his life.[57] The materials included his own research and that of others, as well as articles culled from Hawaiian newspapers and special accounts written for him by Hawaiian scholars who were paid for their efforts. Three large volumes, appearing in eight separate publications, were published as a series of Bishop Museum Memoirs, beginning in 1916 and ending in 1920 (Fornander 1916–1920).

The *Fornander Collection of Hawaiian Antiquities and Folk-lore*, published for the most part in Hawaiian and English, established the then-most extensive body of Hawaiian legends, historical accounts, traditional practices, and chants published. The assembly is large, and drawn from varied sources, many of them noted authorities of their time. These Hawaiian authorities, including Kelou Kamakau, John Papa ʻĪʻī, S. N. Haleʻole, Kepelino, and S. M. Kamakau, are often only indirectly acknowledged, and most of the larger sections of the collection are anonymous.

---

[56] For an example where both the author and date of publication go unacknowledged, see Thrum's publication of the legend of Punaaikoae (Thrum 1912:117–125), which is drawn in entirety from ʻĪʻī, Sept. 4 and 11, 1869, *Ka Nupepa Kuokoa*. For an example of citing date but not author, see Thrum (1919:84–89), which is drawn from the writings of Kamakau, Dec. 29, 1866 and Jan. 5, 1867, *Ka Nupepa Kuokoa*.

[57] Abraham Fornander came to Hawaiʻi in 1838, but did not permanently settle in the islands until 1842. He died in 1887.

Born in Sweden in 1812, Abraham Fornander came to Hawai'i as a whaler and became a Hawaiian citizen in 1847. During his career as a journalist, school superintendent, and judge, he collected cultural and historical materials, publishing a three-volume account of Polynesian and Hawaiian migration and history. His full collection of cultural writings was translated and published after his death (see bibliography). Photographer unknown, ca. 1865, Bishop Museum.

In spite of the variety of sources, however, there is a certain homogeneity to the language style of Hawaiian used throughout most of the collection; much of the Hawaiian narrative material seems to have been rewritten in what appears to be Fornander's personal style or idiolect. Alexander, Thrum, or both then further edited this material for consistency. Because of the multiple sources, anonymity of ethnographic material, and rewriting of text, the *Fornander Collection of Hawaiian Folk-lore* is not included in the canon of Hawaiian authors being considered in this work.

The publication of Fornander's material did fuel a steadily growing interest in Hawaiian culture and lore at the time of its publication and was embraced as a new and important Hawaiian source, yet the Fornander collection has not been as used as a scholarly reference in the same way as the works of the four authors in the canon addressed here. His folklore works and his writings from *An Account of the Polynesian Race*, however, have been incorporated as support materials to the texts in the canon.

MARTHA BECKWITH

During the opening decades of the 20th century, Martha Beckwith, a scholar working with the Smithsonian Institute and Vassar College, added to the small and growing body of Hawaiian literature in English with her publication of legend texts. In 1919, 1923, 1928, and again in 1936, she published translations of Hawaiian legends and wise sayings, some from earlier written sources and others from island storytellers still living at the time.[58] Perhaps because they were viewed as "creative fiction"[59] or the collected and edited "folklore" of 20th-century informants, Beckwith's publications did not become part of the modern canon.

Nonetheless, Beckwith's body of work with Hawaiian materials and her long collaboration with Native Hawaiian scholar Mary Kawena Pukui helped to shape the Hawaiian canon as it is known today. Her presentation of materials

---

[58] Beckwith, Martha Warren, *The Hawaiian Romance of Laieikawai*, introduction and translation by M. Beckwith, published in *Thirty-third Annual Report of the Bureau of American Ethnology to the Secretary of the Smithsonian Institution*, 1911–1912, Washington: Government Printing Office, 1919, 285–666, original text by S. N. Haleʻole, Honolulu, 1863; and Beckwith, ed. *Hawaiian Stories and Wise Sayings*, Vassar College, 1923, republished 1926; *Folk-Tales from Hawaii*, 1928, and *The Legend of Kawelo and Other Hawaiian Folk Tales* (1936). The short stories from Pukui in these texts were edited for republication in *Folktales of Hawaiʻi: He Mau Kaʻao Hawaiʻi*, Bishop Museum Press, 1995.

[59] Haleʻole's *Laieikawai*, a traditional legendary account, was assembled in writing for the newspapers and then published in book form. Although acknowledged as the first published book of indigenous Hawaiian literature, this distinction overlooks the importance of the many serialized newspaper publications.

under the separate rubrics of legend and mythology, history, and culture show evidence of a different epistemological framework than that in which the original materials were found, a point discussed in Chapter 4 with reference to the processes affecting extracted texts.

Martha Beckwith (pictured on the left with an unknown woman) was the first chair of any American Folklore department. Born in 1871 in Massachusetts, she lived in Hawai'i as a child and grew up with a great respect for Hawaiian culture, which influenced her entire academic career. A respected pioneer of folklore studies, she compiled, translated, or edited many books drawn from Hawaiian history and lore. Photographer unknown, ca. 1935, Bishop Museum.

Like Fornander's volumes of folklore described above, Beckwith's books were published bilingually with Hawaiian and English text on facing pages, a rare contrast to the many monolingual English texts about Hawaiian cultural and historical material. Beckwith was hoping to foster bilingual presentation as a norm in translated Hawaiian texts, as indicated in her 1932 publication of a manuscript by Kepelino and in her correspondence regarding future publications planned with Bishop Museum (Beckwith 1932, 1949a, 1949b). A bilingual format was academically valuable, but it was one that the museum and other publishers apparently did not embrace. For over fifty years after *Kepelino's Traditions of Hawaii* appeared, publications of translated works were presented only in English. Bilingual presentations did not reach publication again until the resurgence of interest in Hawaiian created a new demand within the last two or three decades.

Kepelino

In 1932, Martha Beckwith published her translation of an undated manuscript by Kepelino, who was noted in the book for "telling of Hawaiian tradition as it was preserved in the monarchy" (Beckwith 1932:6). Beckwith acknowledged in her introduction that great changes had occurred prior to and during Kepelino's lifetime, which ended in 1878, by which time Hawai'i had experienced one hundred years of Western influence. She nevertheless introduced her translation with this expansive evaluation of Kepelino's work:

> It is evident that the description here given of old Hawaiian worship and of Hawaiian religious conceptions is certainly *uninfluenced* by Christian thought. (1932:7, emphasis added.)

With the publication of *Kepelino's Traditions of Hawaii*, Kepelino, as Malo before him, was given great credence as a first-hand source, especially for providing insight into the continuity of Hawaiian traditions from the early decades of sustained Western contact through the monarchy era. Kepelino's manuscript, like the Fornander collection and Beckwith's legends text, had the added quality of a typescript of the original Hawaiian text on facing pages with its translation, the last bilingual text of its kind produced for nearly fifty years.

John Papa 'Ī'ī

After Kepelino, a quarter of a century passed before another comprehensive work by a Hawaiian author was available to English-language readers. In 1959, as the Territory of Hawai'i was becoming a state, *Fragments of Hawaiian History,*

John Papa ʻĪʻī was raised in the court of Kamehameha I as a retainer and companion for the king's son and heir, Liholiho. He served five kings, and was regarded as a trusted advisor in the innermost government and chiefly circles until his retirement during the reign of Kamehameha V. During his career, he had been an educator, judge, administrator, and commissioner, in addition to his roles on the Privy Council and in the Legislature. His knowledge of the pre-Christian era and his insight into the important events of the past accentuate the importance of his historical writings, most of which were published as memoirs in the newspapers after his retirement. Daguerrotype, photographer unknown, ca. 1851, Bishop Museum.

drawn from the writings of John Papa ʻĪʻī, was published. It presented detailed accounts of his youth in the royal court, the activities of the chiefs, and the traditional practices he witnessed or learned. ʻĪʻī had published his writings in the newspaper *Kuokoa* from 1868 until his death in 1870, and like Malo before him, was appreciated and acknowledged for his insight into the pre-Christian era. His reminiscences included his personal experiences of life in the court of Kamehameha I and carried the credibility of one who had been in the innermost government circles of five kings until his retirement from public service in 1864. Published reviews at the time of the English publication lauded the insight ʻĪʻī brought to the field and linked "his" work as part of the growing, recognized canon:

> Except for the account of the early part of the regime of Kamehameha I which doubtlessly he heard from first-hand sources, his descriptions are based on the actual experiences of a participant or an eyewitness. The accounts are those of normal performances, often very personal and full of detail, rather than the somewhat idealized, objective formulas of Malo, Kepelino and Fornander. (Scobie 1961:253–254)

ʻĪʻī's writings were said to offer, for the first time in translation, historical data about the chiefs, "as seen through Hawaiian eyes" (ibid:254).

Samuel Mānaiakalani Kamakau

In the 1930s, while Kepelino's manuscript was being prepared for print and long before ʻĪʻī's writings had been extracted for translation, work had already begun on the collection and translation of years of weekly columns by Samuel Mānaiakalani Kamakau, the fourth and most published author in the modern canon. Kamakau was a prolific writer, and because of the extent of his writings, and his "florid literary style," the effort to coordinate and complete a collaborative translation project took several years (Kent 1961:ix).[60]

Kawena Pukui and Martha Beckwith completed the laborious editing of various translators' works by 1934, but the manuscript languished for decades, and the first section of the work, *Ruling Chiefs of Hawaii*, was not published until 1961. It took another thirty years to complete the publication of his selected and translated writings from the 1860s as three more separate texts, *Ka Poʻe Kahiko: The People of Old* (1964); *The Works of the People of Old: Na Hana a ka Poʻe Kahiko* (1976); and *Tales and Traditions of the People of Old* (1991). The division of content

---

[60] See Chapter 4 for more details on the processes of publication relating to this text.

Samuel Mānaiakalani Kamakau, of Mokulēʻia, Oʻahu, was born in 1815 and entered Lahainaluna in 1833. Trained as a teacher and a historian, he helped establish Ka ʻAhahui ʻImi I Ka Mea Kahiko O Hawaiʻi Nei, the Royal Hawaiian Historical Society, in 1841 with the sponsorship of Kamehameha III. A teacher and legislator who also held various government offices, he is best known for his prodigious writings about genealogy, history, and culture. Although he wrote in the Hawaiian newspapers for over thirty years, Kamakau's serial columns on Hawaiian history from 1865 to 1871 are his best-known works. Translations of these historical writings have been the source of several English publications. Artist unknown, 19th century, Bishop Museum.

that resulted in these four texts bore little connection to the sequence in which the original serial columns were presented from 1865 to 1871 (see Chapter 4).

The first text, *Ruling Chiefs of Hawaii,* brought together the historical writings of Kamakau from his serial columns of 1865–1871, writings which had long been referred to by such writers as Thrum, Fornander, and Alexander. It was presented as the long-awaited work by the last member to be published of "a trio of outstanding Hawaiian historians" (Spoehr 1961:viii), the other two being ʻĪʻī and Malo. The implication of the completed triad of recognized Hawaiian historians added to the authority of the works by these three men, while obscuring or dismissing the rest of the Hawaiian writers. The new data that Kamakau's historical material added to the field was said to show how "a scholar of Hawaiian ancestry interpreted the history of his people and something as to how he felt about it" (ibid).

Articulation of Texts

Three years later, in 1964, another selection from Kamakau's newspaper accounts was published as *Ka Poʻe Kahiko: The People of Old.* The introduction to this second text describes how the cultural material culled from S. M. Kamakau's historical accounts[61] articulated with the earlier publications of Malo and ʻĪʻī to generate a clearer picture of the "Hawaiian world of old." In her introduction to the book, Dorothy Barrère wrote:

> Davida Malo, in the classic work *Hawaiian Antiquities,* gave a broad outline of the ancient culture; John Ii's personal experiences, recounted in *Fragments of Hawaiian History,* revealed the functioning of that culture. *Ka Poʻe Kahiko* now adds those details which give new depth and meaning to these two works. The three are a composite picture of Hawaiian beliefs and customs as they were in the ancient days and in the transitional period of acculturation to introduced thoughts and concepts. (1964:viii)

---

[61] The "historical" material, like the "cultural" material from Kamakau's serial columns, was originally published in a continuous series from Oct. 20, 1866 to Feb. 2, 1871 as weekly installments, beginning in *Ka Nupepa Kuokoa* and then continuing in *Ke Au Okoa.* The material was extracted, translated and edited for publication as the historical reference text *Ruling Chiefs* (Kamakau 1961). Changes in the text during the process of extraction and editing are detailed in Chapter 4 of this book.

Barrère is a scholar and author noted for her extensive research in Hawaiian-language resources of the 19th century. As her own works reflect, she did not consider these three translated texts, making up "a composite picture," to be the only picture necessary, and one that would be sufficient for all cultural research pertaining to Hawai'i; the objective, rather, was to provide an introductory overview or a point of entry for those embarking on a study in the field.[62] However, an examination of the discourse of sufficiency shows that her comments came to be interpreted literally for decades to follow. For most researchers it seems the texts in hand embodied a sufficiently "composite picture," one, like Houston Wood's "monorhetoric," which contained all the necessary truths.

The limited number of original Hawaiian materials available in English, coupled with the clear assurance that those available were an articulated, complete set, or a "composite picture," helped to establish the sufficiency of those texts discussed in this study. Reviews of *Ka Po'e Kahiko* expounded on how Kamakau's writings worked in contrast and collaboration with the previous publications of Malo and 'Ī'ī :

> Rather than producing an over-all pattern of ancient Hawaiian society like that delineated by Davida Malo in *Hawaiian Antiquities,* or an eye-witness account of its functioning of the type recorded by John Papa Ii in *Fragments of Hawaiian History,* Kamakau is concerned mainly with the fundamental principles which validated the practices of "the people of old." It is therefore complementary to the other two works, and enriches them with further details. (Scobie 1966:248)

Emphasis was given on how this new text, in unison with the two earlier publications, helped clarify the available picture, again addressing a single, more detailed, composite picture:

> The real value of Kamakau, however, lies in the critical way he examines a wide range of magico-religious beliefs, frequently amplifying their description, and giving accounts of their practices. In this manner he confirms and extends much that has been recorded by other Hawaiian writers, as well as filling in gaps, and reduces many obscurities. This is good material which can be adapted readily by students interested in establishing a more complete picture of "the people of old." (ibid:249)

---

[62] Dorothy B. Barrère, personal communication, 2001.

The authority granted to these English publications empowered their adequacy for scholarship and general understanding. The review quoted above, from the prestigious *Journal of the Polynesian Society*, went on to mention the growing number of persons interested in Polynesian material, the difficulty of utilizing the original sources, and the value of their assembly and publication in English. The implication being that the work had been completed, the scattered pieces assembled:

> Many contemporary observations of old Hawaii are hidden in articles in early newspapers and periodicals. They are widely scattered, and frequently in the Hawaiian language. In gathering them together and presenting them in a readily available form, the Bishop Museum is rendering a valuable service to an ever-increasing range of students of Polynesia. (ibid:248)

Ka Poʻe Kahiko was followed about a decade later with another translated portion of Kamakau's columns, *The Works of the People of Old: Na Hana a ka Poʻe Kahiko* (1976). This text also focused on culture rather than history, but it was Hawaiian material culture that framed the selected writings, rather than social systems. Dorothy Barrère, editor of the last three Kamakau publications as well as the ʻĪʻī text, identified links between Kamakau's work on material culture and those of other writers of his time, like Malo, Dibble, and Pogue. She pointed out how, in every instance, Kamakau added a great amount of new data to the existing descriptions and functions of Hawaiian material culture, showing this text to be superior to other writers and encompassing their works. The composite picture was thus enhanced, but its focus was not altered or contradicted, an insight echoed in a review of the book by Donna Dickerson, in *American Anthropologist*, calling it:

> An in-depth ethnohistorical/ethnographic description of pre-European Hawaii, originally written in the nineteenth century as the last remnants of native culture began to vanish. Kamakau provides much valuable data on Polynesian subsistence and agricultural patterns, also technology, language, myth, ritual, calendrics, dwellings and attire. (1977:187)

Finally, in 1991, the remaining translated sections of Kamakau's serial columns were assembled and published as *Tales and Traditions of the People of Old*. Translated and edited nearly sixty years earlier, these selections were again edited for publication by Dorothy Barrère, who acknowledged the diversity of the subject matter as an assembly of earlier omissions (1991:ix).[63] Legends and historical sections of this text had been incorporated piecemeal into English texts for over a century as primary sources for authors such as Fornander, Thrum, and Westervelt.

The presentation of each of the books that became the Hawaiian canon stressed the unique authority of each writer to present his views[64] of Hawaiian history and culture, and emphasized the quality of the translation bringing it into English. Selection and editing of each subsequent text maximized the intertextual support of each for its predecessors, and minimized the potential contradictions or conflicts that could have arisen. Publication of each text by Bishop Museum provided another implicit acknowledgment of the scholarly quality of the resources.[65]

Cultural Authority

The authors whose translated works make up the canon were considered to be remarkable resources by their own contemporaries during their lifetimes. Each of them was acknowledged and honored for their knowledge, and sought out and relied upon as experts by their peers, their governments, and their churches. In each case, the materials that were extracted to become English books were from writings composed at the behest of their contemporaries who insisted that they document the body of knowledge for which they were respected. The cultural authority of four authors is discussed below in the order in which translations of their works were published.

Davida Malo, enrolled in the first class of adult students at Lahainaluna, was a noted scholar and genealogist well recognized by his contemporaries.[66] He quickly came to the attention of the mission teachers for his intelligence, his knowledge, and the respect he gained from the chiefs, as expressed in this note from missionary William Richards, a noted translator and teacher of the chiefs:

---

[63] The critical role of the editor, Dorothy Barrère, in selection of material for inclusion or omission in each of the last four canon texts is a topic worthy of careful consideration, but beyond the scope of this study.

[64] The focus of this study is the written record from the 19th and early 20th century, an archive of native auto-representation that is clearly male-dominated. The miniscule representation of women in the written discourse of the period raises a number of valuable issues that should guide further research in the field.

[65] This is not to say that such presentation was unwarranted. The works of these four authors were carefully selected, translated, and edited according to the standards, systems, and scholars in place under the umbrella of Bishop Museum over the span of nearly a century. The selection of these authors as important resources is unquestioned; it is the isolation of these authors to the exclusion of all other Hawaiian writers that is problematic.

[66] All of the first classes of students at Lahainaluna were made up of adult students, selected by district chiefs and missionary referrals.

> [Davida Malo] is among the most intelligent of the people and a most valuable assistant in translating his knowledge of his own language, is thorough, is able to give authorities for his use of words by reference to ancient meles [songs] and kanikaus [grief chants], is a valuable member of the church, is often consulted by the chiefs on important business and is esteemed by them as a good counselor. (1828a)

Kepelino was considered to be a cultural expert during his life, the son of Namiki, whose interviews made up much of Jules Remy's historical account,[67] which was published in English as *Contributions of a Venerable Savage* (1868). An important cultural resource for his Catholic teachers, a few of his cultural writings were published in *Hoiliili Havaii* in 1858.[68] The manuscript that became *Kepelino's Traditions of Hawaii* was said to be drafted at the request of Bishop Maigret and possibly written down by him following the dictation of Kepelino. Basil Kirtley, a University of Hawai'i English professor, and Esther Mo'okini, a researcher and translator, expressed this about Kepelino:

> [He] belongs with S. M. Kamakau, David Malo, and John Papa Ii in the front rank of native-born preservers and interpreters of the islands' ancient culture. Since his chiefly family (Kahoaliikumaieiwakamoku: to-be-chief-of-the-nine-districts), traced descent from the legendary priest Pa'ao, and was closely related to Kamehameha I, surviving remnants of the old hieratical knowledge inevitably became part of his legacy. (1977:39)

John Papa 'Ī'ī held the esteem of his chiefs and his peers throughout his life and was often heralded as an example of integrity, ability, and knowledge. After meeting with the delegation of Hawaiian missionaries working in the Marquesan islands, Reverend Kekela, a leader of the Marquesan mission effort, wrote of the man in glowing terms:

> Nani kuu pomaikai nui i ka halawai ana me Ioane Ii, a i kuu lohe ana i kana mau olelo ao, a olelo paipai, a mau Haiao, nui

---

[67] J. Remy, *Ka Mooolelo Hawaii. Histoire de l'archipel havaiien (iles Sandwich); texte et traduction précédés d'une introduction sur l'état physique, moral et politique du pays*; Pub. Franz Leipzig, Paris, 1862.

[68] Translation of a portion of this text is in Kirtley and Mo'okini (1977).

ko'u hilahila, no ka mea, ua oi kona makaukau i ko'u, a ua hemahema loa au. (1865)

[I am richly blessed in having met John 'Ī'ī, and upon my hearing his advice, his encouragements and sermons, I am greatly humbled, because his ability is beyond mine, and in comparison I am quite lacking.]

S. M. Kamakau, a younger contemporary of Malo's at Lahainaluna and a fellow founding member of the Hawaiian Historical Association in 1848, was regarded as a leading cultural scholar of his time, meticulous with his large repository of knowledge. John Papa 'Ī'ī, who shared Kamakau's active dedication to history and culture, and wrote columns for the same paper, apparently spoke of him in clear admiration. In a letter by Reverend Elia Helekunihi, an authority on traditional healing, he tells how 'Ī'ī responded to his query regarding the accuracy of Kamakau's historical accounts:

["]He kupanaha keia kanaka["] wahi ia John Ii. ["]Me he la ua ike maka, paanaau na mea apau, na wahi a'u i hele ai me na 'lii Kauikeaouli—Kaahumanu, mehe la oiala kekahi, he uuku loa na mea hemahema.["] (1893)

["This man is amazing," said John 'Ī'ī. "It's as though he personally witnessed and memorized everything, the places I went with the chiefs, Kauikeaouli—Ka'ahumanu; it's as though he too was there. The inaccuracies are miniscule."]

The translations that have come to make up the modern Hawaiian canon have been important sources of Hawaiian historical and cultural information, and the four native authors from whom they are drawn were acknowledged authorities of their time. Each of the canon texts was published under the umbrella of Bishop Museum scholarship[69] and they were each warmly received as new and valuable resources by a growing audience of scholars and general readers. The texts appeared in a sequence wherein each presented new aspects of Hawaiian culture with little overlap or contradiction in the content of the seven English texts.

---

[69] The first book of translations of Kamakau's, *Ruling Chiefs of Hawaii*, was printed by the Kamehameha Schools Press, but was generated by Bishop Museum.

The Hawaiian canon is recognized as an articulated entity; the four authors and their texts are often referred to collectively as a discrete group, again quoting from Moʻokini and Kirtley (1977:39): "Kepelino…belongs with S. M. Kamakau, David Malo, and John Papa Ii in the front rank of native-born preservers and interpreters of the islands' ancient culture." Their works were woven into the fabric of contemporary knowledge through the presentation and acceptance of the initial translated texts described above and the importance of those texts were then normalized. These initial canon texts became primary references for books that became reference texts themselves, developing a process of intertextual validation that continually empowered the canon.

Normalization of the Canon

For decades, scholarly works in fields relating to Hawaiian history and culture have been accepted as rigorous and lauded as such with no recognition of the large body of pertinent texts that remained untapped. Many of these recent works are intricate scholarly reconstructions or analyses of historical Hawaiian perspectives on events and cultural systems, and would certainly have been enriched by the range of resources found in the only locus of public expression among Hawaiians: the newspapers of the 19th and early 20th centuries. The acceptance of research that excludes all but the canon as the foundation of Hawaiian reference has increased the authority of the canon while at the same time obscuring the existence of other resources.

Institutional Validation

The authority of the translated canon sources upon which the modern texts rely is fostered by peer reviews of texts, secondary reference use within other scholarly works, incorporation into curriculum at all levels, and the attained status of these texts as authorities for general reference. For decades, academic reviewers, many in peer-reviewed journals, have praised the "exhaustive" research and "Hawaiian" perspective of new texts in the field which used only the translated Hawaiian canon as their central Hawaiian referents. The reviewers' comments, especially the general agreement among them, provide a guiding force for their audiences of scholars, teachers, librarians, retailers, purveyors, and general readers, indicating, perhaps unintentionally, that use of the canon is completely adequate for excellence. Some examples below illustrate how, as an aspect of validating power, the peer reviews have fostered the continuing generation of authority for these particular texts.

Gavan Daws, awarded the first Ph.D. in Pacific History granted by the University of Hawaiʻi and author of two Hawaiian histories, *Shoal of Time* (1968a) and *The Hawaiians* (with Sheehan 1970), generally dismissed the existence of Hawaiian auto-representational writings. While he acknowledged the historical presence of a native-language press and the ability of Hawaiians to read the newspapers, he implied that either the Hawaiian newspaper writings were not composed by Hawaiians or that writings by Hawaiians did not include cultural insights and perspectives about their world. In 1968, just as *Shoal of Time* was coming out, he stated in an article in the *Hawaii Historical Review*:

> Again, sources on the life of the native community are all but intractable. The Hawaiians were not in the habit of explaining themselves or even exposing themselves in written form (this despite widespread literacy and the existence of a native-language press). In general they did not initiate social action but were acted upon. I claim no special gift of empathy; wishing to understand the Hawaiians I found I could not, and I ended by merely trying to make sense out of what their white contemporaries said about them. (1968b:418)

This perspective is reflected in Daws' texts. In *Shoal of Time*, although he did make use of the translated works of Malo, Kamakau, and ʻĪʻī, his work relied heavily on a mix of observer accounts and archival data.[70] Because of the scholarly climate of the time, reviewers perhaps did not expect Hawaiian resources to be pertinent. Those more knowledgeable about the field might not have recognized any oversight or found any lack of Hawaiian materials, because the Hawaiian sources they would have known were sufficiently represented via the canon. *Shoal of Time* was enthusiastically accepted as "the most complete, full-scale one-volume history ever written of the Hawaiian Islands" (Brown 1969:156). Other reviewers expanded the praise for his extensive research: "Based solidly on primary sources....It could scarcely be bettered" (Hilliard 1970:232). Despite his personal dismissal of Hawaiian writings, Daws was considered to be quite supportive of Hawaiians: "the tendency is to lean over backwards to be fair to the Hawaiians" (Hunter 1969:242). In general, the peer reviews encouraged that reliance on the canon materials as the Hawaiian foundation was sufficient for the

---

[70] Archival records noted here refer to government documents, such as land deeds, census reports, population statistics, etc., in contrast to the manuscripts, letters, and even newspapers that also make up archival collections.

text to be "a thorough account of Hawaiian experience" (*Booklist and Subscription Books Bulletin* 1969:570).

A similar case can be made in regard to Valerio Valeri's book, *Kingship and Sacrifice: Ritual and Society in Ancient Hawai'i* (1985). In contrast to most scholars of his time, Valeri made an effort to learn Hawaiian and carefully evaluated translated primary texts. He cites the Hawaiian language sources he utilized throughout his narrative, notes, and bibliography. His book has become a reference text, often quoted or used as a model by later scholars.[71]

Valeri did go back to the original newspaper and manuscript texts to check translations against original Hawaiian sources, and in referring to those sources he included his own recommendations for wordings, interpretations, and use of existing translations. All the source materials he utilized were those indicated in published translations or in the translations in the Bishop Museum archives. He does not appear to have incorporated any as-yet-unpublished portions of those original texts.[72] Furthermore, outside of the material previously culled and translated, he added no new Hawaiian materials, relying heavily on the writings included within the canon described here and adding only his revised interpretations. His evaluation of Hawaiian sources is limited to those few original sources that existing translations were drawn from, but there is no indication that he surveyed the newspaper material directly in its own broader context.[73] He neither evaluated additional materials, nor did he acknowledge that other Hawaiian resources might be available.

Like Daws before him, Valeri's work was considered by reviewers to be exhaustive, and he was commended by anthropologist Jocelyn Linnekin for "bringing together in a single work all the available evidence pertaining to the Hawaiian sacrificial religion," for addressing "most of the important Hawaiian texts on ritual," and for "relying primarily on original Hawaiian texts describing the rituals" (1986:218).

---

[71] These include Dening, Sahlins, and Kame'eleihiwa, each of whom acknowledge his book as a leading example of primary scholarship in Hawaiian culture and history.

[72] In 1985 the full translations of the original texts by S. M. Kamakau and J. 'Ī'ī were on file at the Bishop Museum archives, but the last portion of Kamakau's work had not yet come to press, and a large portion of the writings by 'Ī'ī were left unpublished in *Fragments of Hawaiian History*. These were not included in Valeri's book.

[73] Valeri's selection of sources is sometimes questionable. For example, in describing the male/female polarity of *kapu*, Valeri (1985:122) relied on Pogue's (1858:24) rewrite of *Mooolelo Hawaii* over the original (Dibble 1838:78) because Pogue asserted that women ate only after men were finished, while the earlier text made no such claim, and actually implied the opposite.

While he did compare the Hawaiian texts and existing translations, many reviews of *Kingship and Sacrifice* indicate that Valeri went much further in researching the Hawaiian sources than he actually did, and that he exhausted all sources:

> Valeri has been indefatigable in searching out obscure historical sources, evaluating them, and reviewing the translations of those that were originally in the Hawaiian language.…The sheer amount of ethnographic data that has been mined, evaluated, and compiled here for the first time is worthy of great praise, for this is a resource book on Hawaiian religion. (Davenport 1987:177–178)

> …comprehensively-researched work…demonstrating the untapped richness of the documentary sources…recollections of literate (?) Hawaiians. (Barker 1987:158)

> Draws on the full range of Hawaiian and European sources. (Kirkpatrick 1986:900)

As pointed out earlier, Valeri did not "search out the obscure" or draw on the "full range," but only investigated those Hawaiian materials that were translated in the canon and a handful of other previously identified and translated texts. Because of his detailed handling of the existing materials, the level of praise thus granted to his work gave greater credence to that limited set of materials which was already available in one form or another, a listing of which he included in his book. Such praise further masks the body of Hawaiian texts left amorphous and undisturbed in the newspaper archives.

By the 1980s, a model of critique seems to have emerged by which scholars evaluated new research by measuring how exhaustively the available canon texts were incorporated or how extensively archival records had been utilized. This effectively disavowed the existence of one hundred years of public, interactive newspaper writing. Subsequent texts by Marshall Sahlins, Gananath Obeyesekere, David Stannard, Lilikalā Kameʻeleihiwa, and others were each reviewed by this measure, whether or not it was clearly acknowledged. Their texts received awards for excellence, and were repeatedly recognized as having excavated *all* of the existing repositories of information.

Reviews of Sahlins' *Islands of History* (1985) praised his extensive incorporation of historical materials, implying coverage far beyond the limited archival records and the canon texts he relied on, calling it, "Excellent use of the accounts of this period, both those kept by crew members, of later Hawaiian accounts of Cook's visit, and of the accounts of Hawaiian mythology and history" (Joesting 1986).

In *Anahulu: The Anthropology of History in the Kingdom of Hawai'i, Volume 1* (1992), Sahlins acknowledged development of a "small canon of published translations," which he extended to include the writings of Fornander and Dibble's *Ka Mooolelo Hawaii,* as well as the archived translations found in the Thrum and Hawai'i Ethnographical Notes (H.E.N.) collections of the Bishop Museum. He recognized the large body of newspapers as an important source of data, but he did not investigate them. Instead, he utilized extensive archival records of the Hawaiian kingdom era, especially genealogical materials, to support his thesis, while making no survey of the large Hawaiian newspaper repository. The reviews generally accepted use of the archival records as representative of how Hawaiians viewed their world, with one reviewer calling the book an "[a]nalysis of the ways indigenous culture organized and interpreted changes imposed by colonialism" (Barieant-Schiller 1993:1669).

How "Natives" Think (Sahlins 1995), containing no consideration of the newspaper writings as the locus of Hawaiian dialogue and expression, was commended for having addressed all of the available sources: "A demonstration of a virtual mastery of the texts themselves" (Friedman 1997), and "a painstaking reconstruction of the events of Cook's visit and Hawaiian memories of him following his death" (Barker 1996).

Obeyesekere's critique of Sahlins, *The Apotheosis of Captain Cook* (1992), won the Louis Gottschalk Award in 1992 for excellence in 18th-century studies without touching any of the range of Hawaiian writings described here. He was praised by reviewers for poring over original materials and for incorporating all that was accessible: "Obeyesekere resolutely adheres to the facts he has culled from the original manuscripts, freed of later distortions and omissions' (Hilt 1993:289). Other reviews made it clear that the full range of materials had been considered, lauding it as a "careful study and comparison of all available seamen's logs and journals and accounts by Hawaiians' (Hanson 1993:762). The bibliography of *Apotheosis* actually contains not a single Hawaiian resource beyond the translated canon texts discussed here.

Another book lauded for the depth of historical research was David Stannard's *Before the Horror* (1989). He generally dismissed or deconstructed Hawaiian sources, and so utilized almost none of the available interpretations offered by Hawaiian writers of the 19th century. As will be discussed in Chapter 4, Stannard referred grudgingly to Kamakau, whom he called, "the one source invariably used by those who bother to cite anyone when claiming that infanticide was rampant" (1989:138).[74]

The responses and reviews of *Before the Horror* are positive on the breadth of his scholarship, even without those Hawaiian sources, calling it an "impressive display of scholarship" (Wells 1990), and "extensively researched,...a far-ranging comprehensive and heavily documented review of all the evidence" (Schmitt 1989:114).

Lilikalā Kameʻeleihiwa, in *Native Lands and Foreign Desires: Pehea lā e Pono ai?* (1992), uses perhaps the broadest range of Hawaiian-language resources of any published scholar. Up through the 1990s, however, the material incorporated into her work is almost exclusively archival land records and letters. She touched the newspaper archive for only two notes, one of which, by referring to Kamakau, regarded material included in his translated works. Because of her insight into the language, genealogy, and culture of 19th-century Hawaiians, her lack of reference to the published writings they produced and the Hawaiian thought represented therein was not considered an oversight in the reviews. Even though familiarity with the Hawaiian newspaper archive had grown with the Hawaiian language movement, it had not yet been integrated into scholarly consideration by the author or the critics. Her text was reviewed as "an act of prodigious scholarship" (Morris 1992), and "a brilliantly exciting and thoroughly researched history" (Osorio 1994).

The reviews quoted above framed the way that recent scholars have been accepted by a more general audience, academic and public, exhibiting how the canon is validated as an adequate foundation for research and analysis. The use that those scholars made of the canon texts and the lack of incorporation of other materials beyond the limits of that canon help to secure the authority of the canon and to further distance and mask the Hawaiian texts that lie beyond it. Reviewers' lack of familiarity with the extensive resources do not note the oversight.[75]

Texts by modern experts who don't step outside of the canon help frame a usage of the canon for its own referential validity as a new "primary" source. The reference qualities of those modern texts affect subsequent writings by others who rely on this authority granted by these experts. Texts like those noted above have become modern foundational references for subsequent researchers and writers who rely on the earlier insights and selected materials. Anthropologist and historian Gregory Dening is clearer than most in acknowledging his use of their texts:

---

[74] "Hoomana Kahiko" (*Ka Nupepa Kuokoa* 1865, Oct. 21). The topic appears in a number of Hawaiian-language news, an example being, but these were not cited by Stannard or others.

[75] Noenoe Silva's text *Aloha Betrayed* (2004, Duke University Press), is indicative of a change in direction for Hawaiian-language scholarship, as discussed in Chapter 5.

> I have not the knowledge to decode all these gestures and symbols. I am a borrower on these points from Valerio Valeri and Marshall Sahlins. (1995:25)

Authors today who rely on the work of noted experts like those above also rely on the sources they incorporated. Thus, some or all of Malo, Kepelino, ʻĪʻī, and Kamakau are invariably found in the notes and bibliographies of modern works in every field related to Hawaiian culture. Published bibliographies like *The Hawaiians* (Kittelson 1985) include no references to untranslated texts. Curriculum guides on Hawaiian culture and history make extensive use of the canon as the only sources by Hawaiian authors drawn from the Hawaiian language. *Resource Units in Hawaiian Culture* (Mitchell 1982), aimed at elementary and intermediate classrooms, but widely used in Island schools at every grade level, includes one or more of the canon authors in nearly every chapter of the book.

In order to fully appreciate the girdling effect that promotion of a narrow canon has upon contemporary knowledge about Hawaiʻi, it is appropriate to survey the actual extent of material available from the period and to consider how the canon texts fit into that larger, currently indistinct, picture.

3 | Beyond the Canon

A limited canon of texts has been generated and fostered as the representation for Hawaiians of the 19th and early 20th centuries. Incorporation of the available resources has been limited to the published translations of four writers from the period, only two of whom were ever published for their peers as part of the vibrant discourse of the time. The presence of a discourse of sufficiency becomes most tangible in a comparison of material used for modern reference against the fuller scope of extant Hawaiian writings. This comparison provides a context of how historical practices—writing, publishing, reading, and public dialogue—were enabled by the then-new technologies of print and literacy. The setting in which those practices developed initially limited Hawaiian participation by framing the kind of language and content that was deemed appropriate for the available venues. As options expanded over time, engagement by Hawaiians was eventually fostered in the creation of the corpus of writings, thus shaping the published discourse through the period.

Hawaiian language newspapers were established as an organ of Hawaiian mission culture, but later became the locus of Hawaiian written dialogue on a national level. The change in control and participation in the production of the newspapers altered both the content and the form of the newspaper repository. A survey of the actual extent of the Hawaiian newspaper corpus, emphasizes how different aspects of the repository, more than simply its size, present critical resources for scholars, researchers, and practitioners today.

The Historical Hawaiian-Language Repository

The range of Hawaiian written works created in the 19th and early 20th centuries is impressive. Surveys of national repositories in the United States indicate that the archive of Hawaiian writings is greater than the sum of written material produced by all Native American societies during the 19th and early 20th centuries.[76] The archival repository in Hawai'i includes hundreds of books, vast manuscript resources, and over 125,000 published newspaper pages. The discourse of sufficiency masks both the magnitude of the repository and the importance of the resources therein.

In the history of Pacific Island societies where the technologies of literacy were introduced, Hawai'i stands apart for its rapid adoption of literacy and zeal for written production. Although the vagaries of archival methods make it difficult to accurately measure, it appears that the Hawaiian published writings also exceed the sum of what all other Polynesian societies generated during the 19th and early 20th centuries, largely due to the extensive newspaper production.

Māori newspapers in New Zealand generated some 30,000 pages of newspapers during the same period, mostly in a small format like the early mission papers of Hawai'i.[77] In the islands of French Polynesia, Catholic and Protestant newsletters were the main publications throughout the 19th century, and a vigorous native-language press did not develop until the 20th century.[78] In Sāmoa, the London Mission Society press began at Leulumoega, Upolu, in 1845, but a government press did not begin until 1905.[79]

In each society, regional historical dynamics shaped the differences in both the production of original materials and the creation or maintenance of the archival repositories, but the massive production of published writings among

---

[76] Stauffer, Robert, personal communication, Oct. 9, 2001, following his research in Native American archive collections for the Hawai'i Newspaper Project, a pilot form of Ho'olaupa'i: Hawaiian Newspaper Resource Project detailed in Chapter 5. See also K. Silva's introduction in *Ka Ho'oilina: The Legacy*, Vol. 1:1, Kamehameha Schools Press, 2002.

[77] Most Māori newspapers were 12"x 9" up to about 18" in height by 1898. For coverage of the historical development of Māori publication, see Curnow (2002:17–41) or visit http://www.nzdl.org/cgi-bin/library.

[78] *Te Vea no Tahiti*, a regional government publication, ran from 1850–1859. The main native-language presses in Tahiti during the latter half of the 19th century were the Catholic *Messager de Tahiti*, 1852–1883, and its contemporary, the pro-Protestant *Oceanie Francaise* (Newbury 1980:209).

[79] *Savali* is noted as the first government press in Sāmoa (Masterman 1980: Appendix 1:17).

Hawaiians in comparison to other indigenous groups calls attention to the unique importance of that resource.[80]

Books

Books in Hawaiian became a literary source as soon as the mission press was functional in 1822, four years before the development of a consistent alphabet and orthography that would shape the language for the rest of the century.[81] *Hawaiian Language Imprints, 1822–1899* (Judd, Bell, and Murdoch 1978) identifies 654 books, from pamphlets to tomes, produced in Hawai'i and abroad in the Hawaiian language between the opening of the presses and the end of the 19th century.[82] Hawaiian-language books continued to be published in the first decade after the turn of the century, with approximately 40 listed in current holdings, but the *Hawaiian Language Imprints* listing contains the majority of the existing Hawaiian-language archive of publications.

Although native speakers were critical resources for the missionaries who created most of the books in the 19th century, Hawaiian direction in the production of books, especially secular books, was minimal, producing less than 4 percent of the books published in their language. Of 654 Hawaiian-language books printed over a span of 80 years, only 23 secular texts are credited, in whole or in part, to Hawaiians. The first, in 1838, was *Ka Mooolelo Hawaii*, edited by Reverend Sheldon Dibble, but acknowledged as the work of Hawaiian scholars at Lahainaluna, including Davida Malo and S. M. Kamakau.[83] Nineteen years passed before a second secular book came out by a Hawaiian author, which was an extensive example text for Hawaiians on drafting a range of legal documents (Kauwahi 1857). A score

---

[80] Foucault's work informs my use of "historical dynamics" in power and knowledge production, White and Tengan (2001) note the shift of representational practices in a Hawai'i setting, and Stillman (2001) refers to the current investigations of archival practices and knowledge.

[81] While the basic writing conventions were agreed upon in 1826 by Protestant mission representatives who largely controlled the presses for decades, these conventions changed over time in the hands of different publishers. One notable example is the Catholic press material, which adopted the letters, *t, v,* and *b* to represent the *k, w,* and *p* found in Protestant and government publications.

[82] Books in this listing include any multi-page publication with the exception of government documents, serial publications (such as newspapers), sheet music, event programs, and such. David Forbes' landmark text *Hawaiian National Bibliography 1780–1900, Vol. 3: 1851–1880* (University of Hawai'i Press, 2001) includes foreign publications about Hawaiian language, local serials and pamphlets, and government documents that are not noted in Bell, but doesn't identify new books in the language after 1900.

[83] Bishop Museum scholar John Stokes (1931) wrote a detailed critique about the manner in which Dibble organized the research and writing that resulted in *Ka Mooolelo Hawaii*, and how the text framed subsequent writings about Hawaiian history, especially those in Hawaiian. Barrère (1976:v) also comments on the impact of this text upon subsequent writings.

of original works or translations over the next 40 years covered a variety of topics, including cultural practice, history, legend, song collections, biographies, and natural science.[84]

There are links between published books and other writings, such as the newspapers and manuscript materials. Dibble's *Ka Mooolelo Hawaii* appeared in sections in the newspaper before publication as a book and then was reprinted in the newspapers once the book became rare. His text also became a model for later serial newspaper histories by Reverend Pogue, S. M. Kamakau, and others. Hawaiian legends, like Haleʻole's account of Lāʻieikawai, appeared in serial form in two

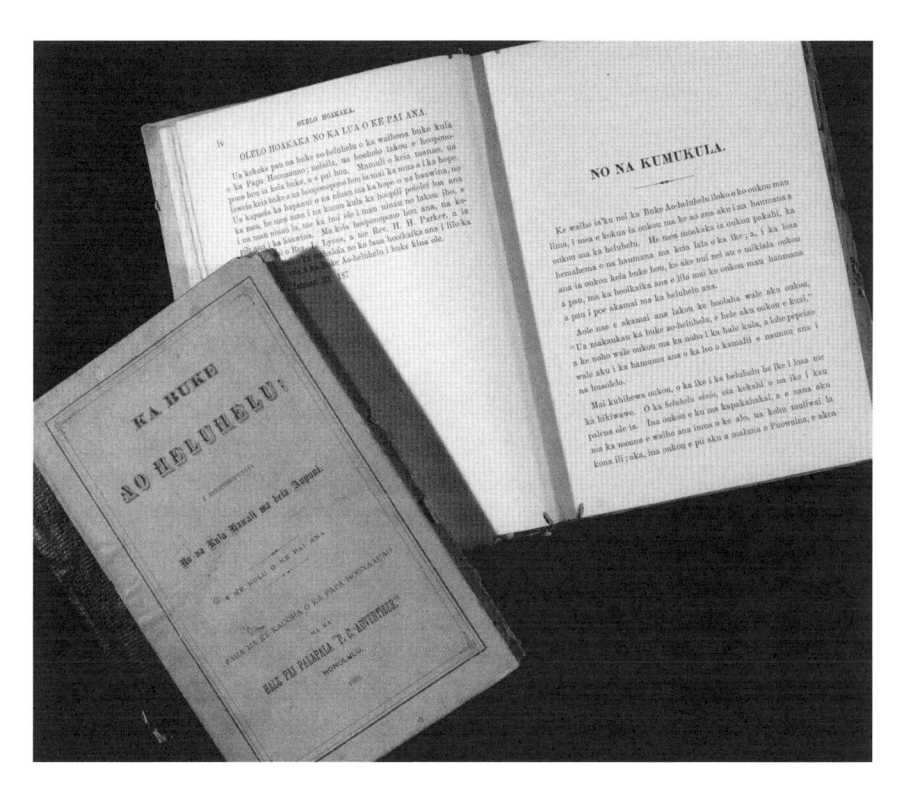

Ka Buke Ao Heluhelu *was a reading text prepared for the common schools which were taught in Hawaiian. Containing translations of poetry and literature from English-language readers and some Sunday School texts, it also includes articles on Hawaiian history, mostly drawn from earlier published texts. Printed by the government in 1871, the book was reprinted two more times over a period of fifteen years and was probably still in use when the last Hawaiian-language schools of the 19th century were made to adopt to English as the language of instruction in 1896. Photo by David Franzen, Bishop Museum.*

---

[84] For a full listing, see Judd, Bell, and Murdoch (1978).

newspapers before publication as a book; foreign legends in translation were serialized in the papers preceding book publication, and several published song books were collections culled from newspapers of the time.[85] While some of the connections between published and unpublished materials are apparent, additional ties continue to unfold with study of the literature as an historical corpus.

Manuscripts

Hawaiian writings were not always created for publication, and the collections of unpublished Hawaiian writings are another rich resource for study. In addition to original manuscripts, archival and family collections contain numerous published texts, such as books, newspapers, and event programs, that have been annotated, corrected, or extended in holograph form, but never made public.

Manuscripts available today in archival collections and those that have appeared in modern publications were mostly unseen by contemporaries of the manuscript author, but some were copied and disseminated on a limited basis during their authors' lifetimes. Davida Malo's manuscript of *Ka Mooolelo Hawaii* was distributed in the form of handwritten copies, among at least a small group of his contemporaries.[86] S. M. Kamakau was said to have referred to manuscript accounts by Malo and others while he composed his history of Kamehameha in the 1860s.[87] Author and translator Moses Manu, also known as Kekahuna'ai'ole, was credited with having written more than thirty manuscript books that were apparently available in some circles (Mahoe n.d.:48).[88] After the turn of the century, Hawaiian historian J. M. Poepoe acknowledged using the unpublished writings of historian S. L. Peleiōhōlani while producing his own serialized historical account, often referring to "*ka S. L. Peleioholani buke kakaulima e waiho nei imua o ka mea kakau.*" [S. L. Peleioholani's handwritten manuscript, situated here in front of the author] (Poepoe 906).

---

[85] For an announcement of a book drawn from newspapers, see *Ka Nupepa Kuokoa,* May 19, 1866, and also see Testa, *Buke Mele Lahui* (1895), where the introduction explains the source of the published song collection.

[86] Two handwritten copies of Malo's manuscript are on file at Bishop Museum, one of which may be the original. The number of handwritten copies that were privately held or once in circulation is not known.

[87] K.U., in an 1878 newpaper article, says Kamakau relied on a manuscript book for his writings, but had stolen it. K.U. is probably John Koi'i Unauna, 2nd generation antagonist of Kamakau, who sparred with Unauna, Koi'i's father, a generation earlier.

[88] Moses Manu, a prodigious writer who published many epic legends in the Hawaiian newspapers, both Hawaiian and translations from English. Born in 1837, little is known of his life aside from his profile as a newspaper writer and translator. Mahoe's manuscript is the only source identifying him by the name of Kekahuna'ai'ole, who was the secretary of the Genealogy Committee established by King Kalākaua.

An 1878 article in *Ko Hawaii Pae Aina* (Aug. 31, 1878) lists experts in the fields of genealogy, oratory, astronomy, architecture, and *"na ike kahiko a pau"* [all the ancient knowledges], whose manuscript texts, in limited circulation, were the important reference sources for such fields of knowledge and incorporated into texts by others. Additional manuscripts on history and culture are acknowledged to be extant, including unpublished writings by 19th-century authors, such as S. P. Kalama, S. L. Peleiōhōlani, Davida Malo, and S. M. Kamakau. It is uncertain whether these private writings were copied or circulated, so their place in the discourse of the time is unknown.

Manuscripts do not allow for the peer review and reaction that is documented with published writings, especially newspapers. As such, manuscript material occupies a different position within the critical public dialogue of the writer's time. Although the writings may be seen as products of the discourse that framed the writer's position, and perhaps connected to his or her public expression elsewhere, these manuscripts generally did not reflect a public aspect of the history of thinking in the same way as circulated writings. Because this study focuses on Hawaiian writings as part of a collective and public field of knowledge, manuscript material is largely outside of that sphere.

The private nature of most manuscripts makes it significant that archival manuscript collections have been the source of two of the modern canon texts: the translations of *Ka Moolelo Hawaii* by Malo and *Kepelino's Traditions of Hawaii* by Kepelino. As manuscript sources, these two texts are not part of the corpus of publicly-shared knowledge and, as such, are not considered in the same detail as are those canon sources from ʻĪʻī and Kamakau, which are drawn from the newspapers.

Manuscript material is of great value, especially as a source for comparison to other resources. Martha Beckwith, in the introduction to *Kepelino's Traditions of Hawaii*, notes the importance of such comparison in her supplements to the translation of Kepelino's work (1932:3). Public and private archival sources contain a large body of unpublished manuscripts and texts that were created during the 19th century, much of which is still unincorporated into modern research.

NEWSPAPERS

Hawaiian-language newspapers make up the largest known repository of Hawaiian writings, a body of material that continues to be incorporated into modern knowledge in a partial and fragmentary manner. Their content, especially the later papers, is particularly pertinent to the social sciences, being, as often described, "a literary form that focused on Hawaiian history and traditions" (Charlot n.d.:Chapter 5, 135ff).

Published in Hawaiʻi from 1834 until 1948, Hawaiian-language newspapers produced about 125,000 newspaper pages, most of which were published after 1861, when a new large format became the industry standard. Of the seventeen Hawaiian-language newspapers published between 1834 and 1861, most were quite small, with the earliest being about letter-size (8.5" x 11"), and some later papers being even smaller. Size was eventually increased, with *Ka Hae Hawaii* in 1856 beginning at 12" high and almost 10" wide, and expanding after its first year in circulation to 15" high and 11" wide, the largest Hawaiian-language newspaper up to that time. The sum of production in the span from 1839–1961 equaled between 3 and 4 percent of the whole.

In 1861, *Ka Hoku o ka Pakipika* and *Ka Nupepa Kuokoa* each began circulation in a large format equal to the largest English paper of the time, the *Pacific Commercial Advertiser*. This set a new norm for Hawaiian-language papers that would continue for the duration of the Hawaiian press into the 20th century. At 23.75" high and 17.5" wide, these papers were about the size of the *Honolulu Advertiser* today.* From 1861 on, most Hawaiian papers printed four-page weekly issues. Occasional special editions were published with more than four pages, and a number of papers expanded to six, eight, or even twelve pages per issue at the end of the 19th century. Some, like *Ka Manawa, Ka Nupepa Kuokoa, Ke Aloha Aina, Ka Nai Aupuni* and others, eventually produced daily publications, a few of which ran for several years.

A notable aspect of these large-format newspapers is that they were far more densely printed than newspapers today. Editors consistently set as much type as possible on a page, allowing little or no space between columns and leaving minimal side and bottom margins. Instead of open space, thin vertical lines separated columns, allowing maximum print space within the usually six-column format. This form was not unique to Hawaiʻi, but is far different than what is produced today. Images were included sparingly, and were considered by some to be "*poho wale*," a waste (Kuapuʻu 1861).[89] Three or even four times more text than is seen in a current *Honolulu Advertiser* was pressed into the same size sheet of newsprint in the Hawaiian papers, giving the equivalent of 10 or even 14 letter-size pages of typescript per newspaper sheet. *Ka Nupepa Kuokoa*, which ran for seven decades, became an industry norm and most subsequent papers matched or exceeded its dimensions. Thus, even allowing for the smaller initial papers, the total production of 125,000 Hawaiian-language newspaper pages exceeds well over one million letter-sized pages of typescript text. The following chart gives examples of newspaper text content:

---

[89] *Ka Nupepa Kuokoa* was an exception, with pictures being one of the newspaper's selling points.
*As of 2010, the *Honolulu Advertiser* became the *Honolulu Star-Advertiser*.

Newspaper [dates]	Size (Height x Width)	Standard Page Equivalent
Ka Lama Hawaii	10.75 x 8	2
Ka Elele	9.25 x 5.75	1.25
Ka Hae Hawaii 1856–3/1857	12 x 10	2.25
Ka Hae Hawaii 3/1857–close	15 x 11	3.5
Ka Hoku o ka Pakipika	23.75 x 17.5	14
Ka Nupepa Kuokoa	23.5 x 17.5	12
Honolulu Advertiser (present)	22.75 x 13.5	4

Table 1. Comparative Newspaper Sizes.

While the smaller early papers were published under the aegis of the missionaries and then the government, many Hawaiian writers participated. By 1861, Hawaiians took an active role as writers, editors, and publishers in the press. Approximately 120,000 newspaper pages, 96 percent of the Hawaiian-language newspaper archive, were produced through 70 different papers over the next eight decades.[90] In the tenuous initial decade of this "native press" beginning in 1861, nearly 6,000 pages of Hawaiian-language newspapers were printed, the equivalent of 60,000 or more typescript pages of writings.[91] Even though the most-cited Hawaiian resources today are translations of writings drawn from this important decade, the sum of those translated works represents less than 2 percent of the body of material created in this first decade of the native press and less than one-tenth of one percent (0.1%) of the whole corpus.[92]

The conditions are not unique to Hawai'i; anthropologist Scott Michaelson critiqued American anthropology for misuse and general dismissal of 19th century Amerindian writings that have been available to researchers for 150 years but still remain unincorporated into modern scholarship. There are many parallels in the setting he described about Amerindian writings and that of Hawaiian writings of the same period:

---

[90] Chapin (2000) offers a listing and general description of all extant newspapers that were printed in Hawai'i. From this list the number of Hawaiian-language papers has been extracted and tallied. Number of pages per issue, issues per year, and opening or closing dates are not always included, and while some newspapers ran up to twelve pages per issue, the average four-page newspaper is used here to estimate the actual number of Hawaiian-language pages created.

[91] Once all extant copies have been checked, this figure could rise to 75,000 or more. These figures would include newspapers up to 1870, encompassing most, but not quite all, of the writings by S. M. Kamakau and J. 'Ī'ī, each of whom continued writing into the opening years of the next decade.

[92] The English publications of works by Kamakau and 'Ī'ī, which were drawn from the Hawaiian newspapers *Ka Nupepa Kuokoa* and *Ke Au Okoa*, equal 1,055 pages, including added notes.

> A surprisingly large and distinctive body of nineteenth-century Amerindian writing on anthropological matters, running parallel to the development of "white" anthropology, is not yet within our sights. (1999:xiii)

The local aspect of this issue was raised over seventy years ago by Kawena Pukui (1937) when she explained to the Anthropological Society of Hawai'i that the newspaper writings by Hawaiians were anthropology, and that the Royal Historical Society,[93] established in 1841, was "A Hawaiian Anthropological Society." Her insights may have drawn some attention to the Hawaiian historical texts, but to little avail. Michaelson elaborated on how such native texts, when they are in some way incorporated, are subsumed and reshaped to fit an already-framed anthropological project, as seen with the Hawaiian canon texts:

> Their texts, then, disappear under the shellac of anthropology, and it is impossible to determine, in the first place, whether anything of these texts poses an alternative to white anthropology because the reading of these texts has been, in a very real sense, predetermined and preconditioned by the overarching anthropological framework. (1999:xiv)

Hawaiian sources, like Amerindian, have been reshaped or ignored, blinding scholars to the actual form and content. The outcome of such misuse or disuse is a decontextualized misreading of the original works, if they are read at all:

> Scholars' lack of information concerning Amerindian self-definition in the nineteenth century results in reading texts only for the ways in which they shore up definitions of whiteness. Amerindians as such play no part in the tale. (ibid:xvi)

Michaelson's observations address the written production of the combined nations of the native peoples of America, while Hawaiians represent a single people. The Hawaiian newspapers make up the largest cache of Hawaiian writings in existence, and this huge collection was written by and circulated nationwide among a fully-literate population. As such, it documents a unique record of Hawaiians' expression and interaction for and among themselves. Although the published record can only partially reflect the intricacies of a society, this repository has the

---

[93] 'Ahahui 'Imi I Ka Mea Kahiko O Hawai'i Nei, and also known as 'Ahahui 'Imi I Nā Mo'olelo Kahiko.

important quality of being a window on the public knowledge and opinion of the period. The size of this window, coupled with most of it remaining unaccessible and untranslated, presents a daunting challenge, but one which promises to be an unparalleled historical resource.

Hawaiian Production of a Written Discourse

The Hawaiian-language archive of 19th and early 20th century writings must be considered in light of historical changes in the kinds of representation that frame the repository. White and Tengan (2001:385) and E. Buck (1993) discuss the re-centering of representation that accompanied the forces of literacy and education, and the historical sequence of written production by Hawaiian writers embodies the shifting processes of these forces that emerged over time.[94] Chapin describes a similar point, that "[a] revolutionary technology acts abrasively and destructively on older forms of culture" (1984:49). She notes a number of forces at work during the first three decades of literacy that shifted representation to include a broader range of the Hawaiian population.

The development of literacy, the technologies of writing and printing, the practices that controlled access to the press, and the motivation of Hawaiians to participate in newspaper interaction all affected representation, determining who was writing and what was being produced for public audiences. These aspects inform an understanding of Hawaiian writings that make up the archival repository.

Literacy

The development of literacy in Hawai'i generally paralleled the technology and production of print. Along with the sweeping wave of foreign innovations, Hawaiians had observed the "technology" of reading and writing in many languages for over four decades, but with few avenues of engaging that technology. With the help of literate foreigners in 1794 and again in 1810, Kamehameha I sent letters to King George III. He signed them "Tamaahmaah" and "Kamaah Amaah," documenting both his awareness and interest in the written word.[95] Kamehameha

---

[94] The impact of such a technological change can submerge or de-center representational practices. See White and Tengan (2001), Buck (1993), and Ong (1982).

[95] Kanepuu (1864) describes the correspondence.

also employed a tutor, John Rives, in 1810 to educate his son, Liholiho.[96] Little is known about the form or duration of the schooling, but *"Ua ao ua wahi haole nei i ke Keiki Alii Liholiho ma ka olelo Beretania me ka palapala"* [The foreigner taught Prince Liholiho in English language, with reading and writing] (Kamakau 1869a). While the seeds of literacy and formal education were planted early, it was some years before they bore fruit.[97]

From their arrival in 1820, Calvinist missionaries worked with Hawaiians to develop a printed form of Hawaiian, opening the door to literacy for Hawaiians in their own language. Students found reading and writing easy to acquire due to an orthography that gave clear correspondence between sound and form (Schütz 1994:173).

During their first years in Hawai'i, the missionaries began teaching classes on each of the major islands under the sponsorship and within the courts of leading chiefs. Their success was rapid, and by 1824, most of the ruling chiefs were not only supporting schools in their lands by sending out the *aloali'i*, court members, who had mastered literacy, but they were also actively urging their people to attend classes and to learn the *pī'āpā*, or alphabet, for reading and writing (Kamakau 2001:22).[98]

Kauikeaouli, Kamehameha III, had exhorted his people in 1825, saying *"'O ko'u aupuni, he aupuni palapala ko'u…No laila, e nā ali'i a me nā maka'āinana, e a'o 'oukou i ka palapala"* [My nation is a nation of literacy…Therefore, chiefs and commoners, you should all learn to read and write] (Kamakau 2001:24).[99] The ruling chiefs of the time followed their king's lead; his personal involvement in fostering education and his own attendance at class was their model. The ranking women also took an active role in the movement to literacy:

---

[96] Kamakau, in *Ka Nupepa Kuokoa*, Jan. 2, 1869, tells of the arrival of Ioane Rive and his being taken on as tutor and *aikāne*, companion, for the young heir to the kingdom, Kalanikualiholiho, who later became Kamehameha II. Kamakau set this as *"mahope mai o ka holo ana mai i ka Peleleu nei"* [while Kamehameha was on O'ahu, after coming on the Peleleu fleet] (1796).

[97] For examples of generative efforts begun prior to the arrival of missionary companies, see Rumford (1993) on the writing system being developed before 1818 by Obookiah ('Ōpūkaha'ia), and reworked by Bingham as the first company of missionaries was preparing to come to Hawai'i.

[98] From *Ka Nupepa Kuokoa*, Apr. 18, 1868, reprinted in Kamakau (2001).

[99] As noted, Hawaiian language appearing in this book is presented in the orthography of the source from which it is drawn. Historical newspaper texts are unmarked, but more recent publications often include the *'okina* (glottal stop) and *kahakō* (macron) used in modern orthography to assist in pronunciation. Some of the newspaper writings of S. M. Kamakau presented here are drawn from the 1996 and 2001 republications of his works, making use of the indices that these reprintings provide as access points for modern researchers.

THE ALPHABET.

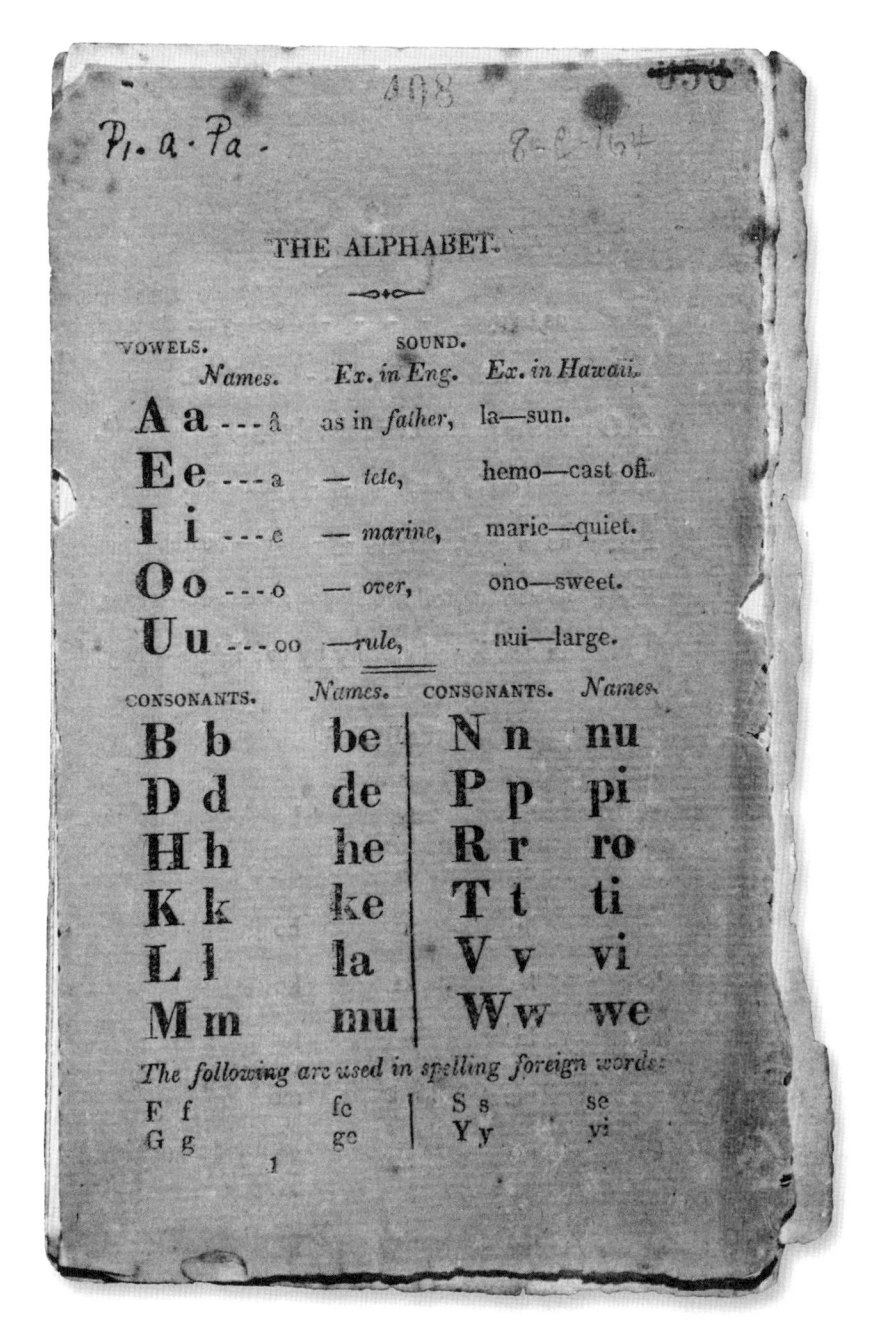

VOWELS.		SOUND.	
	Names.	Ex. in Eng.	Ex. in Hawaii.
A a	ā	as in *father*,	la—sun.
E e	a	— *tete*,	hemo—cast off.
I i	e	— *marine*,	marie—quiet.
O o	o	— *over*,	ono—sweet.
U u	oo	—*rule*,	nui—large.

CONSONANTS.	Names.	CONSONANTS.	Names.
B b	be	N n	nu
D d	de	P p	pi
H h	he	R r	ro
K k	ke	T t	ti
L l	la	V v	vi
M m	mu	W w	we

The following are used in spelling foreign words:

| F f | fe | S s | se |
| G g | ge | Y y | yi |

The Alphabet *[Ka Piapa]* was a 16-page pamphlet introducing the written language to a fluent population. The first page shows the sound of vowels and how they join with the consonants (12 consonants were in use before a consistent 7 were chosen.) The text then introduces familiar words and phrases. 2,500 copies were printed in 1822, while literacy was expanding from royal courts to countryside. Photo by David Franzen, Bishop Museum.

'O Ka'ahumanu, 'o Kekuaipi'ia Nāmāhana, 'o Kīna'u, 'o Kalanipauahi, 'o Kekāuluohi, 'o nā kaikamāhine a pau a Ka'ahumanu a me nā ali'i a pau, ua kīkīko'ele 'ia a pau loa i ke a'o palapala; ua hele nui nā ali'i 'elemakule a me ka po'e 'auwae pōlea e nome mai ka waha i ka pa'ana'au i ka ui, ka lile a me ke akua ma ka mauna 'o Sinai. He hana kupanaha kā kēia mau hana i kōkua 'ia mai e ke akua. (Kamakau 2001:25)[100]

[Ka'ahumanu, Kekuaipi'ia Nāmāhana, Kīna'u, Kalanipauahi, Kekāuluohi, indeed all of Ka'ahumanu's young women and those of all the chiefs, they all perfected their literacy; the elderly chiefs went in great numbers and the toothless ones, whose mouths ruminated while memorizing the articles of faith, the group recitations, and the story of the Lord on Mount Sinai. These were truly amazing efforts assisted by the Lord.]

Kamakau points out that on seeing the quick mastery of literacy by those in their own courts, the high chiefs, led by Ka'ahumanu, sent native teachers out to all the lands they governed, quickly spreading literacy from Hawai'i to Kaua'i. The effort was already well under way by the mid-1820s when formal mission schools were opened in the rural districts, and much of the adult population had already mastered basic literacy:

'A'ole lakou i a'o aku i ka po'e o'o, ua 'ike kahiko nō lākou i ke a'o 'ia e nā kumu kula o ka wā kahiko, 'o ia ho'i nā kumu a'o pī'āpā. (1996:249–250)

[They didn't teach the adults, who had long known how, having been taught by the teachers of long ago, those [native] teachers who taught reading and writing.]

---

[100] From *Ka Nupepa Kuokoa*, Apr. 25, 1868, reprinted in Kamakau (2001).

In taking an active role in the spread of literacy, the king and chiefs were executing their traditional roles as the central authorities over knowledge, a move that would eventually shift authority beyond their control.[101]

In 1828, Laura Fish Judd, wife of the mission doctor Gerritt P. Judd, wrote about Hawaiians being such enthusiastic learners of reading and writing that many of them were equally adept at reading text that was held upright, sideways, or inverted (1880:17).[102] This skill was necessitated by the relative lack of printed material for the number of readers and the need for several persons to share a single text. With several readers circling a single book, only the holder of the text would have a direct view of the page.

At about the same time, William Richards commented that the limited resources for literacy motivated "industrious" Hawaiians to simply memorize entire books (1828b). In 1831, just three years after these observations, Lahainaluna College was established on Maui as a center of higher learning. The chiefs made use of the new college to further train their own teachers (Kamakau 2001:25).[103]

A nationwide zeal for the *palapala*, or written language, produced rapid results. Kamakau, in his serial history of the nation, reflects that by the mid-1820s one could already ask "*Aia la mahea ka poe ike ole i ka heluhelu?*" [Where would one find folks who do not know how to read?] (1868a, Jan. 18). For a decade or more, the focus was on adult students, with general education for children beginning in 1832 (Day and Loomis 1997:22). By 1834, missionaries reported 20,000 natives, or nearly one-fifth of the population, actively attending schools at a ratio of 3 adults to each child (Schütz 1994:174).

In 1839, just over a decade after her initial comments, Mrs. Judd compared Hawaiian literacy to other societies and estimated the percentage of literacy among Hawaiians to be "greater than in any other country in the world, except Scotland and New England" [sic] (1880:62). The bible was fully translated into Hawaiian by that same year, standardizing the language throughout the kingdom in the same

---

[101] See Wist (1940:1–5) on traditional chiefly roles in knowledge production. Also see Buck (1993:128) on the de-centering of chiefly power over knowledge that resulted from literacy:

"Although Hawaiians continued to pass on their traditional knowledge and cultural practices within the confines of the family and local communities (particularly in areas removed from Honolulu), 'the regime of truth' that had resided with the *aliʻi* in their compounds and the priests in the *heiau* was subverted by the education offered by the missionaries and encouraged by such *aliʻi* leaders as Kaʻahumanu. The long-held assumption that *aliʻi* and priests were discursively qualified to exercise power over knowledge—to say 'what counts as true'—dissolved in the new cultural order of Hawaiʻi."

[102] For vignettes on Hawaiian enthusiasm for reading and writing, see also Day and Loomis (1997:16). An extension of this sharing occurred later with newspaper being handed from reader to reader. Editors complained of the practice because it diminished sales, and encouraged each reader to subscribe for themselves.

[103] Original text in *Ka Nupepa Kuokoa*, May 2, 1868.

way the King James' version had affected English usage elsewhere (Wist 1940:21–22). Twenty years later, in 1859, just prior to the opening of the native press, the *New York Tribune* reported that the literacy of the Hawaiian population had even surpassed that of New England (Day and Loomis 1997:31).

Perhaps more important than global comparison was the national mindset; Hawaiians considered themselves to be a literate people. Kamakau, as quoted earlier, spoke of the rarity of non-readers by 1825. Sam Damon, publisher of *The Friend*, comments in 1856 that all natives could write (*The Friend* 1856). The acknowledgment of full literacy was general among Hawaiians and their foreign contemporaries. Thus, as Hawaiian writers took an active role in writing and publishing text for national distribution, they were aware that they were writing for, and reading along with, a fully-literate populace. As the press became the locus of national dialogue, such a mindset would affect the care invested in writing and the importance placed on what was read.

Print in Hawai'i

Hawaiians had been introduced to reading and writing prior to the arrival of the Calvinist mission of the American Board of Commissioners for Foreign Missions (ABCFM) in 1820, but the coming of the first company of missionaries marked the beginning of formal education, the development of a preliminary alphabet, and the printing of Hawaiian texts in Hawai'i. From its beginning in Hawai'i, printing technology, unlike literacy, was the domain of the ABCFM and its local agency, the members of the Sandwich Islands Mission. The first press in the islands was set up by the mission in Honolulu and began printing in 1822. They established a second press at Lahainaluna in 1834 for both production and training in the printing trade. Directly through the mission presses and eventually through schools and government liasons, the mission community maintained general control of most Hawaiian-language printed matter for the next quarter of a century.

By 1830, the Sandwich Islands Mission had printed nearly 400,000 copies of 28 different tracts, pamphlets, and books (Day and Loomis 1997:22). In 1834, *Ka Lama Hawaii* was the first newspaper in Hawai'i, establishing a newspaper industry which produced a series of mission newspapers. Production of printed material soared, and by 1858, the mission print shops had generated thousands of different publications, including bible translations, hymnals, inspirational stories, textbooks, legal documents, tracts, and newspapers in the Hawaiian language.[104] American presses added to this number, supporting the mission with tracts and books to supplement local production.[105] Local commercial and government

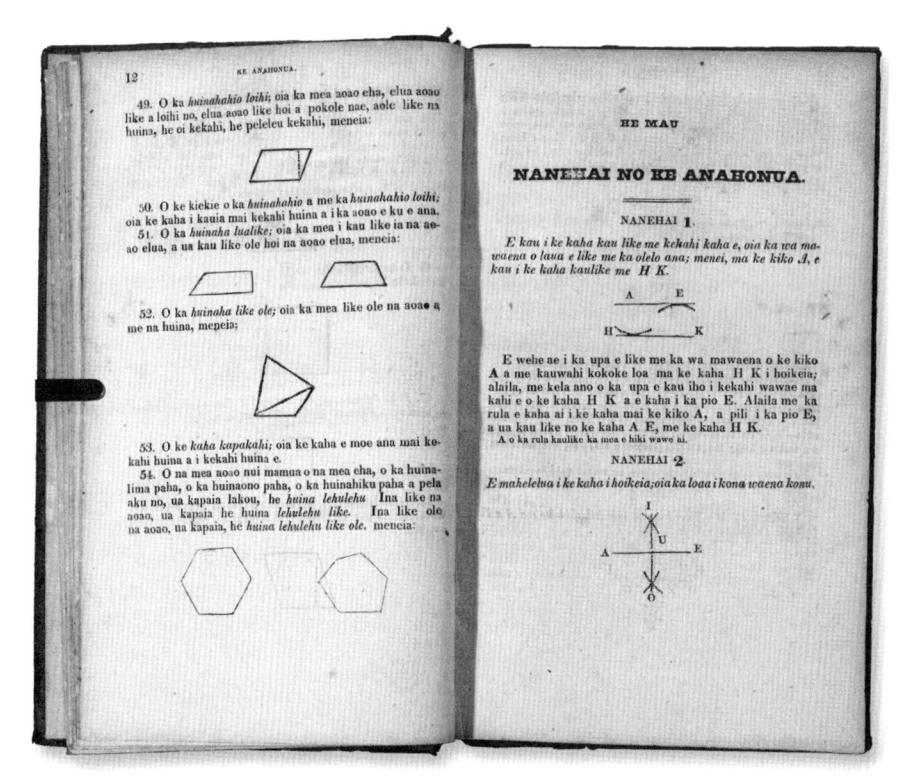

Pages 12–13 of "Ke Anahonua. Oia ka mea e ike ai ke kumu o ke ana aina a me ka holo moku. He mea ia e pono ai ke kulanui." [The surveyor. So one will know the foundations of surveying and sailing. Appropriate for the college.] Hawaiian language adaptation of Nathaniel Bowditch's The New American Practical Navigator. Translated by Lorrin Andrews, engraved by S. P. Kalama, and published by Lahainaluna Press, 1834. An upper-level math text with sections on geometry, trigonometry, measuring heights and lengths, land surveying, and principles of sailing, with tables of latitude and longitude. Photo by David Franzen, Bishop Museum.

---

[104] The recorded figure of production is 113,017,173 pages, but does not include texts printed in New England and shipped to Hawai'i to support the mission's endeavors. The Honolulu offices of the mission press closed in 1858 and the Lahainaluna press was dismantled a year later, leading to contracted printing thereafter (Day and Loomis 1997:26).

[105] Elisha Loomis returned to New England in 1827 to oversee printing for the Hawaiian mission, and is credited with 15,000 copies of each of the gospels of Matthew, Mark, and John (Day and Loomis 1997:14). Rev. E. W. Clark later took over the N.Y. production of Hawaiian texts.

printers eventually increased this amount even further, continually adding newspapers and books to stimulate and supply a Hawaiian market.[106]

While most early printed material in Hawaiʻi was generated from the mission presses, other groups also produced books, tracts, newspapers, and journals. In 1836, two years after *Ka Lama Hawaii* began, the *Sandwich Islands Gazette and Journal of Commerce* marked the start of an English-language commercial press. This first English newspaper was started in an effort to expand a local printing industry and to oppose the mission monopoly (Chapin 1996:19). Following this first foreign-language paper, *The Sandwich Islands Mirror and Commercial Gazette* began in 1839, after which came *The Polynesian* in 1840, and *The Friend* in 1842, the forerunners of what became a continuous line of English newspapers (Chapin 2000:127). English journals like *The Hawaiian Spectator* (1838–1839) appeared sporadically as well. English periodicals serviced a small, but growing, population of foreigners, while mission publications in Hawaiian addressed the larger population.

After twenty years of Calvinist dominance in Hawaiian religious and secular education and publishing, there was a growing Catholic presence. Catholics gained a stable foothold in the Islands following the forced acceptance of a Catholic influence in 1837. Catholic production of Hawaiian-language material actually began in 1831 while the first priests were in temporary exile from Hawaiʻi, but Catholic presses began local publication of Hawaiian-language tracts in 1841 and newspapers in 1852 (Day and Loomis 1997:30). The English and Catholic publications were weekly, monthly, or quarterly, and of various duration, but each added to the mass of print being made available.

By the mid-1850s, presses were generating millions of pages in copies of books, tracts, and newspapers for a native population of just over 65,000,[107] but Hawaiian writers composed little of that body of published material. At least half of the Hawaiian-language books that were produced during the 19th century were published by this time, but less than 5 percent of the eventual newspaper production had come into print by the end of the 1850s. Native writers had minimal representation in print prior to the beginning of a secular and independent Hawaiian-language press, because, until that time, publishing in Hawaiʻi came under the aegis of the mission. The experience, training, interest, and confidence that developed on the part of Hawaiians in regard to the printed word during these first decades laid the foundation for a flood of native writing that was to come, especially in the newspapers.

---

[106] See *Ka Hae Hawaii* (1861).
[107] Schmitt (1977: 25, 35). The census recorded a population of 65,647 for 1860, a steady decline from roughly 142,000 in 1825.

Newspapers as Locus of Discourse

The rapid achievement of literacy by the Hawaiian population was remarkable, but for over thirty years, from the 1820s through the 1850s, the level of literacy far exceeded their published writings. Along with literacy, the mechanical skills of typesetting, plate engraving, and printing were taught directly to mission apprentices and different aspects of printing made up standard courses of study at mission schools, especially Lahainaluna (Day and Loomis 1997:20). This training produced a skilled labor force for the printing industry, but for decades, foreign missionaries and businesses controlled much of the content and form of publication.

Hawaiians provided translation, information for content, and labor for the printing of books and newspapers, but initially received texts rather than generated them. Calvinist, and eventually Catholic missionary teachers copiously produced books, tracts, newspapers, and most printed material in order to propagate their faiths and to educate the Hawaiian people in the ways of Europe and America.

By mid-century, Hawaiians took a more active role, mostly in newspapers. For the remainder of the century, they would be only minimally represented in published books, while newspapers went on to become the central venue of Hawaiian participation in the written record. The start of the independent Hawaiian newspapers in 1861 initiated what was to become a continuous presence of Hawaiian publishers, editors, and writers for the next nine decades.

A Shifting Paradigm of Representation

Publication of Hawaiian newspapers, beginning in 1834, opened a new venue for spreading information. The first mission paper, *Ka Lama Hawaii*, serving the students at the newly-established Lahainaluna College stated clearly that the dissemination of knowledge was its primary goal:

> He mea ia e hoolaha i ka ike i kela mea keia mea e pono ai na haumana o ke Kulanui, he mea hoi ia e ao aku i ka maikai o ka naauao mamua o ka naaupo, a me ka aoao maikai o kanaka ma na aina naauao, a he mea ia e hoike i ka pono o ka ke Akua olelo, i maluhia keia pae aina, a i pomaikai hoi keia aupuni. (*Ka Lama Hawaii* 1834a)

> [It [the paper] is a means to disseminate information about everything the students of the College need, it is also to teach the goodness of knowledge over ignorance, and the good aspects

of people in enlightened lands, and it is a means to display the righteousness of God's word, so that this archipelago may be peaceful and the nation be blessed.]

Lorrin Andrews reported that *Ka Lama Hawaii* was "a channel through which the scholars might communicate their own opinions freely on any subject they chose" (1835), but such communication was carefully guided by mission mores and editorial selection for more than twenty years.[108] Though the earliest mission papers allowed readers to submit their writings, there was a narrow range of content deemed appropriate for publications, and reader participation was further limited by the small space available in the letter-sized publications, which did not expand for two decades, until the late 1850s.

More general and secular coverage of local and foreign news began appearing in the initial English newspapers from 1836 on, as the publishing industry developed. The Organic Acts of 1846–1848 set up a government arm of publishing official documents and government involvement with the newspapers grew through regular subsidy, beginning with *The Polynesian* and extending to Hawaiian-language papers with *Ka Elele*. From that point on, Hawaiian newspapers followed suit in regards to expansion of content by including a limited number of secular articles, but the selection of appropriate news was still guided for many years by the missionary objectives of proselytizing and educating.

During those first two decades of the newspapers' existence, editors of Hawaiian and English papers requested that native writers share cultural information and historical accounts through the mission, government, and business newspapers, but response was limited, mostly appearing in the mission press. Genealogical and historical information was printed occasionally, and *kanikau*, or dirge poems, were published if they were for someone of importance and composed in "good taste."

In the mission papers—such as *Ka Lama Hawaii*, *Ke Kumu Hawaii*, and *Ka Nonanona*—and even in the early years of the government-sponsored *Ka Hae Hawaii*, requests for cultural or historical information were often couched in statements about how sharing such information would allow readers to appreciate the progress of the Hawaiians from "*na'aupō*," or ignorance, to "*mālamalama*,"

---

[108] Schütz (1994:172) discusses how the ABCFM demanded the power of censorship over all published writings.

or enlightenment of civilization and religious awareness.[109] This early request in *Ke Kumu Hawaii* for stories about the ancient chiefs exemplifies the deprecating manner in which material was usually solicited:

> ...ike pono kakou i na mea e pono ai a me na mea e hewa ai, i na mea e pomaikai ai a me na mea e poino ai ma Hawaii nei. I maopopo hoi, ua oi aku ko kakou pono mamua o ka lakou. (Bingham 1835)[110]
>
> [...so that we accurately know the right and wrong things, things by which people here in Hawaiʻi are benefited or harmed. This would make it clear that our virtue is superior to theirs.]

Even dedicated converts to Christianity must have chafed at the thought of submitting materials intended to ridicule their own ancestors and histories. That tension became a discursive force which, like technical power over the presses, limited Hawaiian presentation. The surge of cultural material following the initial secularization and later independence of the Hawaiian press makes such a case seem very likely.

Public Press

The opening in 1856 of a more secular weekly Hawaiian newspaper, *Ka Hae Hawaii* (The Hawaiian Flag), was seminal in developing the newspapers as a central venue for written expression and interchange among Hawaiians. This paper opened the budding technology to a new level of access for the broader Hawaiian audience. Still limited by size and constricted as the organ of the missionary-influenced Department of Public Instruction, *Ka Hae Hawaii* encouraged more interaction by readers than ever before. *Ka Hae* covered a broader range of content than its predecessors, often including detailed cultural and historical accounts. Such articles were fitted in among the mission reports, educational articles, and "wholesome" news

---

[109] The clear reifying of cultural practice during this period, and the consistent identification of the old pagan way as *hewa* (wrong, evil) and the new Christian way as *pono* (right, righteous) is a rich area of study that would inform research into Hawaiian representational practices from the beginning of literacy to the present.

[110] This request from Hiram Bingham was directed to Kepooloku, a noted genealogist of the time, but is similar to many other examples of the period.

that Richard Armstrong described as the basis of the paper (Chapin 1996:29).[111] The more secular focus of the paper generated a new level of responsiveness from readers whose letters and articles then further added to the breadth of content.

The tenor and purpose of the majority of articles in *Ka Hae Hawaii* remained basically Calvinist, and those that didn't directly convey an educational, governmental, or spiritual message were often preceded or followed by an editorial framing, such as *"E heluhelu oukou a noonoo i na mea lapuwale o ka poe kahiko"* [You should all read and consider the frivolous things of the ancients]. The year-long serial publication of Pogue's rewrite of *Ka Mooolelo Hawaii*,[112] supported by the newspaper and planned for subsequent book publication, was presented with this editorial statement:

> He mea ia e lealea ai ka poe naauao; he mea hoi ia e maopopo ai ka pilikia o ka noho ana, iloko o ka naaupo, a me ka pomaikai o keia koho ana, iloko o ka malamalama (*Ka Hae Hawaii* 1858).
>
> [It is something that will delight educated people; it is certainly a means by which the difficulty of life in a setting of ignorance becomes clear, as does the blessing of this choice, of being in enlightenment.]

Though still flavored by Calvinist proselytizing, *Ka Hae Hawaii* allowed for and cultivated reader interaction. Every issue of *Ka Hae Hawaii* contained letters from readers on an unprecedented variety of topics. Usually quite short, two to four paragraphs, these addressed local affairs and oddities, reports of accidents, deaths, illness outbreaks, and commentary on recent events or government actions. Letters from readers and those generated by neighborhood agents of the paper were still quite limited in scope and size, but the presence of such individual input encouraged others to respond. Such a stimulus appeared at a time when literacy had become practically universal among Hawaiians, and no other avenue for general public expression had yet been established.

---

[111] J. Fuller was listed by Moʻokini (1974) as the editor of *Ka Hae Hawaii*, but the paper was under the direction of Richard Armstrong, known as Limaikaika. Armstrong arrived in Hawaiʻi in 1832 with the fifth company of missionaries of the ABCFM, but resigned from the mission in 1848 to take the post of Minister of Public Instruction.

[112] Several books and many serial columns in the papers carried the title *Ka Mooolelo Hawaii*, or the variant spelling *Ka Moolelo Hawaii*, generally meaning "Hawaiian History."

Through *Ka Hae Hawaii*, the Ministry of Public Instruction actively cultivated appreciation among Hawaiians as an audience for general-interest newspapers. *Ka Hae Hawaii* announced that its goals included educating the Hawaiian population, informing them of government business and laws, developing their awareness of local and global events, and, importantly, increasing the interest among them for newspapers (*Ka Hae Hawaii* 1861). This effort apparently responded to a growing demand on the part of Hawaiians, which Samuel Damon, editor of *The Friend*, mentioned in regards to the opening of *Ka Hae Hawaii*:

> For years the natives have been left to glean all foreign and domestic news from the pages of a small paper issued from the press of the American Mission…The Hawaiians are famishing for useful information upon various secular subjects, education, agriculture and mechanical trades. (*The Friend* 1856)

The effort was successful during its six years in print; in 1861, *Ka Hae Hawaii* stopped publication, stating in its final issue that its goals had been met and that the Hawaiians had become *poe puni nupepa*—"a people who craved newspapers" (1861). Not only had Hawaiians become an avid reading audience, but they were beginning to collectively generate the content. Hawai'i was poised to shift and re-center the production of public discourse.

The Hawaiian newspapers were kept affordable, and had stayed that way for decades through mission or government funding. The early, small-format mission papers were supported by the Calvinist mission at minimal or no cost to readers, as were the few papers published by the Catholics. *Ka Nonanona* (1841) cost 12.5¢ per year, and *Ka Elele Hawaii* (1848) set its rates by social status: 25¢ a year for commoners; $1 for chiefs and foreigners; 50¢ for others of importance.[113] The government-funded *Ka Hae Hawaii* began as a weekly in 1856 for a price of $1 annually, rising to $1.50 when its size increased after a year. *Ka Hae Hawaii* was still far smaller and cheaper than the English papers of the time, *The Polynesian* and *Pacific Commercial Advertiser*, which cost $8 and $6 per year, respectively.[114]

---

[113] *Ka Elele Hawaii* was officially a government newspaper, but was considered an organ of the mission.

[114] *The Polynesian* began publication again in 1844, after a 2-year hiatus. The subscription price was reduced to $6, and later that year the paper began to receive government subsidy to print the laws and announcements.

Subsidized newspapers like *Ka Hae Hawaii* generated an audience, but they also developed a readership accustomed to an affordable press.[115] In 1856, H. M. Whitney announced his plan to produce a large, independent weekly Hawaiian newspaper of good quality at $4 per year, but it was cancelled for lack of subscribers, a lesson not lost on publishers of the time. His idea of an independent paper came about later in a small monthly format at 25¢ a year.[116] When the first two independent Hawaiian papers, *Ka Hoku o ka Pakipika* and *Ka Nupepa Kuokoa*, emerged in 1861, they kept their subscription cost at a low $2 per year, apparently following what the market would bear. That cost, for weekly issues of Hawaiian language newspapers, remained the same until 1948, when *Ka Hoku o Hawaii* ended publication.[117]

With the cost of papers remaining relatively constant, the improved network of communication became an attractive quality of newspapers. While a few months for the spread of global news may seem unimaginable today, it reflected a new level of advancement in the early 19th century; *Ka Hae Hawaii* boasted about the worldwide speed and power of the press:

> Ma Ladana paha, ma Nu Ioka paha, ua hanaia kekahi mea ino loa, a hala na malama me ka hapa, ua kukala ia ka inoa o ka lawehala ma na aina pau o ka honua nei. (1857)

> [In London, or perhaps New York, some evil deed is carried out and within the passing of a month and a half, the name of the perpetrator is announced in every country in the world.]

While news from abroad still took a month or months to travel, local news began to appear regularly in *Ka Hae Hawaii*, and readers could share local news and ideas from all islands on a weekly basis, a speed and regularity that seemed almost conversational in comparison.[118] Ready access to local news, along with

---

[115] For comment on how a regular subscription of $2 would maintain independent press, see *Ka Hae Hawaii* 1861.

[116] Whitney announced his intentions in *Ka Hoku Loa O Hawaii* (Whitney 1856) (contained in the *Advertiser*) and the need for 200 subscribers, but the paper never appeared in the proposed format. The eventual monthly *Ka Hoku Loa* (1859–1864) was edited by Rev. H. H. Parker.

[117] While weekly subscription rates remained at $2, daily papers, usually Monday through Saturday, rose to $8/year. The price was anachronistic, for $2 in commodities in 1864 had changed greatly by 1948.

[118] Twenty-first century communication via the internet, which was a foundation for L. Cruz' 2003 dissertation, would be analogous to the Hawaiian newspapers of the 1860s in the way the new technology was embraced by the public for its accessibility and the emerging possibilities of engaging one's audience.

the ability of readers to respond to published writers, opened a new space for interaction, one that Hawaiians adopted and developed into a regular center of communication and expression. This new venue provided a public setting resonant with an oral tradition, allowing for public validation, negation, or correction of those presenting their writings. *"Ina ua loaa ka wahahee, ua kinai ia e ka oiaio e kuhikuhi ana i ke ano o ka wahahee"* [If falsehood is found, it is erased by truth revealing the nature of the falsehood] (*Ka Hae Hawaii* 1857).

Later independent Hawaiian newspapers garnered a subscription base of smaller size, with 2,700 copies printed of *Ka Hoku o ka Pakipika* (1862, Oct. 10: 2) and 3,000 for *Ka Nupepa Kuokoa* in 1862 (1861, Nov. 1: 2), their first full year of production. This level of subscriber support is from a Hawaiian population of approximately 65,000 at the time.[119]

The expanding content, affordable cost, and reliability of the only secular Hawaiian newspaper of the time promoted increased readership, as did the direct efforts of the government to cultivate interest in the newspapers.[120] Subscriptions to *Ka Hae Hawaii* doubled during its six-year run, from about 1,500 paid subscribers in 1856 to 3,000 in 1861, equal to two of the local English-language newspapers of the day, the *Pacific Commercial Advertiser* and *The Friend*. The actual number of copies printed probably far exceeded subscriber numbers: *The Friend* and many of the mission newspapers were distributed for free to some sectors, and other newspapers printed extra copies to be sold individually or given away. *Ka Hae Hawaii* would likely have followed the established practices in order to generate new readers.

Māori newspaper scholar Jenifer Curnow points out in regard to Māori papers that publication numbers do not accurately reflect readership, as the vernacular papers were shared among family and community, expanding the readership geometrically (2002:18). The same was true for the Hawaiian-language papers, judging by articles and anecdotal accounts. Editorials criticized the sharing of papers as undermining the newspapers viability. Hawaiian-speaking elders born in the early 20th century recount how the whole newspaper was read aloud to family members and then passed along from house to house.[121] *Ka Hae Hawaii* and its successors undoubtedly reached far more readers than the numbers would indicate.

---

[119] The population had diminished from roughly 142,000 in 1825 (the last census prior to the 1834 advent of Hawaiian newspapers) to 65,647 by 1860 (Schmitt 1977:25, 35).

[120] *Ka Hae Hawaii* frequently contained articles directly espousing the virtues of newspapers as a source of progress for the Hawaiians. Examples abound; see *Ka Hae Hawaii* (1861).

[121] Many Hawaiian native-speaking elders of the late 20th century, as children, were expected to read aloud to older family members from the bible and from the Hawaiian newspapers. Kamuela Kumukahi, personal communication, June 24, 1995.

The expanding size of the paper provided more content to interest the readership and also allowed more room for articles and letters from those readers, building both interest and interaction.

Ka Hae Hawaii was published until December 25, 1861, shortly after the independent press emerged. An editorial in its closing issue explained that the strategy of government subsidy and support had been successful enough that the paper would be retired. The closure of Ka Hae Hawaii was a direct result of the establishment of the two independent papers, Ka Hoku o ka Pakipika and Ka Nupepa Kuokoa, and its closure was an effort to support these private endeavors.

The strategy that nurtured the newspaper venue had generated a discerning audience, and dissatisfaction with the form and content of Ka Hae Hawaii helped shape the new Hawaiian press:

> Hoohalahala pinepine mai kekahi poe i ka Hae Hawaii, no ka uuku o kona kino, aole lawa na mea hou a me na manao maikai maloko ona; aole paiia na mele, a me na kanikau e like me ka makemake o ka poe nana i kakau. (Ka Hae Hawaii 1861, Nov. 6)
>
> [People have frequently criticized the Hae Hawaii for its small size, which cannot contain sufficient news or good opinion; chants and dirges are not printed as per the wishes of those who composed them.]

The new, larger format of the independent papers made every attempt to overcome the criticism that had been leveled at Ka Hae Hawaii, an intentional reshaping of the paradigm of knowledge production for the Hawaiian-speaking population. The form of the independent papers was enlarged, with expanded news, receptiveness to a broad range of material, letters and opinion pieces, serial stories and frequent inclusion of chants and dirges.[122] In the opening issue of Ka Hoku o ka Pakipika, the change was lauded:

> No na makahiki he kanaha i hala ae nei, aole o kakou he nupepa nui a kulike hoi me ka makemake o ka lahui Hawaii, kahi i hiki ai ia kakou ke hookomo i ko kakou mau manao ponoi, nolaila, aole i loheia na mea akamai me na mea lealea, a

---

[122] Kanikau, or dirge chants, were published for a fee, by line length, usually $2 for 50 lines. For example, see Ka Nupepa Kuokoa, Jan. 30, 1864, p. 1.

ko kakou manao i hookupu ai, ua waiho keia mau mea ma ka papa, me ka manao ole ua loaa ia kakou kekahi wahi naauao iki, a ua nele loa kakou i ka nupepa ole e hoihoi ai, a ua hoka loa ka makemake o ka poe maa i na manao maikai no kahi ole e hiki ai ia lakou ke hoolaha ae i na manao o lakou. (J. B. Keahiakawelo 1861).

[For the last forty years, we have had no major newspaper that accorded with the wishes of the Hawaiian people, where we could submit our own personal thoughts, and therefore wise and fun things, and ideas that we have generated have not been heard, they have been left on the floor, without thinking that we have gained some bit of education, so we have completely lacked a newspaper in which we could take interest, and the interests of those who are accustomed to intelligent thoughts have been thwarted by having no place where they can disseminate their insights.]

Keahiakawelo's comments were expressed on behalf of *Ka Hoku o ka Pakipika*, but his support for change was apparently widely shared. This note, published in the same week by H. M. Whitney, editor of *Ka Nupepa Kuokoa*, offered its own slant:

O na Nupepa ka ai hanai i ka pololi o ka manao. Malaila e kena ai ka makemake, e mahuahua ai ka ike. Aole e maona ka manao i na pepa liiliii e like mamua. E kanaka makua ana o Hawaii nei, e ake nei e like ko lakou ike me ko na haole. (1861)

[Newspapers are the sustenance of intellectual hunger. It is there that desire can be fulfilled and knowledge developed. The mind will not be satisfied with small papers like before. Hawai'i is maturing, and desires that their knowledge be equal to those of foreign lands.]

Writers, many of whom had never been published prior to the advent of the independent press, filled both of the new, large-format newspapers with staff editorials and submissions from the reading public.

Along with a great increase in contributing writers, the enlarged and independent papers allowed for the steady presence of serialized narratives, including both native and foreign historical accounts, legends, and cultural descriptions, which immediately became mainstays of the newspaper format. The newspapers' stated openness to all writers and topics generated an abundance of unsolicited articles and fostered the normalization of letters of response. Staff writers, those submitting their works, and the general readership were well aware of the importance of what had become a discerning national audience. This cautionary note, from a debate between two writers in the opening issues of both *Ka Hoku o ka Pakipika* and *Ka Nupepa Kuokoa*, clarified the setting at the outset of the independent press:

> Mai manao oe he 12 wale no mea nana e noonoo mai kau mau olelo a me kau mau hoakaka ana, aole, aka he Lahuikanaka okoa, no ka mea, aia o Hawaii; o Keawe; o Maui, o Kama; o Oahu. O Kuhihewa; o Kauai; o Manokalanipo; o lakou ka poe nana e apono mai a e ahewa mai, ke pono a ke hewa kau alakai ana. (Waianuenue 1861)

> [Do not assume that only twelve [a jury] will consider your statements and explanations, no; an entire nation of people will do so, for those of Chief Keawe's isle, Hawai'i, and from Kamalālāwalu's domain, Maui, of Kākuhihewa's land of O'ahu, and there in Manokalanipō's realm, Kaua'i, they are who will approve or condemn regarding whether your direction is right or wrong.]

1861—The Independent Hawaiian Press

The independent press greatly expanded the range of Hawaiian representation beyond what had existed previous to that time, and the surge of Hawaiian participation indicates a major shift in the power over knowledge. As such, it exemplifies the kind of break in continuity and inconsistency in historical sequence that Foucault addressed as a point of entry for investigation, an area of the field that would pose new challenges to historical inquiry in identifying those discontinuities, ruptures, and transformations. The details of this transition deserve careful investigation.

The material contained in the sudden expansion of Hawaiian writings in the 1860s has been noted, extracted, and investigated from many perspectives, but after a century of research, such efforts are still preliminary. No study to date has addressed the importance of changing strictures on content and form throughout the period in question, or the activation of national dialogue and published public discourse in a newly-literate society. Documentation and analysis of the whole spectrum will inform many topics, including the relationships between orality and literacy, the demographic and representational practices the newspapers enabled, and the resulting forms of subjectivity.

Historian Helen Chapin recognized the importance of this transition when she addressed the emergence of the native press as the outcome of "literacy joined to a newspaper technology, conferring empowerment" (1996:59). Chapin identified general themes that appeared to set the independent Hawaiian papers apart from what she considered establishment papers after 1861, and political historian Noenoe Silva (1999, 2004) further distilled those distinctions in her work, but both studies are still preliminary observations about the larger body of material.

Chapin credits the newspaper *Ke Au Okoa*, which began in 1865, with setting many of the patterns that would guide the content and arrangement of subsequent Hawaiian papers, but the earliest independent Hawaiian papers, *Ka Hoku o ka Pakipika* and *Ka Nupepa Kuokoa*, exhibit that such patterns were being established from the genesis of the independent native press. Editorial positions and reader responses to content and form were common, as seen in the dialogues discussed below. Examples of those interactions are presented in this editorial, which gave excerpts from numerous letters and reasons why they could not all be printed, while emphasizing the collective nature of the newspaper:

> He nui no na leta e hiki mai nei no ko kakou pepa, e hiki ana paha i ka haneri a oi ae, i kela pule, keia pule. A ina e paiia ua mau palapala la a pau, mahea la auanei kahi kowa kaawale e komo ai o na mea maikai e ae? Ua maopopo no ia makou me ka olioli nui, ke kumu o ka hiki nui ana mai o na leta, mai na welau mai a pau o keia mau Mokupuni, oia no ke kaulana nui o ko kakou nupepa nei. (*Ka Nupepa Kuokoa* 1862, Sept. 6)

> [Many letters arrive for our paper, a hundred or more each week. If they were all printed, where would we find room for other good things? We here know, happily, that the reason for the flood of letters from all corners of these islands is due to the great renown of this paper belonging to us all.]

Limited space continued to restrict what could be printed, and even with the larger size and expanded boundaries of content in the independent press, widespread Calvinist mores still affected editorial decisions. In 1865, when W. P. Alexander submitted his students' essays on ancient religion to the *Kuokoa*, he advised the editor, L. H. Gulick, to censor them as necessary. Gulick printed the essays, but because the original submissions are not archived, the level of editing imposed on the printed articles is unknown. Alexander's caution signifies some of the pressures that were still very extant on publication.

> ...it will be necessary for you to expurgate occasionally, the essays I send to you. Indeed, Hawaiian antiquity cannot be recorded intelligently without much we should hesitate to print.—I leave that to you—W. P. A. (Kirtley and Mookini 1977:69)

In her text *Aloha Betrayed* (2004), Noenoe Silva analyzes the opening of the independent native press in 1861 as an embodiment of a resistance movement. Using the published editorials and interchanges involved in the opening of the independent newspapers, she illustrates the criticism leveled at *Ka Hoku o ka Pakipika* as the first independent *Hawaiian* newspaper, and the kinds of opposition the paper faced from religious and economic sectors. The presence of such opposition was particularly vitriolic at the advent of *Ka Hoku o ka Pakipika,* but other Hawaiian-language papers also experienced such opposition, as shown in later defensive editorials and commentaries that defended their positions and practices.[123]

The dynamics of the first years of the native press are inherently complex, and understanding those dynamics is made more difficult by the distancing of language and time. Although resistance is a factor in the emergence and growth of the independent Hawaiian press, it is one of many, and indicates no single focus. The articles in the papers of the day pinpoint many challenges that Hawaiians faced at the time and exhibit an array of responses to those challenges.

In presenting the writings of this period to my own students, I use the term "movement of insistence" to describe the vitality and confidence of the newly-expanded Hawaiian presence in the newspapers after the start of the native press. Letters, editorials, and sequential dialogues of the period addressed topics of an ever-increasing range, from economic policies to ancient religious practices. Throughout the period, articles abound containing issues of self-determination, documentation of the past, future planning, re-evaluation of traditional practices, and the importance of Hawaiian consideration and decision about those issues. The sudden appearance of myriad voices do not seem to indicate a renaissance or sudden renewal of interest, but rather a new-found point of access to participate in the processes affecting the lives of the readers and writers. Describing the

---

[123] See, for example, Kuaana (1866), *Ka Nupepa Kuokoa* (1867), and *Ka Nuhou Hawaii* (1873).

variety of writings as evidence of a "movement of insistence" retains an analytical flexibility, while incorporating other themes like those recognized by Chapin, Silva, and others.

Orality and Newspapers

In the first half of the 19th century, Hawaiians were still moving from orality to literacy, a form of societal process that Walter Ong describes in *Orality and Literacy* (1982). He states that characteristics of an oral society remain extant for generations following the adoption of literacy and print, continuing to shape the worldview of those generations and the manner in which that view is expressed in their writings.

Ong describes residual features of orality found in newly-literate societies, like the collective nature of knowledge and the sense of shared sources for creative works. In Hawaiʻi, cultural aspects like these integrated more easily with the venue of newspapers than with books. Coming from an oral society, Hawaiians were accustomed to a system where shared knowledge and memory could be validated or refuted through presentation and peer dialogue. Collective memory and public presentation allowed for the comparison of chants, genealogies, histories, and legends for completeness and accuracy, processes that were common in the newspaper interchanges. Chiefly authority over the validation of knowledge was diminished with the advent of literacy, further empowering the general public to participate in the forum that the newspapers provided.

The dynamic of collective validation became a force within the newspapers only after interaction had become normalized in the later independent press. Aside from scattered arguments between known scholars, there was little room for it in the first decades of the newspapers during the earliest literate period of Hawaiʻi. Once culturally-pertinent dialogue flourished in the newspapers, the oral nature of the society became more fully engaged.

Issues regarding personal ownership of knowledge were rare indeed, but validation of collectively-owned information and of the authority to present such information appeared in early papers and became common topics of published interchanges as time passed.[124] Discussion arose in those early papers about the propriety of publicly disseminating certain kinds of information.[125] Later criticisms

---

[124] Issues of knowledge ownership were not apparent within Hawaiian newspaper discourse, although the matter of copyright did arise in 1869 when S. M. Kamakau's writings began to be translated into English in *The Polynesian*, resulting in Kamakau securing a copyright for his serial column.

[125] See Unauna's critique of S. M. Kamakau, presented in Chapter 4 of this text.

centered on accuracy of content and the credibility of individual writers when presenting shared knowledge of history, legend, or practice. Legends, historical notes, or genealogical material presented in the newspaper could be critiqued by readers who would correct published work, silence the writer outright or mount a defense of that material.[126]

In spite of radical social changes during three-quarters of a century of continued intercourse with foreigners, oral traditions of Hawaiian society were still strong at the time the independent native press began in the 1860s, and the content of the press offers examples of their continuation. Ong speaks to the conflict between writing and the oral tradition, whereas writing creates "discourse which cannot be directly questioned or contested as oral speech can be because written discourse has been detached from its author" (1982:79). He goes on to point out how "[a] text stating what the whole world knows is false will state falsehood forever, so long as the text exists." The Hawaiian oral systems that were still in place were activated by these powers of the published word, and while Ong's point about distance between author and audience was especially true of books, it was less rigidly so in the case of newspapers, especially the Hawaiian newspapers, which allowed for a slow, but near-oral form of interaction.

The gap between author and audience was spannable only through response and dialogue. Correcting or refuting other writers allowed the finality of printed text to be diminished, especially as newspapers were frequently bound and kept for reference.[127] This gave the newspapers a continuing context of dialogue for readers of the time.[128] Taken in isolation, pieces of that dialogue appear factual, final, and uncontested. In using these writings today, Ong's observations about the finality of print must be considered along with the oral practices and interactions that shaped the written repositories of the newspapers. The intertextuality of the newspapers, the cross-reference between articles and even between different newspapers informs our understanding of the resource. Careful consideration of the full assembly of all writings by individual authors or about particular topics grants new

---

[126] See, for example, *Ka Hoku o ka Pakipika* (1862) which denies that there is a single authoritative version of any legend, as well as Unauna, A. (1842) and Kamakau (1843) (on authority to publish chiefly genealogy).

[127] Newspaper publishers regularly printed offers to bind subscribers' full year of newspapers, as well as offering for sale bound copies of the previous year's papers. For examples, see *Ka Nonanona* (1845), Kanepuu (1856), and *Ka Elele Hawaii* (1848).

[128] Historian Noelani Arista, in the introduction to the 2007 reprint of *Kepelino's Traditions of Hawaii*, addressed how the Hawaiian intellectual traditions of the kingdom era are documented in the written and published discourse of the time, but have yet to be fully researched and understood by modern scholars.

recognition to voices and issues of the period. The extraction of any portion of that material from its context of dialogue and peer response or from the full range of a writer's works is problematic in a number of ways, a point discussed in Chapter 4.

GROWTH OF PARTICIPATION

The change in scale of the number of Hawaiian voices represented in writing is apparent when comparing the transitional paper *Ka Hae Hawaii* with the subsequent independent press that it helped to generate. Running for over five years from 1856–1861, mostly in a mid-size format, *Ka Hae Hawaii* published approximately 1,000 newspaper pages. This would equal four to five times that number of letter-size pages of text.[129] Letters or articles by Hawaiian writers outside of the scope of government or mission business make up less than 10 percent of the whole, perhaps 100 pages of newspaper, equivalent to as much as 600 (letter-size) pages of general discourse in this somewhat-independent budding venue. This was within, of course, the continuing frame of direct mission and government oversight, but these articles submitted by readers included a range of topics, from local events to opinion pieces about government or religion.

From 1861 to 1870, the three Hawaiian newspapers *Ka Hoku o ka Pakipika, Ka Nupepa Kuokoa,* and *Ke Au Okoa*[130] produced six thousand broadsheet pages of text. The large format makes this sum equivalent to well over 60,000 letter-size pages of material, most of which was produced by Hawaiian writers.[131] The thousands of articles from the decade of the 1860s represented a new scale of Hawaiian writers and a newly-independent setting.

By the 1860s, the Hawaiian staff of the papers produced most of the editorial and serial content of *Ka Hoku o ka Pakipika* and *Ka Nupepa Kuokoa.*[132] Two characteristics of this transition from mission to Hawaiian control are:

---

[129] The 1,000 typed pages is an estimate. *Ka Hae Hawaii* published approximately 300 four-page issues, regularly increasing its size and by the last years of publication had expanded to about six letter-size pages of text per page. Each full page of these later issues of *Ka Hae* contains over 13,000 characters, while an 8.5 x 11" sheet of double-spaced 12 point type is about 2,000 characters per page.

[130] *Ke Au Okoa* was a government-sponsored paper, but followed closely the norms that had been set by the two previous independent papers, *Ka Hoku o ka Pakipika* and *Ka Nupepa Kuokoa,* and eventually merged with *Kuokoa* in 1873.

[131] *Aha Elele*, not considered here, was another Hawaiian-language paper, published by the government only during the 1864 constitutional convention. Religious papers of the decade include *Hooiliili Havaii, Hoku Loa, Na Helu Kalavina, Ka Hae Kiritiano, Ke Alaula, Ka Hae Katolika,* all of which would have been affected by the presence of the independent press, but which are not being considered in this discussion. See Chapin (2000) for more information.

[132] *Ka Nupepa Kuokoa* was edited by H. M. Whitney and *Ka Hoku o ka Pakipika* also had a *haole* editor, G. Mills (Mila), but the writers were mostly, if not all, Hawaiian.

Ka Hae Hawaii [*The Hawaiian Flag*], published weekly from 1856 to 1861, increased Hawaiians' engagement in the production of newspapers. Government sponsored through the Department of Public Instruction, the paper encouraged readers to submit news and articles, and expanded its size to accommodate the additional content. As the independent press emerged in 1861, Ka Hae ended publication, announcing that it had succeeded in making Hawaiians a "poʻe puni nupepa," a people who loved newspapers. Photo by David Franzen, Bishop Museum.

(1) the number of articles or letters directly addressing some aspect of Hawaiian culture, and (2) the number of letters submitted and published from the reading audience.[133] A comparison of establishment (mission/government) and independent papers illuminates the extent of the transition.[134] The appearance of articles directly addressing cultural topics soared from an average of less than one per issue in mission/government papers to 9 or more as the norm for *Ka Hoku o ka Pakipika,* 5 per issue in the opening years of *Ka Nupepa Kuokoa* and 2–3 per issue in *Ke Au Okoa.* Likewise, an average of 4 signed letters in earlier government and mission papers rose to twenty as the average in each issue of *Ka Hoku,* and 10 or more per issue in *Ka Nupepa Kuokoa.* The government-supported *Ke Au Okoa* maintained an average of 4–5 signed letters per issue, similar to the mission and government papers, although the letters were of greater length and included a much broader range of topics. While the size difference of the papers must be taken into account, the increased presence of Hawaiian interaction is apparent.

CONTENT AND FORM AS REFLECTION OF ORALITY

Many of the forms and processes of communication documented in the Hawaiian oral tradition by early observers, such as oratory, recitation, chant, and protocols, were continued for generations after literacy became widespread. Evidence of this retention is incorporated into the letters and articles for the newspapers, especially in the latter half of the 19th century.

Letters and articles generated from the readership expanded what had, in earlier papers, been mostly the product of the newspaper's own writers and editors. Usually edited into some level of consistency adopted by individual papers, such materials from the reading audience often contained content or form that extended beyond the boundaries of the paper's own norms. These materials provide unique insight into the discourse of the period by giving glimpses of the way the population beyond the newspaper offices expressed themselves in this venue.

---

[133] "Cultural aspect" is a subjective description; for the purpose of this survey, only those articles whose topic directly addressed a cultural practice or Hawaiian historical event, whether generated by the paper or in a submitted letter, have been considered for this count. Regarding letters, those signed by the editor, publisher, or submitted as signed reports from a government or mission office were not included in the tally. *Ka Elele* (1848–1849), *Ka Hae Hawaii* (1856–1861), and *Ka Hoku Loa* (1859–1864) were reviewed as mission or early government papers, *Ka Hoku o ka Pakipika* (1861–1863), *Ke Kuokoa* (1861–1870), and *Ke Au Okoa* (1865–1870), were considered as independent and post native-press examples.

[134] One issue per year in each of the newspapers was surveyed for this overview.

Poetic forms of address, which showed skill and preparation on the part of the speaker while bestowing respect on the person addressed, mostly appear in these reader-generated pieces. Poetic greetings and closures were sometimes included, usually in truncated form, during the first decades of the press, but became far more common in newspapers after 1861. During the opening decades of the mission and government press, these formalities were absent, and it is unclear whether they were deleted, edited, or self-edited into a form of Hawaiian language more commonly produced by the mission institutions: simple, direct, and functional.

The signed letters from readers in the mission papers often launch directly into the content, with no greeting at all, and with no closure other than a name. Some letters open with a simple *"Aloha oe"* [Greetings], or *"Aloha oe e Ka Elele"* [Greetings to the newspaper *Ka Elele*], and close with a name or with *"na'u, na X"* [by me, by X]. Even an early cultural dialogue in *Ka Nonanona* between S. M. Kamakau and A. Unauna on the propriety of printing traditionally privileged knowledge was framed in this terse form of opening address and closure (Kamakau 1842b, 1843; Unauna 1842). Occasional letters offer fuller, not necessarily more poetical, forms of address: *"Aloha oe e ka mea hoopuka'ku i ka Elele, a me ke Kuhina Aopalapala, oia hoi ke Kuhina Kalaiaina, me olua ka malu me makou ka pomaikai, a me ka lanakila"* [Greetings to the publisher of the *Elele*, and to the Minister of Education, namely the Minister of the Interior, with you two being the governance, and with all of us being the benefit and the success] (*Ka Elele Hawaii* 1848, Jun. 8).

Such eloquence was rarely included at all in earlier newspapers until *Ka Hae Hawaii* enlarged its format, and even then it was uncommon. It is uncertain whether the minimalist and functional style of language used in early papers was the work of editors, dealing with the restraint of space or if such language was generated by the writers with an understanding that the mission papers and the language therein belonged to a separate, simplified cultural sphere. The more complex language forms that appeared with increased participation by readers is one more similar to formal language in speeches and salutations of the time than the terse, clear language of mission papers.

When literacy was introduced, Hawaiians did not have a standard form for letters or written narratives. Such forms were taught along with literacy in formal schooling and appear in most of the writings of the mission and government papers. The writings submitted to the 1860s newspapers show a new and extended mixture of traditional oratory and modern Western written forms rather than a replacement of the older traditional forms by newer styles of presentation. The greeting and closure shown below, offer small, common examples:

E ka Hae Hawaii e—Aloha oe: E hiki paha ia oe ke lawe aku i ka makana a Kapuulena ma na kihi eha o ko Hawaii nei pae aina, i ike mai o'u hoa o ka naauao. (Kealakai 1861)

[O Hae Hawaii–Fond regards to you. Perhaps you could carry this gift of the sulphury Puʻulena wind of my land to the four corners of this island chain, so that my enlightened companions may know.]

He ma'u keia wahi mamala manao ua nui a lawa, ke hoi nei ke keiki o ka la ulili wela o Kaimuki, ke pa mai nei ka makani kolonahe o kuu aina la he moae. Me ka mahalo. (Kalanikuihonoikamoku 1865)

[This little fragment of thought, of little merit but perhaps not worthless, has gone on long enough, and this child of the dazzling hot sun of Kaimukī returns, for the gentle breeze of my land, the trade wind, beckons. With appreciation.]

Poetic and deeply-cultural language of Hawaiian oratory became more apparent as the secular press developed, and flowery greetings and closures became common after 1861 in letters to the native press, even though space was still problematic. When mixed with Western styles of expression, the formal, even archaic, oratorical language is sometimes understandable today, even after more than a century of cultural change, but entire sections are often composed in language that is obscure or even opaque to modern readers.

The formal language of oratory relies for its meaning upon a foundation of cultural knowledge, and "the cultural institutions in which utterance was deeply embedded" (Ong 1995:10). Familiarity with the cultural institutions that illuminated meaning would have been more universal in the reading audience of the period, and the frequent presence of complex oratorical forms in the post-1861 newspapers speaks to the continuity of such cultural knowledge, contradicting some of the historical resources that focus on the change and loss of such cultural fluency.

In the following example from 1865, a writer's closure lists ocean (*kai*) characteristics coupled with word-play on relationship terms like *kai-kuaʻana, kai-kaina* (elder sibling, younger sibling) to acknowledge how fellow readers of *Ke Au Okoa* must comprehend for themselves the enveloping sea (*kai*) of news from the East, be it good, troubling, familiar, or strange. While the following translation attempts to show the general implications of the text, the full meaning of these references would have been grasped only by persons of the time who shared a deep insight into traditional metaphor and analogy, perhaps not even the whole readership of the period:

> Nolaila, e oʻu makamaka o Ke Au Okoa, na hoa loliii o na po loloa, hoa hookele o ka la makani, kahi a ka ihu e honi aku ai i na mea aala o ka welau makani i lawe loa ia mai ka Hikina loa mai, a loaa ka mea a loko e olelo iho ai, he kai nui, he kaikoo, he kai piha, he kai emi, he kai make, he kai lana malie, he kai ku, he kai oni, he kai okilo hee, he kai malolo, he kaikoeke, he kaikuaana, he kaikuahine, a he kaikuano, he kai paeaea, a pela aku. Ke hooki nei au i ke kakau ana ke wehe mai nei ka welau makani o Lahaina nei he maaa, ke holo mai nei ka oluolu a loaa au malalo o ke kumukukui o Puehuehu nei. (Nailiili 1865)

> [Therefore, my friends of Ke Au Okoa, pleasurable companions of the long nights and fellow navigators of the windy days, where one could catch the scent brought from afar in the East on the fringes of the breeze that would stir the heart to reflect, saying it is a grand sea, a raging sea, a high tide, an ebb tide, a neap tide, a calm sea, a stormy sea, a rocking sea, a glassy sea, a flying-fish sea, an in-law, an older brother, a sister, a sea of solitude, a smooth sea, etc. I close off writing at this point as the zephyr of Lahaina, the breeze called the Maʻaʻa, emerges, and comfort hastens to find me, here in the shade of the candlenut trees in Pūehuehu.]

Such extensive poetic language continually presented a problem for the limited space of the newspaper, and many letters and chants were left unpublished for lack of room. While the editor selected general letters for publication, a charge of $1 per column was set for the publication of *kanikau*, or poetic dirges, as well as for announcements and advertisements.

> He mau hanele ka nui o na Kanikau e waiho nei ma ko makou papakakau, a ua hiki ole ia makou ke pai ia mau mea a pau, no ka nele i kahi kaawale ole, ina paha he paumi ae ka nui o ka makou pepa. (*Ka Nupepa Kuokoa* 1862, Apr. 19)

[There are hundreds of dirge poems left on our desk, and we are unable to print them all due to lack of available space, even if our paper were ten times its size.]

As submitted letters increased, editors issued occasional pleas to their readers to curtail both the length and poetic language of their writings. One editorial in *Ka Hae Hawaii* gave multiple examples of the poetic openings of letters, saying that such decorative speech was cumbersome for the paper, and that many such letters were simply not printed (*Ka Hae Hawaii* 1860b). The early editors of *Ka Nupepa Kuokoa* often complained in general that letters were too numerous to all be printed and that many were written *"Me he mea la, ua kipa kino mai ma ko makou keena kakau, e kamailio ai"* [As though they had dropped into the office to chat] (1862, Apr. 19). *Ke Au Okoa* gave examples of openings and closings that were too poetic to be useful, asking readers to *"E kakau iho i na hua e hoomaopopo ai na manao io, a pau ia, e hooki ae"* [Write words that clarify the actual content, and when that is done, stop] (1869, Apr. 22).

Polynesian orature was a strong tradition, and a similar use of traditional oral arts in combination with foreign, or *pākehā*, forms of presentation was identified by Jane McRae in her work with the Māori newspapers of the 19th century (2002). She comments on how the older oral arts were juxtaposed with, rather than replaced by, Western written forms, a combination which is also apparent in the Hawaiian examples. While style and length of language that was both personal and deeply cultural was an ongoing dilemma for the editors, the continuous appearance of such poetic forms shows that such language continued as a norm. It exemplifies the writers' appreciation of oratory and reflects the thinking processes of the native population of the time.

Orality and World View

The presence of traditional oratory and similar cultural forms in turn-of-the-century writings provide indicators that cultural structures often described by later researchers and historians as being gone by that time were still extant in the late 19th century.[135] Educator Manu Meyer, in her work on Hawaiian epistemology (1998), posits that an entire new world view has overlain or fractured an earlier Hawaiian cultural framework of knowledge built on such cultural perspectives.

---

[135] It is noted in the next chapter (pp. 136–138) that even in the translated works of Hawaiian authors from the period, cultural practice they described as ongoing was presented in translation as a thing of the past.

She does not attempt to clarify any form of that earlier framework, and having been subsumed, its characteristics would be difficult to isolate and identify. There is, however, the possibility that analysis of the historical frames of reference like these in the newspapers would allow for insight to world views and perspectives of the times by providing for comparison material with current knowledge and practice.

One field of study, of many that could be researched in the Hawaiian press, would be how *kuleana*, or privilege and responsibility, altered over time. *Kuleana* regarding appropriate times and settings for speaking would provide an example. Once defined by relative social position and genealogical standing, a whole range of *kuleana* were altered through the constitutions and laws enacted by the monarchy, granting equal status to subjects and protecting the rights of free speech for all. The fact of written and published expression further affected how these rights were practiced.

While new legal rights changed the foundations of *kuleana*, and newspapers shifted the venues, the transitions did not diminish the importance of publicly validating or correcting collective knowledge, and the processes for handling such knowledge did not undergo complete change. The lively, extended dialogues that appeared in the papers establish documentation about the earlier settings and subsequent transitions over time. Identifying such indicators of an earlier epistemology would support the recognition, comparison, and reintegration of past and present *kuana ʻike Hawaiʻi*, Hawaiian world view.

Dialogue in the Press

Dialogue between individuals within the newspapers and between individuals and the newspapers themselves can be traced in a nascent form to some of the later mission papers of the 1840s.[136] Initially dealing with the topics deemed appropriate in those papers, such as genealogy or history, the fields of dialogue expanded over the years to a much broader range, although still bounded by what was considered appropriate for public discussion.[137]

Some of the longest-running topics began with mission editorials censuring particular Hawaiian practices, such as idolatry, native medicine, or hula. As personal expressions began to expand in the paper, they usually supported the established

---

[136] Kamakau's 1842 interchanges with Unauna, detailed later in this text, are examples.

[137] Some examples of inappropriate material are clarified: "*i ko makou manao ana, aole he mea kupono, ka hoolahaia o na hihia ohana imua o ka lehulehu*" [in our opinion, it is inappropriate for family problems to be broadcast in public] (*Ka Nupepa Kuokoa* 1862, Apr. 19). It is likely that other whole fields were excluded with little or no comment.

position, expounding on the topic or describing local instances of transgression, but as the number of letters increased, differences in opinion about dealing with such issues became apparent, generating reader responses to individual writers and initiating ongoing discussion within the newspapers. Writers openly argued with previously published letters, and challenged the reading public to offer their opinions, like the following letter in *Ka Hae Hawaii* about the government's role in handling prostitution and adultery:

> Auhea oukou, e ka poe paio, no ke aha la ka mumule o ka waha? Ekemu mai, i lohe nui ke kini o kakou i na mea e pili ana i na aoao elua o keia wahi manao. (M. 1860)
>
> [Where are all of you, O argumentative ones, and why the silence? Speak up, so that the multitude of us can hear the things pertaining to the two sides of this particular subject.]

Another issue that garnered strong public interaction was that of native medical practitioners. Sporadic letters and editorials appeared in Hawaiian papers for at least a decade prior to the 1858 publication in *Ka Hae Hawaii* of a seven-part serial column on the ancient practice of native medicine entitled "Ka Oihana Lapaau Kahiko" (Kalama 1858–1859). The series was the first large presentation in a decade-long, continuous dialogue on the topic of native medicine in *Ka Hae Hawaii* and its successors, *Ka Hoku o ka Pakipika*, *Ka Nupepa Kuokoa*, and *Ke Au Okoa*.[138]

Scholars today are beginning to recognize the particular importance of such extended published dialogue, yet the analysis is still incomplete. Collette Leimomi Akana (2002) presented a year-long section of these letters in annotated translation showing a widespread disapproval of the practice of native medicine, but consideration of the decade-long sequence of letters indicates that opinion was mixed, and that far more than general disapproval was involved as well. The dialogue both led to and reflected a social movement that resulted in a renewed viability of native healing practices, a system for licensing of native healers, and the establishment of a national department of health.

Initially, writers pointed out that while foreign doctors had been successful in treating certain illnesses, Hawaiian healers would better serve particularly

---

[138] Coverage on issues relating to native practices continued throughout the entire span of Hawaiian-language papers.

Hawaiian ailments.[139] Trained doctors and medicines were also scarce, especially in rural districts, so native healers were often the only available option. Persistent criticisms regarding individual native practitioners increased, interspersed among the more general censure of the practice from the Christian community, as the newspapers became a forum for discussing Western and native medicine in light of population decline. The national dialogue on this topic and the availability of the newspapers as a centralized place to report charlatans provided powerful tools for change, allowing for the revitalization and the collective regulation of the field of traditional healing.

Letters denouncing individuals as *kahuna hoʻopunipuni*, false practitioners, or *kahuna wahaheʻe*, lying experts, allowed the writers to publicly identify imposters in the field, usually by name and full description, so that skilled practitioners would not be wrongly maligned by the general censure. This public policing of the healing arts provided renewed confidence in the reliability of native healers. Supporters and satisfied patients could defend a healer who was wrongly accused of fraud, while those accused who had no acknowledged record of success or satisfied clients to publicly defend them quickly saw their credibility destroyed and their practice finished.[140]

The public opinion expressed both documented and impelled contemporary social action.[141] In 1859, as this public interaction went on in the papers, Crown Prince Lot Kapuāiwa issued licenses to *kahuna lāʻau lapaʻau*. After some years of ongoing debate, a conference of healers was held on Maui in 1866 to establish a system for validating expertise.[142] Then in 1868, amid continued opposition by foreign and mission sectors of the population, Lot, now King Kamehameha V, established the official licensing of traditional medical practitioners through a newly-established Hawaiian Board of Health (Akana 2002:35).[143] The dialogue on native medicine provides evidence for the role of newspaper discourse in shaping government action and the converse impact of action upon public discussion.

---

[139] A letter by J. Nākoʻokoʻo (*Ka Nupepa Kuokoa* 1870, Jun. 11) gives a good example of this argument, but many examples exist in papers of the period.

[140] Waimanalo (1863) is a good example of such a defense of a maligned practitioner.

[141] This quote by Esther Moʻokini was an overview statement, but applies to the particulars presented above: "Hawaiian language newspapers were not only reflections of politics and culture in its many dimensions; but primary instruments of movements and individuals, and influences on events, trends and attitudes. Hawaiian newspapers are, therefore, indispensable sources for every aspect of our history." (1974: xiv)

[142] The conference, begun in December of 1866, extended into 1867. The proceedings of that conference are published in translation in *Must We Wait in Dispair* (Chun 1994).

[143] Also see Bushnell (1993:110) who covers the development of the Hawaiian Board of Health. See Chun (1994) regarding the proceedings of Maui conference.

Ancient Religion

A similar protracted public interchange appeared for decades in the newspapers on the subject of *hoʻomana kahiko,* ancient religion, and the practices that were related to religious ritual, including the hula and native medicine. Beginning with editorial and pedagogy pieces in the mission press about the evil nature of pagan practice, the topic continued to appear in the secular press, often expressing the outward disdain or despair of the writer. In this example, from an article about *hoʻomana kiʻi,* idol worship, the writer denounced the practice in his opening, but went on in the article to include a great level of detail, including deity names and ritual sequence:

> Lapuwale maoli keia hana. Kainoa ua pau ka pouli, a ua hiki mai la ka malamalama i Hawaii nei. Aole ka! eia no ka ke mau nei no ia hana lapuwale. Ahea la e pau ai ia hana o ko Hawaii nei. I koʻu manao, aole no e pau ana a hiki wale aku i ka pau ana o ka honua. (*Ka Hae Hawaii* 1860a)

> [This activity is truly worthless. One would have thought the darkness was over, and that enlightenment had come here to Hawaiʻi. Not at all! Here such wretched news continues on. When will this practice be ended here in Hawaiʻi? In my opinion, it will never stop until the end of the world.]

Ancient religion continued to be a frequent topic after the opening of the native press in 1861. Articles noted where some particular religious act or ritual had been witnessed, with most writers expressing disapproval of perpetuating the ancient beliefs. Chants and prayers connected in any way to ritual use were often left out completely, criticized, or included with disclaimers, lest they be mistakenly perceived as being encouraged by the newspaper.

From January 5 to December 30 of 1865, *Ka Nupepa Kuokoa* ran a 33-part extended series on ancient religion called "Hoomana Kahiko," presented with the stated goal of showing the fallacy of such practices and to bring an end to those practices still being observed. One of the articles that seemingly generated the "Hoomana Kahiko" series made note of those who were still involved in old religious ritual and urged *Ka Nupepa Kuokoa* to quickly provide information "*i ike mai ai keia poe e noho ana i ka pouli*" [so that these people living in darkness may see] (Hukilani 1864).

The series, by various students in Lorrin Andrews' divinity class at Lahainaluna, began less than two months later, and ran for much of the year 1865, generating a number of reaction letters during its run. The co-editor of *Ka Nupepa Kuokoa* at the time, missionary L. H. Gulick, showed concern about the extent of "idolatry" dialogue fostered by his paper, for in the following year the paper was reticent about printing an article which contained a prayer to ʻaumākua, or guardian spirits. Preceding that article was this editor's note:

> Aole makou i manao e hoopuka i keia pule i na Aumakua, i mea e ao ai i ko makou poe opiopio mahope o ia hana uko ole a na kupuna o kakou, oiai ua ike kakou a pau i ka noho ana o keia wa, aole i like me ka wa mamua. Ke hoikeike nei makou i keia me ka hookamani ole, i mea e ike pu iho ai kakou a pau i ka lapuwale maoli o na pule a ko kakou mau makua—Luna Hooponopono. (Gulick in Kalaaukumuole 1866)
>
> [We did not intend to publish this prayer to the family deities so that our young people will learn those useless endeavors of our ancestors, whereas we all recognize that life today is not like previous eras. We present this without pretense, that we all may see the true worthlessness of the prayers of our forefathers — Editor.]

The long-running discussion in the Hawaiian papers on ancient native religion is invaluable for the insight it can provide us today about the diversity of opinions expressed from within the Hawaiian and resident foreigner population over the span of decades. The variety of coverage on this topic is also important for the inclusion of details and descriptions of religious practices, terms for actions and materials, names of deities and their realms, and areas and times in which historical practitioners were observed.

Perpetuation

One of the most far-reaching exchanges in the 19th-century papers concerned the broad field of documentation and perpetuation of traditional knowledge. This multi-faceted topic often overlapped and broached into many fields, like medical practice and religion mentioned above, as well as farming, fishing, and others. The century-long concern over the loss of Hawaiian knowledge generated a massive amount of written cultural material: genealogies; histories; legends; chants; riddles; extensive categorical listings regarding stars, plants, fishes, sites, winds, rains, clouds, deities; and innumerable other fields of cultural knowledge.

Like most of the discursive production of the period, the early, smaller papers had limited room for such expressions, but the issue of documentation began there and expanded as the discursive space grew with the size and intentions of the papers. Whether the published information was being censured or celebrated, there was a general acknowledgment that heritage information should be documented while knowledgeable persons were still living and before the rapid pace of change and depopulation swept such knowledge away. Mataio Kekūanāoʻa, Hawaiian statesman and father of Kamehameha IV and V, addressed the chiefs in urging that traditional knowledge be documented lest it be lost:

> …o ka olelo kahiko o keia mau aina aole i pai ia. Auhea oukou e na lii malama aupuni, e ae ana i ka naauao, e ae mai oukou, e pai ae na moo kuauhau kupuna ma ka olelo honua, no ka mea o ka olelo kahiko no ia o keia mau aina, malia paha o pau oukou i ka hala e aku, nalo wale loa ka olelo kumu o Hawaii nei mai ka mole mai. A i ole e pai ia la ea! he hoailona ia no ka na lii malama i ka mea kahiko… (*Ka Lama Hawaii* 1834b)

> [… the ancient language of these lands is not printed. Hearken O governing chiefs, agreeing to wisdom, give your consent that the ancestral genealogies be printed in the indigenous language, because that is the ancient language of these lands. You may all pass away, and the source language of Hawaiʻi, from its very taproot, will disappear completely. To avoid that, let it be printed! as a sign of the chiefs' concern for the things of old.]

A genealogist and historian, Kepoʻokūlou had one of his genealogies published in *Ke Kumu Hawaii* (1835, Aug. 19), which Hiram Bingham then framed with the statement, "*I maopopo hoi i na kanaka a me na keiki a pau ma Hawaii nei ma ia hope aku*" [So the people and children of Hawaiʻi today and in the future may understand]. S. M. Kamakau closed his 1842 writings on history and genealogy with, "*I mea e maopopo ai i keia hanauna; a ia hanauna aku ia hanauna aku*" [In order that it be understood by those of this generation and all successive generations] (1842a). Writing for over three decades, Kamakau frequently referred to perpetuating knowledge of the past, opening an 1865 editorial with this statement:

> He mea maikai loa ka imi ana i na mea i haule a nalowale o na mea kahiko o Hawaii nei; a ke imi nei kakou e loaa mai me ka

pololei, a e lilo ia i waiwai na na hanauna mahope aku nei i ka
wa pau ole. (1865c)

[It is very worthwhile to seek what has fallen away or disappeared concerning the ancients of this land, Hawaiʻi; and we are seeking in order to acquire those things accurately, for they will become something of great value to future generations for all time.]

Many such exhortations expressed a general concern for generations to come, but some clearly defined those future generations, by decade and century. J. H. Kānepuʻu, in addressing the need to publish legends and *mele* in full, ended that editorial with,

E makemake ana ka hanauna Hawaii o na la A. D. 1870, a me A. D. 1880, a me A. D. 1890, a me A. D. 1990. (Kanepuu 1862)

[Hawaiian generations of the 1870s, 1880s, 1890s, and the 1990s will be wanting this.]

While there are many examples in the interim, this commentary from forty years later, by historian and editor J. M. Poepoe was part of a passionate plea for continuity of knowledge and the teaching of history to successive generations:

A o ke kanu mau ana aku o ia moolelo iloko o ka opio a kanaka makua wale ae oia, he hoomau ana aku no ia i ke aloha mawaena o ka hanauna hou a me ka hanauna i nalo aku, a e nalo aku ana hoi ma ka welelau komohana o keia ola ana. Ua olelo ae o Hoapililoihi (Longfellow) he mea pono ma ka nee ana imua me ke au o ka manawa: E waiho iho i hailona ma ka puʻe one o ke au o ka manawa i loaa ai ka ike i ou mau hoa e nee mai ana, he alahele no keia ua hele mua ia, a loaa no ke kupaa ana no ia nee ana aku imua. (Poepoe 1906b)

[The continual cultivation of that history in the young people until they are mature adults is a perpetuation of love and regard between this new generation, those who have gone on before, and those yet to pass at the furthest reaches of this existence. Longfellow stated that we must, as we move into the future:

Leave a trace upon the sands of time, so your fellows who will follow may find it, and know this to be a path already traveled, garnering in them the determination to forge on ahead.]

The emphasis on documenting knowledge for future generations expressed by those above and many others is inherent in much of the published material.

The number, range, and completeness of legends, historical accounts, chants, and such that appeared in the Hawaiian-language newspapers expanded greatly after the independent newspapers opened. Legends and stories, which began to appear in abbreviated form early on, grew into irregular serial features in *Ka Hae Hawaii* and then became a standard feature in almost all subsequent Hawaiian papers. The same kind of expansion occurred with the additions, corrections, and supporting or censuring opinions that, a century and a half later, can help today's readers understand such heritage knowledge and its place in the society of the time.

The extensive interchanges that generated and framed the ever-growing body of published cultural knowledge were common in the independent press, and often included intertextual referents connecting different articles and even multiple newspapers to a single discussion. For instance, the presentation of legends and histories were quickly cut short when critiqued for incorrectness, appended when additional information was known, or retold again in full when variations of the accounts were available.[144]

Writers frequently referred to previous issues of a paper, or to an issue or issues of other newspapers of the time in order to link multiple references into a single narrative response. It was common, in fact, for serial stories or single articles appearing in one newspaper to be the subject of commentary or addendum in another. Serial legends or narrative accounts that began publication in one newspaper often moved to a second paper, sometimes with no pause, recap, or explanation. The interchange of any reaction articles would then respond to the changed locus of presentation.[145] Such intertextuality poses yet another challenge to any attempts at fully understanding or utilizing the written resources while the whole of the repository remains relatively uncharted.

---

[144] See Koko (1865), where he cuts his account of Lonoikamakahiki after criticism from Haleʻole (1865). Koko is further criticized for not finishing the story (Na Keiki o Kukuimalu 1865). The epic account of Pele and Hiʻiaka appears in over ten variant accounts in subsequent newspapers, beginning in 1862 in *Ka Hoku o ka Pakipika*.

[145] Examples would include Haleʻole's *Laieikawai*, which began in *Ka Hoku o ka Pakipika* and moved to *Ka Nupepa Kuokoa*, Kamakau's *Moolelo o na Kamehameha*, which moved from *Ka Nupepa Kuokoa* to *Ke Au Okoa*, and Hoʻoulumahiehie's *Hiiaka*, which began in *Hawaii Aloha* and moved to *Ka Nai Aupuni*.

The only portions of today's canon texts that were published for a Hawaiian audience of the authors' peers were the serial columns of Kamakau and 'Ī'ī. They wrote in the 1860s and early 1870s. None of the intertextual dialogue that framed the original writing has been incorporated or acknowledged in the texts that have become the modern canon. The complexity of the cultural content in the writings of the time, the cultural forms that framed them, the extended dialogues of the discourse, and the intertextual alignments of their presentation all reveal the problematic nature of isolating any portion of that fabric without an understanding of the threads that run through it.

4 | Misrepresentational Texts

The actual corpus of Hawaiian-language writings is both massive and complex, and efforts to date at incorporating that material or analyzing its content are still preliminary. This chapter addresses certain writings of Kamakau and ʻĪʻī, canon texts translated from the newspaper corpus and considered "representational," i.e., embodying the whole. However, analysis shows that these texts are neither representative, nor could they possibly replace the extensive, poly-vocal, and largely unutilized body of historical Hawaiian auto-representation that exists. Dependence on these works throughout the broadest range of modern scholarship is pervasive today, appearing and reappearing in scholarly and popular literature through direct or secondary reference to this canon. Such widespread use grants representational status to these texts and, in effect, replaces a broader scope of Hawaiian writers.

Reliance on the canon texts is problematic, not only because of what they leave behind in the way of context and other writings, but also for the impositions they place upon current fields of study. These few texts inadequately represent the larger body of works from which they are extracted, and they also inadequately represent even their own authors and original content, being recast, through translation, editing, and reorganization, into new Western-style reference texts.

As translations, these texts acquire their own integrity as resources, but the focus of this study is the relation of those texts to their original sources and the further link to the larger body of Hawaiian writings of the 19th and early 20th centuries.

Of the authors of the canon texts mentioned above—Malo, Kepelino, ʻĪʻī, and Kamakau—only the last two were alive when their works were originally published.[146] Their writings are reviewed in detail here.[147] There are many differences between the original newspaper writings of Kamakau and ʻĪʻī and the form in which those writings were published as English books. The changes enacted upon the texts and the processes generating those changes are examined here.

Samuel Mānaiakalani Kamakau

Samuel Kamakau's works are available today in English as four separate texts: *Ruling Chiefs of Hawaii* (1961); *Ka Poʻe Kahiko: The People of Old* (1964); *The Works of the People of Old: Na Hana a ka Poʻe Kahiko* (1976); and *Tales and Traditions of the People of Old* (1991). These were all drawn from serial columns that appeared weekly in two consecutive newspapers, starting in *Ka Nupepa Kuokoa* and later moving to *Ke Au Okoa*. The series appeared in three sections during a span of five and a half years, from June 16, 1865 to February 2, 1871. The first series was titled "Ka Moolelo Hawaii," or "Hawaiian History," and ran for 16 weeks.[148]

A year later, he began the series that ran weekly for the next four and a half years. Originally titled "Ka Moolelo o Kamehameha" [The Story of Kamehameha], the name changed as time passed and content of the column progressed, becoming "Ka Moolelo o Na Kamehameha" [The Story of the Kamehamehas], and eventually returning to the 1865 title, "Ka Moolelo Hawaii" [Hawaiian History], as the third phase of this continuous sequence began.

---

[146] While many articles by Malo and Kepelino appeared during their lifetimes, those writings are not part of the translated works available today, and are not included among the texts addressed in this study. Their translated works were drawn from manuscript materials that were not part of the public discourse of their eras. Some of David Malo's manuscript that was later translated as *Ka Moolelo Hawaii: Hawaiian Antiquities* (1903), was published in *Ke Au Okoa* two decades after Malo's death, but that posthumous publication is not comparable to the writings of Kamakau and ʻĪʻī who published during their lifetimes for their contemporaries.

[147] A similar analysis of the publications of Malo and Kepelino would be beneficial, but is beyond the scope of this work.

[148] Jun. 15, 1865 to Oct. 7, 1865. The first installment was actually titled "No ke Kaapuni Makaikai i na wahi Kaulana a me na Kupua, a me na 'Lii Kahiko mai Hawaii a Niihau" [Concerning a Tour of the famous places and the supernaturals and ancient chiefs from Hawaii to Niʻihau], which was maintained as a subtitle for the rest of that series.

Ka Nupepa Kuokoa, *October 20, 1866,* published the first installment of S. M. Kamakau's "Ka Moolelo o Kamehameha I" which would appear as a weekly serial for the next five years. The material in the four English versions of his writings was drawn from this column series. Photo by David Franzen, Bishop Museum.

Although S. M. Kamakau had been writing for the newspapers since 1838, journalism was his passion, not his career. Employed in many fields, including teacher, judge, civil servant, and legislator, Kamakau probably gained little or no income from his writing until the 1860s, when he became a paid serial columnist for the newspapers *Ka Nupepa Kuokoa* and then *Ke Au Okoa*.[149] He asserted, though, that he had a responsibility to write and document the history that was known in full to so few, and which he felt was remaining at the time in his hands alone:

> Ua noonoo nui koʻu poo i ke ao a me ka po, a ua makaukau no au e hoopiha. No ka mea, owau wale no ka mea i koe mai o ka poe i ike i ka moolelo kahiko o Hawaii nei. (1868b)

> [My mind has pondered day and night, and I am indeed prepared to bring it to completion. For I alone remain of those who knew the ancient history of this land, Hawaiʻi.]

He published regularly for 33 years, from 1838–1871, and produced nearly 400 articles, most of which dealt with cultural description, history, legend, and social critique.[150] His work stands out among 19th-century writers in Hawaiʻi for the extent of his published writing and for the position he held as a respected voice among his peers, although not one free of criticism. The events and forces in the course of his career shaped his literary position and the content of his writings, as discussed below.

Shaping the Hawaiian Text: Criticism and Debate

Critiques informed the content of Hawaiian writings. The dialogue-like quality of the newspaper interaction, especially by the 1860s, presupposed a responsive readership that was knowledgeable about oral tradition and printed resources. As mentioned earlier, it was a readership that was sensitive to authority issues in regard to what was appropriate for publication and who was qualified to present it. Criticism came quickly upon those who were deemed unqualified

---

[149] Kamakau was paid $1 per column when his serial column appeared in 1865 in *Ka Nupepa Kuokoa* (Kamakau 1865d), but the income was unreliable. He mentioned insufficient payment in a letter to W. Chamberlain in 1868, and informed him that he planned to write instead for *Ke Au Okoa* (Kamakau 1868b).

[150] An appendix of Kamakau's published works is included in the backmatter of this text.

to have their writings made public. Those who couldn't overcome their critics curtailed their writing.

Kamakau, more independent and adamant about his qualifications and authority than many other writers of his time, tackled his critics zealously and derisively.[151] As one of the new group of scholars educated at Lahainaluna College, he jostled in the newspapers for position as a spokesperson for his people and considered himself a repository of historical and cultural knowledge.[152] While early and continued interchanges never stopped him from writing, they may have made him more cautious about accuracy and may have kept him from dealing with subjects in which he had less mastery.

In response to some of his earliest writings, Kamakau received angry critiques about the correctness of his historical and genealogical knowledge. Issues were also raised about his right to share what was deemed to be privileged information with a general readership. A. Unauna, a noted genealogist for Kamehameha II and III, was one of his early, strident critics.

In the opening to an extended genealogy, which he published in 1842 as his first detailed cultural piece, Kamakau wrote:

> Ke kuauhau no na Kupuna kahiko loa mai o Hawaii nei, a hiki mai ia Wakea. Mai ia Wakea mai a hiki mai i keia manawa a kakou e noho nei, i mea e maopopo ai i keia hanauna; a ia hanauna aku ia hanauna aku. (1842a)

> [Here is the genealogy of the most ancient ancestors of this land, Hawai'i, coming down to Wākea. From Wākea it continues to our present time, so as to be clear to this generation, to the next generation, and to following generations.]

A. Unauna quickly submitted this critique under the heading "No Ke Kuauhau" [Concerning Genealogy]:

> I ka wa kahiko he olelo kapu loa keia, aohe e haawi ia aku i ke kanaka e, i kana keiki no e haawi ai.

---

[151] Little of the overtly sarcastic and derisive commentary included in Kamakau's original writings is included in the edited English translations, masking the strident and adamant style seen in the Hawaiian text.

[152] Kamakau entered Lahainaluna in 1832, began teaching there in 1836, and stayed on the staff until 1846.

Aole e loaa keia olelo i ka makaainana; aole i na kanaka kuaaina; aia o na lii ka mea e loaa ai. E ninau aku i kanaka o ke kuaaina, aohe e loaa; ina ua loaa i ke kanaka he kanaka alii no ia; no ka ike i ke kuauhau nae ia. Na kanaka i hanau alii, no ke lii; aole na kanaka kuaaina e noho ana me ke lii nui; o ke aikane a me keiki hookama ko ke kuaaina mau kanaka noho me ke lii nui. He ninau ia nae ko laua; o ka ike i ke kuauhau ka mea e hemo ai ka pilikia o na mea e hakaka ana, i ka i ana mai a ka mea i ike "o kou kaikuaana no keia, na mea oe, na mea keia," a ike laua, pau ae la ka pilikia....

Auhea oe e Kamakau kuauhau nui o Lahainaluna, ke ninau aku nei au ia oe ma kau palapala kuauhau i hookaulana mai ai oe i kou makaukau i ke kuauhau. (1842)

[In ancient times this was a very sacred subject, never to be given to another, to one's own children would it be granted.

This subject is not acquired by the common people, nor by the country people; only through the chiefs was it gained. Inquire of the people of the countryside, nothing will be found; if it [such knowledge] came to a person, that was a chiefly person, but the rank is apparent because of their knowledge of genealogy. Those born of chiefs belonged to the chiefly ranks, that is not so with the country-folk who reside with the high chiefs; the *aikāne*[153] and the *keiki hoʻokama*[154] are the kinds of country people who reside with the high chiefs. Their positions, however, are subject to question; knowledge of genealogy is what removes problems of those who are in dispute, as when a knowledgeable one states "this is your older sibling, you are the child of so-and-so, and that one is the child of so-and-so," and when they acknowledge each other, the problem is over....

Take heed, O Kamakau, great genealogist of Lahainaluna, I am asking you about your printed genealogy by which you've made famous your genealogical skill.]

---

[153] *Aikāne* indicates an intimate, same-gender companion, not necessarily a sexual relationship, but more than common friendship or alliance.

[154] *Hoʻokama* is an adoptive relationship, often after childhood, where the adopting party does not have primary care in the upbringing. It is a familial relationship established through mutual agreement rather than blood relation or child-rearing.

Unauna then went on to question specifics within the original genealogical account.

In the same issue of *Ka Nonanona* where Unauna's letter appeared, a letter from Kamakau addressed typesetting errors in the genealogy he had submitted, giving the editor, Armstrong, a specific list of errors that should be corrected (Kamakau 1842b). In his next article, appearing in a following issue of *Ka Nonanona*, Kamakau responded condescendingly to Unauna about his critique of Kamakau's authority and depth of knowledge. His reference to books written by the ancient deity Wākea and his use of "U" instead of Unauna's full name are examples of pointed sarcasm and insult aimed at Unauna. The first makes fun of Unauna's claim to traditional knowledge and the shortening of his name to "U", or "'Ū", refers to him by that one-letter word, meaning, among other things, "moan" or "groan":

> Auhea oe e Unauna, ka haumana kuauhau a Auwae ka mea i ike, a maopopo loa maloko o ko mau buke kahiko loa a Wakea i kakau ai.
>
> E Unauna e, e noho mua ilalo, e noonoo, e pelu iki mai, e heluhelu iki iho, e noonoo iki ae a maopopo loa; alaila e kakau iho me ke akamai.
>
> Mai kuhihewa i ka laau pakuikui a ka poe lawaia, a hei i ka pa, aole i ka mole o ke kamanialii....
>
> Auhea oe e U. ka mea i ike a i ao ia ma ke kuauhau, a ua like ka ike me na hoku o ka lani i uhi ia e na ao ua i ka po. Aole au i ao ia ma keia mea; o ka pu a me ka pauda, ka mea e lele ai ka poka. O ka naauao a me ka noonoo, oia ka mea e lele ai ka manao, a nana no i paipai i ka lima e hana a e kakau. (1843)

> [Take heed, O Unauna, genealogy student of 'Auwae,[155] the knowledgeable one, as is clear in your ancient books which Wākea[156] wrote.
>
> Unauna, sit down first, to think, bend a bit forward, read a bit, think a bit more until it becomes clear, then write intelligently.

---

[155] 'Auwae was a noted genealogist during the reign of Kamehameha I.
[156] Wākea is one of the original progenitors in Hawaiian genealogies, a sky father who mated with Papa, the earth mother, to eventually give birth to the sacred lines of chiefs. Mention of Wākea as an author is a sarcastic pretense about Unauna's claim to knowledge of old.

> Don't misconstrue the thrashing stick of the fishermen and snag the mouth of the net, or tangle in the deep pocket of that net of chiefly pretense....[157]
>
> You should pay attention, U., who knows and who was trained in genealogy, with knowledge like the stars of the heavens, covered by rain clouds at night. I wasn't trained in this subject; guns and powder are what make bullets fly. Intelligence and thought are what make ideas fly, and those are what encourages the hand to act and to write.]

Kamakau goes on to introduce his opinion that serious thinking and personal intelligence supercede the limits of oral tradition, of learning directly from another and accepting that single source. He uses Kauakahikahāola and his peers, famed genealogists and orators from the time of Kalani'ōpu'u, king of Hawai'i Island in the late 18th century, to validate his authority.

> E Unauna: Ua kakau au i keia kuauhau ma ko'u noonoo ana a ma ko'u akamai iho, aole ma ko hai manao, aole ma ke ao ana i ke kuauhau; me ke akamai wale no ka hana ana.
>
> Aka i kuu manao, ina e ala hou mai o Kauakahiakaola ma, ka poe kuauhau mai ka po mai e olioli lakou i keia, no ka mea, ua pau ia lakou i ka nalowale; olioli lakou ke ike hou....
>
> Auhea oe e Unauna ka haumana kuauhau a Auwae. Ua maopopo loa ia makou i na haumana o ke Kulanui kou ike a me kou akamai: ike ae nei makou ia oe, pakela loa aku ka poe ma Honolulu, a ma Amerika a me Beritania, a ma na aina naauao a pau loa ia oe. (1843)

> [Unauna: I wrote this genealogy through my own thought processes and my own wisdom, not through someone else's opinions, nor by training in genealogy; by intelligence alone was the deed done.
>
> But in my opinion, if Kauakahiakaola[158] and his peers, those genealogists of antiquity were to arise, they would rejoice at this, for it disappeared with them; they would rejoice to see it again....

---

[157] A reference back to Unauna's own letter, about knowledge being used by non-chiefs to imply their status.

[158] Probably Kauakahiakahāola, the orator and genealogist of Kalani'ōpu'u.

Listen, Unauna, genealogy student of 'Auwae. We, the students of the College,[159] understand clearly your knowledge and wisdom: we know you, and that the people of Honolulu, and in America and Britain and in all the enlightened lands are far superior to you.]

After proclaiming that educated folk are all superior to one like Unauna who was mentored in the traditional fashion, Kamakau clarifies his stance that a new scholarly approach to genealogy is preferable to the "ignorant method" of old practiced by Unauna.

E U. e, Aole o'u makemake e hana pololei loa e haalele i kekahi mau keiki, a ma na keiki wale no i ku i ke aupuni wale no e kakau ai. Ua ike oe i ke kuauhau a Kepookulou, ma ke kumu Hawaii. Maopopo anei? Pau anei ka pohihi malaila? Ina paha heluhelu kekahi kanaka a paa naau loa ia kuauhau, a ninau mai kekahi mea e ia ia, "Ehia keiki a Umi?" Olelo aku oia "hookahi, o Keliiokaloa, a o Kukailani kana keiki aku, a o Makaualii kana keiki aku a o Iwikauikaua kana keiki aku, a o Keakealani kana kaikamahine, a o Keawe kana keiki aku," alaila ninau hou oia, "Pakahi wale no anei lakou i na keiki?" Alaila heaha kana olelo ilaila? He hoka.

O ke kuauhau ma ka mooolelo Hawaii, ua maopopoia ia makou, ua pau kekahi hemahema, a nolaila makemake makou e lohe i kekahi mea hou e maopopo ai e pakui hou aku a manamana loa.

O na kuauhau a ka poe i kapaia he poe akamai, ua hana pololei lakou, aole hoomanamana, ua hookoa ia na manamana; ua kapaia he kuauhau okoa kela mana keia mana; aka he hana naaupoia i ka manawa kahiko. O ka mea hou ka i oi aku mamua o na mea kahiko. (1843)

[U., I have no desire to work in direct genealogical line and leave behind some children, writing only about the children who ruled. You saw Kepo'okūlou's genealogy, in *Ke Kumu Hawaii*. Was it clear? Was the confusion taken care of there? If someone should read and memorize that genealogy, and

---

[159] Lahainaluna.

another asked "How many children did 'Umi have?" That person would respond, "one, Keliiokaloa, and Kukailani was his child, then Makaualii was his, and Iwikauikaua was his child and Keakealani was Iwikauikaua's daughter, with Keawe being her child," and the other would ask again, "They each had only one child?" And then what is that one's response? Bafflement.

Genealogy in Hawaiian history is understood by my group and me; some flaws have been taken care of, and so we want to hear new things to grasp, to add on and to branch out extensively.

The genealogies by people called wise, they followed in direct descent, not identifying branches of the family line, the branches were separated out; each branch was called a separate genealogy; but that was an ignorant practice in ancient times. The modern style is what is superior over the ancient ways.]

Kamakau then derides Unauna's authority to assert genealogical connections and challenges him to draft this broader form of genealogy without relying on Kamakau's own works. He includes a challenge to write the personal histories of the chiefs as well as the lists of their names:

Auhea oe e, U. O na mea au i ike ai, ua hookomo wale ia me ke kuleana ole e pili ai, e kakau iho oe i na inoa o ua mau mea la au i ike a na'u, na ka mea i ike ole e hooponopono aku, me ka hawawa; a nana na kanaka mai keia pae aina aku, a hiki i na aupuni naauao....

Eia kekahi. E hana mai oe i kuauhau pololei loa, aole e komo iki kekahi inoa o ka'u kuauhau iloko, aole hoi ma na mana a'u i hoakaka ai; i mookuauhau e wale no; E hoomaopopo mai no hoi i ko lakou noho ana? Alaila, lilo oe i mea akamai loa; ua like oe me Petolemo ke kanaka naauao no Aigupita. (1843)

[You should listen, U. The things you know, you include with no authority to adjoin them, you write the names of those you know and I, the unknowledgeable one, will correct them, haphazardly; and all the people, here and abroad in the enlightened lands, will observe....

This too. You should draft a direct-line genealogy, not including any name from my genealogical works therein, nor any of the branches I identified; make a separate genealogy. You should also clarify their ways of life. Then you would become wise; you'll be the peer of Ptolemy, the sage of Egypt.]

In closing, Kamakau warns Unauna about playing with things beyond his own limited powers. He also points out how Unauna can "heal the wounds" of his ailing work, and threatens humiliation if he doesn't mend his ways:

> Auhea oe e Unauna he mea nui keia, he mea nou e naauao ai; a e lilo ai oe he mea noonoo nui loa. Aka he palupalu ke kai a me ka wai, aka, ea, he nui na kanaka i palemo aku ia lua; a o ke gini i kona aleale maikai ana ma ke kiaha, i kou nana ana, i kou hoao ana ia mea, e nahu mai no ia me he nahesa la, a e pa mai me he moonihoawa la.
>
> O kau mau mea hoi i hai mai nei he mau mea kuhikuhi ia i ko makou nana ana, aka, ea, akahi no nae a paa kona hakahaka, i kou hoakaka ana mai ma ka nupepa hoolaha ike.
>
> Eia no ka mea e paa ai kona mau hakahaka, o ko imi mai i na ninau i hoakaka ia'ku nei mamua, oia ka laau lapaau, o ka nini ikaika hoi ia e ola'i kona mau palapu eha. Mai kuemi, mai unu iho, mai kekee, mai kulou ilalo, e ala ka maka iluna.
>
> Aka i loaa ole ea, e akaaka makou, na haumana o ke Kulanui ia oe, me ka henehene. "E hele oe mai hana hewa hou aku." (1843)

[Listen, Unauna, this is important, something to make you wise; and something that will make you philosophical. It's true, sea water and fresh water are soft, but, hey, many have drowned in those depths; gin ripples nicely in a glass, when you look, but when you taste that stuff, it'll bite like a snake and sting like a scorpion.

What you have stated, a mere supposition, in our observations, but, now the gaps can be filled by your clarifying them in an educational newspaper.

Here's what would fill its gaps, your researching the questions explained above first, that is the remedy, a powerful balm that will cure its aching sores. Don't back away, don't pull in, don't twist around, don't bow down, let your eyes look up.

But if you don't get it, aha! We, the students of the College, will laugh at you and tease, saying "Go and sin no more."]

Criticism didn't disappear because of Kamakau's adamance, but went on throughout his career, becoming a regular feature of the newspaper venue. As mentioned in the previous chapter, the critical dialogue in which Kamakau took part honed both his own contextual knowledge and that of the populace. He responded on a regular basis and there is a large body of letters that embody his manner of dealing with critics. His tone was often cynical and sarcastic, or even vicious, asserting the quality of his knowledge, the superiority of his training, and his own authority to present a given topic while demeaning the critics' rights and qualifications to do the same.

Two decades after his tangles with Unauna, he sparred on a regular basis with the son of Unauna, John Koi'i.[160] In *Ke Au Okoa*, Koi'i critiqued Kamakau's initial historical writings in *Ka Nupepa Kuokoa* (Kamakau 1865a)[161] that included genealogy of the chiefs. Koi'i writes:

> Ua hemahema io no anei o Davida Malo, i ka mookuauhau ana i hoopuka ai ma ka buke a Pogue? Aole anei o kau ka hemahema loa? Ua ao maoli ia anei oe i ke kuauhau? Aole paha ea? No ka buke no hoi paha a Kaunuohua, ka wahine a Kalauwalu laua o W. L. Moehonua, kau wahi kuauhau ea? (Unauna, J. 1865)
>
> [Was Davida Malo actually incompetent in the genealogy he published in Pogue's book? Isn't yours the truly defective work? Were you really taught genealogy? It's not so, is it? Your bit of genealogy probably comes from the book of Kaunuohua, wife of Kalauwalu and from W. L. Moehonua,[162] doesn't it?]

Kamakau responded in *Ke Au Okoa*,[163] listing problems with Malo's text, acknowledging having seen Kaunuohua's book only to add corrections, and

---

[160] John Koi'i, possibly Koi'i or another variant, signed his letters with several forms of his name: J. K. Unauna, J. Koii, John Koii, and John Koii Unauna.

[161] This series was included in the English text *Tales and Traditions of the People of Old* (Kamakau 1991).

[162] Moehonua was a noted genealogist and the others mentioned are apparently his peers.

[163] Koi'i's critique in *Ka Nupepa Kuokoa* and Kamakau's response being in *Ke Au Okoa* is a common occurance of the intertextuality of the time.

repeatedly condemning J. Koi'i Unauna for his inability to understand cultural knowledge that is like a "fish of the deep":

> Ke olelo aku nei au ia oe, he i-a keia no ka moana uliuli, he aho lau, ku i keia ko-a, aole e hiki ia oe, he ihu pohue. I luu iho oe, ku ko maka i ka iliohalawena, i elieli iho oe, hawahaba ko lima, i na'ana'u iho oe, umiaumia ko lua i nalo, puu ka auwae, no ke aha? No ka 'ike ole. (1865e)

> [I say to you, this kind of knowledge is a fish of the deep ocean, needing a long line; it comes together in this fishing spot, but you are incapable, as a bobbling, gourd-nosed surface diver. If you do dive, your face gets stuck in worthless dog-fur seaweed; if you dig down, your hands get smeared with excrement; when you try to exhale, your diaphragm squeezes to collapse out of sight, with the chin left jutting out, and why is this? Because of ignorance.]

Especially in the early years of his career, Kamakau established himself as a rather brazen new scholar, combining traditional knowledge with a more scholarly method which he learned from his Lahainaluna teachers. His position, however, changed over time. In later works he lauded the sources of the lore he collected, and went on to publish genealogies in the direct linear style that he earlier denounced when addressing Unauna and his other critics. Both the Hawaiian and English publications of Kamakau's writings include many examples those genealogies in the model he once refuted in his initial letters to Unauna.

While his critics were numerous through the years, Kamakau held his position as a cultural and historical scholar through his tenacity and through his displays of expertise. His writings were widely accepted as authoritative, a position supported, in part, by his ability to address his critics directly and decisively. His authority was bolstered by his being retained as a paid columnist,[164] and by the tacit approval of the many knowledgeable people of his time who could have derided his work and didn't. Legislator and writer E. Helekunihi recalled a quote from John Papa 'Ī'ī, who responded to a question about Kamakau's accuracy:

> He kupanaha keia kanaka. Me he la ua ike maka, paa naau na mea a pau, na wahi a'u i hele ai me na alii, Kauikeaouli –

---

[164] See Kamakau (1865d).

Kaahumanu; me he la o ia ala kekahi. He uuku loa na mea hemahema. (1893)

[This man is amazing. It is as though he personally saw and memorized everything, the places I went with the chiefs, like Kauikeaouli and Ka'ahumanu; it's as though he was there as well. The errors are very minimal.]

Intertextual Writing

The dynamics of criticism and approval actively shaped the content of Kamakau's writings, but the passive influences calls to mind comments that Greg Dening made about his own writing. He said the work of many others unconsciously reflect "an endless litany of those whose spoken mind cannot be unspoken and to whose sentences I respond even if I have not read them" (1989:139). Kamakau, too, built upon and added to the writers of his time and to earlier writings, and although he rarely acknowledged his sources, some guiding forces are obvious.

In 1838, American missionary Sheldon Dibble published *Ka Mooolelo Hawaii*, the first historical account of Hawai'i to be written and circulated in Hawaiian.[165] Adult students of the new Lahainaluna College generated the history, having been trained by Reverend Dibble in a colloquium setting to gather and write up historical and cultural information through interviews with knowledgeable elders. This landmark text was soon translated into English as *Hawaiian History* (Tinker 1839, 1840), and then rewritten by Dibble in English (1843). Twenty years later, the text was redrafted in Hawaiian by Pogue, again called *Ka Mooolelo Hawaii* (1858).

Kamakau, who acknowledged being one of the student researchers and writers of the original *Ka Mooolelo Hawaii*, used the format and expanded the material from these publications into his own later writings, adding to them, but not usually relying on direct incorporation. His writings both reflected and depended upon readers being familiar with the Dibble, Pogue, and other texts of the time.

---

[165] The text was published in sections in the newspaper *Ke Kumu Hawaii* prior to publication as a book, reprinted in full in later papers once the book had gone out of print.

Similarly, "Hoomana Kahiko,"[166] a multi-author series on religious practices, appeared in *Ka Nupepa Kuokoa* just prior to the opening of Kamakau's "Ka Moolelo o Kamehameha," and Kamakau was able to rely on his readers' familiarity with those descriptions in his own subsequent account. His coverage of the topics that had appeared in "Hoomana Kahiko" was then minimized, and for the most part, corrective and additive rather than primary. He assumed the readers already had access to the pertinent information because of the cross-referential nature of the Hawaiian newspapers. There are many examples of earlier or contemporary writings that Kamakau commented upon, added to, or assumed to be referential texts for his audience, including a published indirect dialogue between Kamakau and ʻĪʻī, which is discussed in a later section of this study. Dorothy Barrère mentions how Kamakau opened his 1865 "Moolelo Hawaii" series as an amplification of Davida Malo's *Moolelo Hawaii* manuscript text (1976:v).

Kamakau's works of the late 1860s, his part of today's canon, were not only influenced by the writings of others, but also by his own earlier writings in the course of his long career. One example is an instance in 1869 where he quoted his own published letter of 1845 to Kamehameha III.[167] Rather than including direct repetition of his earlier note to the king, he expanded his original comments in his rewrite, adding historical details in the process. In regard to re-using his own earlier material, Barrère notes that Kamakau "repeated and embellished—and occasionally changed—some of his accounts" (1991:x).

Kamakau also wrote articles apart from his serial columns to inform the contemporary reader about his longer works. Such commentary, sometimes included in his editorial writings, help to frame how Kamakau saw his own material and how his readers should understand his limitations, his strengths, and his goals in writing Hawaiian *moʻolelo*. Just after his initial serial column in 1865, and prior to initiating "Moolelo o Kamehameha," Kamakau presented an extensive view of himself in relation to other historians and genealogists, and revealed that while most of his written records were destroyed in a fire a decade earlier, he could rely on his memory for most of the detail (1865c). In the same article he invited those who could add to his work to contact him via the editor of *Ka Nupepa Kuokoa*, L. H. Gulick. None of the editorial commentary that Kamakau received from or provided for his reading audience has been included in the modern translations of his works.

---

[166] "Hoomana Kahiko" was the title of a serial column by various authors on topics of ancient religious practice. The series appeared in *Ka Nupepa Kuokoa* from January 5 to December 30, 1865, with a few weekly lapses and a summer hiatus. A number of related articles, commenting on, and adding to "Hoomana Kahiko," appeared during and following the publication of the series.

[167] Kamakau (1845). Reprinted in "Ka Moolelo o Na Kamehameha" (Kamakau 1869d, Jul. 1).

Such a long view of all of Kamakau's writings would be what Foucault would recommend, to study the *œuvre,* the sum of a single writer's production, as something that goes beyond genre, incorporates the writer's personal history, and informs the understanding of any individual writing that the author generates (1972:23–25). A clear compilation of the nearly 400 Kamakau-related articles by Kamakau would shed a bright light upon any analysis of his individual works. Two bibliographies of his writings have been attempted (Thrum 1917, Chun 1993), each one partial, a product of the minimal research tools available when such compilations were undertaken. A more extensive bibliography of Kamakau's writings is appended in this narrative. Although much expanded, it is still certain to be incomplete.

The forces mentioned above affected Kamakau's writings as forms of self-editing, conscious, and subconscious, that changed what he actually put on paper. From the point when he finished writing, however, other processes, like editing, extraction, and translation came to bear, each affecting the extent and the character of the material available to us today.

Editorial Constraints

Little documentation is available about the editing that was imposed on Hawaiian writers of Kamakau's era by the newspapers, the main venue for publication. There is, however, a rare body of original holograph material by Kamakau at the Hawaiian Historical Society (1868d). This material, 142 pages written for the serial column "Ka Moolelo o Kamehameha," appears to have been handwritten by Kamakau and then edited prior to submitting it to the editor of *Ka Nupepa Kuokoa*.[168] The changes mostly include choice of articles (*ka, ke, nā,* etc.) and spelling of proper names.

Comparison of the submitted handwritten text and the published material appearing in *Ka Nupepa Kuokoa* shows a second level of consistent editorial changes in addition to those which were marked on the holograph manuscript. The latter changes, appearing only in the published newspaper, may have been done to galley copies prior to printing the paper. The sections compared showed that these final changes imposed no alteration of content, but rephrasing and minor clarification of subjects regularly occured. Short examples below show the level of unmarked editorial changes made after the corrected manuscript was submitted. A strike-through represents material deleted from the edited manuscript form and brackets show additions, which are then mirrored in the English translation.

---

[168] The corrections on the manuscript appear to be in the same hand as the original holograph.

S. M. Kamakau's handwritten manuscript was edited by hand prior to being typeset for publication in the newspaper. The edited holograph, when compared with the published columns, indicates that further editing occurred after the manuscript was submitted. Courtesy of the Hawaiian Historical Society, Honolulu.

"O na olelo huna, me na olelo ohumu no ka pono a me ka hewa, no ke ola a me ka make, o kela ano me keia ano, o ko ka lani me ko ka honua; ua ike e [no] o Kaiana, aole mea huna e nalo iaia. Aole oe e pilikia i na'lii, [no ka mea], ua ike no o Kaiana i ka lakou mau olelo huna." ~~Aka, ua kaaninipo loa o Kaahumanu~~ [O keia mau olelo a Kamehameha, aohe hoolohe ia aku e Kaahumanu, no ka mea, ua lilo loa oia i ka uwe haalipo] i ke aloha i kona kaikunane. Ua hoole mai no hoi o Kamehameha, "Aole keia e pilikia au e hookaumaha nei." (Kamakau 1868a, Sept. 12)

["Secret talk and criticisms about right or wrong, life or death, of this or that kind, heavenly and earthly, Ka'iana already [indeed] knows them; nothing secret escapes him. You won't have trouble from the chiefs [because] Ka'iana does know their secret talk." ~~But Ka'ahumanu was completely overwhelmed~~ [These statements by Kamehameha were not heard at all by Ka'ahumanu, because she was absorbed in tearful lament] for love of her brother. Kamehameha opposed it, saying "This which you grieve over will not become a problem."]

Another example of editorial clarification, again with impact on style but not content:

Ua nui ka poe i lawe pio ia mai a he nui [no hoi] ka poe i holo i ka nahelehele; a he nui na'lii [kane a me na'lii wahine i] pio, ~~he nui na 'Lii wahine~~ [Oia no] o Kapooloku ma. (Kamakau 1868a, Sept. 19)

[Many people were taken captive and many [indeed] were those who fled to the forest; and many were the [male] chiefs [and female chiefs who were] taken captive, ~~and many chiefesses~~. [Namely] Kapo'oloku and her companions.]

In addition to standard editorial changes, some material was deleted as unsuitable or unwieldy. An entire segment of Kamakau's serial column was deleted by what appears to be the editor's order. That portion dealt with Catholicism, and how Hawaiians interpreted the new religion in relation to the older native practices. The segment was never included in the newspaper series or in the English translation. In another example, a *mele* nearly 300 lines long, submitted with the Kamakau holograph writings but not appearing in the series, may have been dismissed as too long for the flow of the series.[169] Printing parts or short excerpts of longer *mele* was not unfrequent,[170] but the deletion of whole content areas is almost completely undocumented. These archived holographs represent only a small fraction of the 5-year series appearing in *Ka Nupepa Kuokoa* and *Ke Au Okoa,* and while the material is too scant for extrapolation, the deletion of apparently unsuitable topics and the cutting of long chants implies that there was active editorial constraint on Kamakau's series, and on the totality of his writings.

Self-edited and further constrained by his publishers, the printed work of Kamakau reflects the contribution he was able to include in the published dialogue of his time. It was a piece in the larger scope of a discourse produced by Hawaiians who created a space for that presence in the Hawaiian-language newspapers. Modern understanding of Kamakau's contribution has, however, been affected by a number of more recent changes to his body of work. These latter changes are more easily documented than those of his own time and include the process of extraction, the subsequent translation, the reordering, and the editing of his writings for English publication.

Shaping the English Text: Extraction and Decontextualization

Recognition of Kamakau as an important author and historian resulted in a project initiated in 1923 by the Historical Commission of the Territory of Hawaii. Seventy-eight "chapters" drawn from *Ka Nupepa Kuokoa* and translated by John H. Wise were reported in 1924 to have been of "considerable use" to the Commission and "others interested in Hawaiian history" (Historical Commission of the Territory of Hawaii 1925:14).[171] It's not clear who had access to these initial unpublished translations, but the subsequent translation work and preparation for printing was continued in collaboration with the Bishop Museum:

---

[169] Although the holograph has the word "Printed" written on the front, a three-line excerpt of that *mele* text is all that appeared in the entire run of Kamakau's serial column. Both the deleted text and the *mele* are referenced in the Appendix.

[170] For example, Kanepuu (1862) wrote about the deletion of material from stories and *mele*.

[171] It was apparently one of the earliest projects of the Historical Commission to have the material copied and translated for use by the Commission and "others who may wish to consult it." Kamakau's writings at the time were noted as being "buried in the files of the native newspapers, the *Kuokoa* and the *Au Okoa*." John Wise was a Hawaiian senator and considered an authority on Hawaiian language and culture. The report does not clarify whether he translated the extracted chapters or coordinated the effort, but he was in charge of the initial translation project. Historian R. S. Kuykendall was the Executive Secretary of this Commission, and certainly one of those who made use of the initial translations.

> In 1931 Bishop Museum sponsored the systematic translation of all of Samuel Kamakau's articles on Hawaiian history and culture that had appeared in the weekly newspapers *Kuokoa* and *Ke Au Okoa* from October 20, 1866, to February 2, 1871. (Barrère 1964:vii)

The full impact that the process of extraction had upon the clarity of Kamakau's writing cannot be detailed without much more study of the synchronous articles, editorials, and critiques that contextualize his work, but the general importance of such an extraction is readily acknowledged. The introduction to one of the English translations of Kamakau's work comments on how his writings, in general, were more comprehensible to those of his own era:

> Kamakau wrote at a time when his people still retained much knowledge of the changing culture, and many of his allusions and half-explanations, easily comprehensible to them, appear tantalizingly indefinite and incomplete today. (Barrère 1964:vii)

He wrote to a populace that was far more culturally informed than the current reading population and more able to grasp the content he covered. While that is apparently true, the matrix of printed material among which Kamakau's writings appeared helped to provide valuable clarification and reference for the benefit of the reading audience of his time. Extraction of his writings from that cross-referential foundation is part of what makes his writing so "tantalizingly indefinite" today.

The decontextualizing of Kamakau's writings diminished their clarity, and would have done so even if they had been kept intact as a whole, sequential body of writing. Subsequent translation, reordering, and editing, all processes which can certainly add new insights and intelligibility, also acted, step by step, to distance the source material from the reach of the modern reader. Each process imposed changes on the original, and the impact can be recognized by comparing Kamakau's Hawaiian text with the English publications available today. These processes created a new and different resource in English, one that has its own value and may represent the original, but should not replace it.

Translation

> Translation has always been one of the most powerful ways to regulate knowing because it is a tool in the hands of someone

with superior knowledge, i.e., the translator who knows both languages. Whoever needs the translation knows only one language and is therefore at the mercy of the translator. The power relationship between the two is one of dependency on the part of the monolingual reader. (Morris 2003)

The process of identifying material for translation and the delineation and selection of that material to be drawn from the original matrix is the initial act of translation. The process of extracting Kamakau's writings from the newspapers was initiated in the 1920s by the Historical Commission, then completed in collaboration with the Bishop Museum. Isolated from the newspaper columns, Kamakau's three-part cultural/historical series totaled roughly 1,500 pages of typescript.[172] The short series, "No ke Kaapuni Makaikai" resulted in a 70-page typescript; the "Moolelo o Kamehameha" sequence entailed more than 900 typed pages, and the continuation of the series under the title "Ka Moolelo Hawaii" then added another 500 pages of typescript to that sum. John Wise began translating this body of text and the remainder was divided among numerous translators, including Mary Kawena Pukui, Thomas G. Thrum, Lahilahi Webb, Emma Davidson Taylor, and others (Kent 1961:ix).

Not all persons who were approached to assist in this effort were equally qualified to do the task of translation and interpretation. Asked to translate five issues of Kamakau's columns, Mary Low of Hulihe'e, Kona, was hesitant and agreed to attempt only a couple. She wrote back to say she couldn't do it, even with the help of elderly Hawaiian friends—"It is too bad the work was not started earlier when those knowing the ancient Hawn. language were living" (1931a and 1931b). Others of uncertain ability apparently didn't decline. Father Reginald Yzendoorn, a Catholic historian, completed the five issues he'd been sent, but with gaps in the translation of passages that he acknowledged were beyond his understanding. The questions he raised show a general unfamiliarity with the subject of sacred symbols, but he noted "...I hoped that I would find some old Hawaiian able to explain the meaning of certain terms." He didn't find such a resource, but persisted, apologizing for submitting a less-than-complete translation: "I am sorry not to be able to give better satisfaction. It salves my pride that educated Hawaiians do not know any better" (1931).

---

[172] The three series include: "No ke Kaapuni Makaikai i na wahi Kaulana a me na Kupua, a me na 'Lii Kahiko mai Hawaii a Niihau," "Ka Moolelo o Kamehameha," and "Ka Moolelo Hawaii." Reference here to page counts refers to typescripts of the columns prepared for production of *Ke Kumu Aupuni* (1996), *Ke Aupuni Mō'ī* (2002), and future untitled republications of Kamakau's texts.

Because the translation efforts resulted in various levels of completion and included multiple styles, Mary Kawena Pukui reviewed and reworked the different sections into a more uniform narrative, an apparently difficult process. Martha Warren Beckwith commented on the collected translations in a letter to Caroline Curtis:

> Some of the translations were helpful, like Mary's [Kawena Pukui], Mrs. Taylor's, and Thrum's, but only in spots, and much was incoherent. Ask Mary! She was particularly scornful. (1949a)

The resulting manuscript was worded and annotated by Beckwith with Kawena Pukui's help.[173] The stated goal of translation as a research tool according to Beckwith was "not for popular consumption, but in order to put into the hands of ethnologists who do not read Hawaiian or who have no access to the original text, a version as nearly literal as possible of Kamakau's text" (1939). The task was mostly completed by 1936, some twenty-five years prior to its eventual publication, although Caroline Curtis' letters to Beckwith in 1949 imply a drawn-out closure to the process, which finally came to press in 1961.[174]

The divergence from the stated goal of a literal translation to the greatly altered eventual publication described below reflects more on the processes involved than on the work of the principal translator, Mary Kawena Pukui. Pukui was certainly the most highly-lauded translator and interpreter of Hawaiian material of the 20th century, with a career that spanned decades and resulted in many publications and resources. While other processes were involved in the discrepancies that appear between original text and published translation, translation issues played a significant role as well.

Translation is by its nature a subjective and highly contested process. Lawrence Venuti addresses the problems in this overview:

> Translation never communicates in an untroubled fashion because the translator negotiates the linguistic and cultural differences of the foreign text by reducing them and supplying

---

[173] D. Barrère (1964:vii) writes this about the process: "As in the case of the history series, the culture series was translated piecemeal by a group of Hawaiian scholars and the translations were gone over by Mary Kawena Pukui, the main contributor, and Martha Warren Beckwith, Professor of Folklore, Vassar College. Their work was completed in 1934 and is a completely literal translation, worded and annotated by Miss Beckwith."

[174] See Bishop Museum (1936) and Beckwith (1949a).

another set of differences, basically domestic, drawn from the receiving language and culture to enable the foreign to be received there. The foreign text, then, is not so much communicated as inscribed with domestic intelligibilities and interests. (2004c:468)

Tejaswini Niranjana, in *Siting Translation: History, Post-Structuralism and the Colonial Conquest,* problematizes translation "as a significant technology of colonial domination." She urges translators to avoid presenting their translations as a crystallization of knowledge, or as "direct, unmediated access to a transparent reality" and counsels them,

> ...to inscribe heterogeneity, to warn against myths of purity, to show origins as always already fissured. Translation, from being a "containing" force, is transformed into a disruptive, disseminating one. (1992:20)

Larry Kimura, noted Hawaiian-language scholar, addresses the problem of translation in light of English and Hawaiian:

> In discussing the role of Hawaiian in Hawaiian culture, it is also well to remember that American English is a vehicle of its own culture and that English words carry their own connotation and history. Whenever Hawaiian is translated into English, the English words used add cultural connotations to the idea conveyed, while eliminating intended connotations and meanings of the original Hawaiian. (1983:182)

This subjectivity of translation has been widely acknowledged, and critiqued from numerous perspectives, including feminist, Marxist, post-modernist, etc.[175] There is, however, a general agreement within translation theory that two broad types of translation can be identified: "direct" or "literal," as opposed to "oblique" (Vinay and Darbelnet 2004:128), also referred to as "formal" in contrast to "dynamic" (Nida 2004:153). Direct, literal, or formal translation aims at careful handling of the words and phrasing used in the original texts with attention to transmitting details and structures therein. Oblique, interpretive, or dynamic translations try to bring the essence of the text into the target language, either

---

[175] For a good overview of translation studies in this century, see Venuti (2004b).

through transmission of concepts or through attempts to mirror the impact in the target language. Between the poles of these contrasting styles, many interim forms and styles are recognized, influenced more or less by one or the other major types. Any style of translation reconstitutes and reframes text, a process that is inherently contestable.

> It is important to recognize the inevitability of difference between translations, for all too often translators are accused of betraying the original, of diminishing it or distorting it, as though some perfect single reading might exist and result in a perfect idealized translation. (Bassnett 1997:2)

The particular choices made during the processes of translation for Kamakau's works are not analyzed at length or contested in this study, but translation problems do exist, so a few examples are included here. Mistranslations are additional elements of the processes affecting these works that again undermine the reliability of the English text as a critical resource, and as a sufficiently representative text.

Because the original manuscript of Kamakau's extracted writings was so massive and was handled by a number of differently qualified translators, it would have been nearly impossible for Kawena Pukui to align the translation styles into a consistent form and at the same time check the accuracy of each turn of phrase in the text. Misunderstandings, typographical errors, or oversights did slip in through the process. The following is one example, where a section of Hawaiian text got tangled in translation, reading like this in the original:

> Mahope iho, ua loheia ka mea nana i lawe ke keiki oia hoi o Naeole. No laila, ua haawiia o Naeole ke kahu hanai o ke keiki. Ua hoonoho aku o Kalaniopuu i kona kaikaina ia Kekunuialeimoku i makua hanai no ke keiki. (Kamakau 1866b, Oct. 20)

A formal, or literal translation of this text would read:

> Afterwards, it was heard that the one who took the child was Naeʻole. Therefore, it was granted that Naeʻole be the guardian of the child. Kalaniʻōpuʻu appointed his younger brother, Kekūnuialeimoku, as a foster parent for the child.

The published English translation, however, omitted the name of Kalaniōpu'u and referred to Kalani'ōpu'u's younger brother as Nae'ole's sister. The text in *Ruling Chiefs* reads:

> After it was learned that Nae-'ole was the person who had taken the child, he was made the child's guardian, and his younger sister, Ke-ku-nui-a-lei-moku, was appointed his [the child's] foster mother. (Kamakau 1961:68–69)

The published English text overlooked the reference to Kalani'ōpu'u, changed the gender of his younger brother, Kekūnuialeimoku, and put him, as a female, in the Nae'ole lineage, rather than Kalani'ōpu'u's own. This multi-pronged oversight deleted Kalani'ōpu'u's role in the appointments, but more importantly it wrongly attributed a chiefly male of Kalani'ōpu'u's ruling line and foster father of Kamehameha as being a foster mother from Nae'ole's less noble lineage, an historical and genealogical reference that has been perpetuated in subsequent publications (Ahlo, Walker, and Johnson 2000:15).

A mistranslation of text about the first Catholic baptism in Hawai'i has produced misinterpretation regarding the intentions and roles of the chiefs at a highly-analyzed point in Hawaiian history, the overthrow of the *kapu* system. An article by Roland Perkins relies on the English texts to show how Hawaiian historical accounts developed over time, from *Mooolelo Hawaii* (Dibble 1838) onward. Perkins gives emphasis to the reference in *Ruling Chiefs* about the intentions of Kalanimoku to "rule as Pope over the islands," as though the addition of this detail is particularly sinister (1980:72). The stated intentions of Kalanimoku are actually completely absent from the Hawaiian text and only appear as a mistranslation in English. The Hawaiian text given in Kamakau's column echoes and adds to what had been included in *Mooolelo Hawaii*, reads:

> I ka noho ana a na 'lii a me na 'lii wahine a me na aialo o na 'lii; ia manawa ku mai la kekahi moku i Kawaihae, e holo ana i Nu Holani no Farani mai, a he kahuna Katorika Roma maluna oia moku a ua bapetizo ia o Kalanimoku e ua kahuna *Pope la maluna o ka moku*. O John Young Olohana ke kumu o ia Bapetizo ana, no ka mea, ua ninau o Kalanimoku ia John Young Olohana i ke ano o ka hana a kela Kahuna i hana mai ia Kalanimoku. Ua olelo mai o John Young Olohana oia ka poe kahuna o ko lakou mau aupuni, a o ke Akua oiaio ma ka lani. (Kamakau 1867, Nov. 2, emphasis added)

A full, literal translation would be:

> During the residence of the chiefs, the chiefesses and the members of the royal court; at that time a certain ship landed at Kawaihae, sailing from France to Australia, and there was a Roman Catholic priest on board the ship and Kalanimoku was baptized by this *Catholic* priest *on the ship*. John Young Olohana was the reason for the baptism, because Kalanimoku had asked John Young Olohana about the nature of the duties of that priest who then attended to Kalanimoku. John Young Olohana replied that those were the priests of their lands and of the true God in heaven. (emphasis added)

This excerpt was published in *Ruling Chiefs* as:

> At this time there arrived at Kawaihae a ship from France on board of which was a Roman Catholic priest. When Ka-lani-moku learned from John Young that this man held office from his government as a priest of the true God in heaven he had himself baptized by the priest *as pope over the islands*. (Kamakau 1961:225, emphasis added)

This translation misinterprets the word "Pope," used in the Hawaiian text as an adjective, to mean Catholic, or papist, and translates it instead as a noun, from which is extrapolated Kalanimoku's intentions to act as "Pope over the islands." *Moku*, meaning island or ship, is affected by this understanding, changing the interpretation from *papist on board*, to *Pope over the islands*. No mention is contained in the Hawaiian text about Kalanimoku's aspirations to be a pope, but the publication of that mistranslation in the English text has already crept into other historical analyses of the time.

One more example where the English translation is misleading is drawn from the closure to a section describing wanton behavior of ancient times and comparing it to the changing era following the arrival of Captain Cook:

> Ke mau nei no hoi ka moe lehulehu, e like me ka wa kahiko.
> (Kamakau 1867a)

The text would literally read like this:

> Numerous sexual liasons are still ongoing, just as in ancient times.

This summation was translated and published in *Ruling Chiefs* to read:

> Today, licentiousness is more common than formerly. (Kamakau 1961:235)

But the original line actually contains no sense of comparison or expanded licentiousness; it only refers to the continuation of such behavior. The difference is minor, but incorrectly documents Hawaiians', or at least Kamakau's, perceptions about historical and cultural change or continuity.

As could be expected, small errors in the typescripting and translating process occurred, like an instance where *puaa* (pig) was misread as *puna* (spoon), resulting in an English reference to a stolen spoon when the original text told of a stolen pig (Kamakau 1961:282). With an original text already aged and fragile, and thousands of lines to transpose and translate, such small changes seem insignificant, but the accumulation of such errors undermine the overall reliability of the resulting English text.

The study of translation particulars like these becomes a separate project, but their presence highlights the problematic nature of reliance on the English text as representational access to the author and the larger body of original Hawaiian writings. In addition to the subjective nature of translation, the process also allows additional human error to further distance a reader from primary sources.

Reordering

> We are living in a strange kind of dark ages where we have immense capability to bring together information but when we gather this data, we pigeonhole it in the old familiar framework of interpretation, sometimes even torturing the data to make it fit. (Deloria 1995:231)

Reordering of text has far-reaching implications in the transformation of the material that Kamakau originally presented to his peers. The most massive reordering of content occurred at the initial development of the English manuscript, dividing Kamakau's collected columns into two separate fields. A distinction made between "history" and "culture," took place after the process of initial translation:

> Two manuscripts resulted; one, containing his historical material, was published in 1961 by The Kamehameha Schools, under the title *Ruling Chiefs of Hawaii*...The other manuscript contains Kamakau's account of the material and social culture of the Hawaiians before and during the early period of acculturation to Western ways,... (Barrère 1964:vii)

The distinction is decidedly foreign, i.e., Euro-American, in concept. While the English language has clearly different meanings for terms like history, legend, and culture, Hawaiian language does not share the same semantic boundaries. The Hawaiian word *moʻolelo*, used throughout the titles and narrative of Kamakau's series, is a single concept in Hawaiian conveying multiple meanings, encompassing what in English would be considered as history, ethnography, myth, legend, account, description, tradition, etc.:

> *moʻolelo*. n. Story, tale, myth, history, tradition, literature, legend, journal, log, yarn, fable, essay, chronicle, record, article; minutes, as of a meeting. (From moʻo ʻōlelo, succession of talk; all stories were oral, not written.) *Puke moʻolelo aupuni*, public records. (Pukui and Elbert 1986:254)

Or in an orthography and definition of Kamakau's era:

> Moo-o-le-lo, *s. Moo* and *olelo,* discourse. A continuous or connected narrative of events; a history. *Luk.* 1:1. A tradition. *Mat.* 15:2. In modern times, the minutes of a deliberative body; a taxation list. (Andrews 1865:395)

Kamakau composed his series as a continuum under the rubric of *moʻolelo*, and titled it as such, "Ka Moolelo o Kamehameha I," meaning the "moʻolelo" of or about Kamehameha I. He often referred to his project as a *moʻolelo* in his narrative (1867a, Feb. 16). Early on in the "Moolelo o Kamehameha I" series, a writer using the name Luna Auhau critiqued the wording of the title in a letter to *Ka Nupepa Kuokoa*, saying it was too narrow to address the breadth of the subject matter, but his recommendation for a broader title that would encompass all the various topics Kamakau was covering still relied on the Hawaiian understanding of the word *moʻolelo*. Luna Auhau's recommendation was:

> Ka Moolelo o ke au ia Kamehameha I. O ke kumu o kuu manao ana pela, aole pili keia mau mea e hoopuka ia nei i ka moʻolelo o Kamehameha I wale no; i na mea e pili ana i na alii e ae kekahi, ia Kalaniopuu, a i na mea e ae he nui wale. No laila kuu kanalua i kela poo. (1867)

> [The Story about the era of Kamehameha I. The reason for my thinking that way is that these things being published do not pertain to Kamehameha I alone; they regard things pertinent to the other chiefs, to Kalaniʻōpuʻu and to many other persons or topics. From there comes my concern about that title.]

Kamakau wrote *moʻolelo*. He often included references or even whole sections from other story forms, like *kaʻao*,[176] *moʻolelo kaʻao*,[177] and *mele*[178] of all kinds, but he used those references and information to illuminate what he termed a *moʻolelo*. *Haʻi moʻolelo*, the recounting of histories and stories, both oral and written, often includes explanatory asides about the characters, the practices, or the settings that are involved in a generally chronological story sequence. Kamakau saw himself as a *haʻi moʻolelo*, one who tells the stories, or even more so as a *kākau moʻolelo*, a writer of *moʻolelo*, a formal, self-proclaimed title that he used often.[179] In his preface to the Fornander collection of cultural writings (Fornander 1916:1), Thomas Thrum, publisher and translator, referred to Kamakau as *the historian*, and in the same sentence lists Kepelino and Haleʻole[180] without any descriptors, intentionally setting Kamakau apart from his contemporaries in the field.

Kawena Pukui worked with Martha Beckwith to articulate the various translators' works, but Beckwith seems to have taken responsibility for deciding which content was "historical" and which qualified as "cultural." She is also credited with the wording and annotating of those two manuscripts (Barrère 1964:vii). Those parts of Kamakau's *moʻolelo* that were considered to be history were published in *Ruling Chiefs of Hawaii* (Kamakau 1961). The portions viewed as being something other than history were relegated to the second manuscript,

---

[176] Traditional legends or well-known tales, historical or mythical.

[177] Story sequences which include fabulous or legendary accounts.

[178] Poetic compositions, of which there are many varieties, including genealogical, personal, geographical, etc.

[179] See, for instance, Kamakau (1869d, Jul. 1).

[180] Z. Kepelino is discussed as one of the canon authors in Chapter 2 of this text. S. N. Haleʻole was a noted historian, newspaper writer, and the author of *Ke Kaao o Laieikawai* (1863), which is acknowledged as the first published book of Hawaiian literature.

which would later be subdivided into three subsequent publications.[181] Thus, whole sections of his original text were unavailable in English for a span of thirty years, a reordering that was mostly unacknowledged and the extent of which was de-emphasized.

No mention is made in the 1961 English text of *Ruling Chiefs* of such a division, or that the book contained only a portion of Kamakau's original Hawaiian text. The ease with which modern readers and scholars could assume *Ruling Chiefs* to accurately represent Hawai'i's foremost native historian certainly helped to foster the unquestioning acceptance of the English text as a canon resource. After thirty years in print without acknowledgment of it being a portion of the original, the new preface in the 1992 reprint edition of *Ruling Chiefs* indirectly addressed, for the first time, that the book was part of the larger scope of Kamakau's original writings. The reference to "excerpts" does not clarify the levels of change imposed on the original, but it does acknowledge a larger body of work by the author:

> This book, *Ruling Chiefs of Hawaii*, is only one of four edited volumes of Kamakau's extensive writings translated into English. The excerpts presented in *Ruling Chiefs* focus on the political history of our people. (Kame'eleihiwa 1992:iii)

Following the publication of a second portion of Kamakau's writings as *Ka Po'e Kahiko: The People of Old* (Kamakau 1964), folklorist Katherine Luomala made a reference about the reordering of Kamakau's writings in a review of the second published portion. The reorganization, imposing order and "continuity" to a text that seemed to "jump about" in a Western sense, is addressed in a way that diminishes the importance of the change by pointing out that original source dates are included:

> The editor has rearranged Kamakau's order, but has given the newspaper sources for those who wish to consult the original. Kamakau jumped about at times from subject to subject and the new arrangement gives continuity. (1966:502)

---

[181] Kamakau, S. M., *Ka Po'e Kahiko: The People of Old* (1964); *The Works of the People of Old: Na Hana a ka Po'e Kahiko* (1976); and part of *Tales and Traditions of the People of Old: Nā Mo'olelo a ka Po'e Kahiko* (1991). Most of the material that resulted in the 1964 and 1976 publications was prepared in 1939 as a single text, submitted in draft form as *History of Hawaii, Part 2: Traditional beliefs and customs*. This text, arranged in chapters that correspond to the 1964 and 1976 publications, was credited as being translated and edited by Martha W. Beckwith and Mary Kawena Pukui, but didn't get published in this form. (Bishop Museum, MS SC S. M. Kamakau, Box 8.1)

One powerful example of the difference between the original sequencing of Kamakau's Hawaiian *moʻolelo* and the reordered English *history* has far-reaching implications for cultural analysis today. In the course of his chronology, Kamakau described Kalaniʻōpuʻu and the battles he led on Maui during the time of Captain Cook's arrival at Waimea, Kauaʻi. Prior to introducing Captain Cook, Kamakau spent four full weekly columns explaining the Hawaiian mind-set of the time concerning foreigners and the existence of foreign lands (Kamakau 1866b, Dec. 22, Dec. 29; Kamakau 1867, Jan. 5, Jan. 12, Jan. 19). His sequencing of the narrative therefore situates Cook's arrival as part of a continuum of Hawaiians' understanding about historical contact with the world beyond the horizon—not as an unprecedented, isolated event.

Kamakau opened this part of his narrative by introducing the widespread traditional knowledge about names and places in Kahiki, a general term for any land outside of the Hawaiian archipelago. From there came the gods, eventually making their way to Hawaiʻi, becoming progenitors of islands, supernaturals, and humans. From Hawaiʻi they sometimes traveled again to other lands, but always returned to the Hawaiian Islands.

Kamakau then introduced ancestral figures such as ʻUlu, Hema, Kahaʻi, and others, whose legendary sailing exploits included places in the Pacific, Asia, and even Europe (ibid). He detailed the stories of dozens of chiefs, navigators, and priests, some originating in Hawaiʻi, others coming from afar, and still others who share origins both in Hawaiʻi and abroad. These heroes are credited for their travels back and forth between Hawaiʻi and lands beyond; their stories recall their feats, the wonders they witnessed, and the lands they knew. These seafarers sometimes returned with living proof of their adventures, such as rescued parents, amazing beings like *kupaliʻi*, little people, or *pilikua*, giants, as well as new plants, implements and cultural practices (Kamakau 1866b, Dec. 22).

He then dedicated a partial chapter to the *haole*, or foreigners, who apparently made accidental landings on these shores. From the arrival of a boat *Ulupana* in the time of the chief ʻAuanini to the arrival of Captain Cook, over a score of outsiders, fair of skin and shiny of eye, were recounted as having come ashore on different islands. Many of them stayed and married into Hawaiian families, where their lines are still acknowledged (Kamakau 1867a, Jan. 19). Only after presenting this context did Kamakau enter into an account of Cook's arrival at Waimea, Kauaʻi.

These contextual sections were all omitted from the "historical" text *Ruling Chiefs*. They were relegated to the "cultural" portions of the reordered manuscript text, and not published until thirty years later, in the book of remainder sections, *Tales and Traditions* (Kamakau 1991:90–122). During this thirty-year gap, anthropological analyses by major figures in the field, such as Valerio Valeri (1985),

Gananath Obeyesekere (1992), and Marshal Sahlins (1995), were completed and published. The exclusion of this particular material in Kamakau's original sequence leaves an important gap in their considerations. Each of these scholars posed theories about the individual and collective perspectives of Hawaiians during the period of transition that Kamakau addressed, but none investigated his original writings (or the other writings of his time) as resources. Each relied heavily on the reordered English translation of Kamakau as one of the few Hawaiian sources they consulted.[182] The extensive bibliographies of their publications reference a broad array of observer accounts and theoretical works, but include no material from the archive considered here, aside from very rare consideration of material already brought to their attention either in *Ruling Chiefs,* or in the Hawai'i Ethnographical Notes (H.E.N.) of the Bishop Museum.[183]

Editing

Dorothy Barrère, in *The Works of the People of Old*, acknowledged an editorial decision that again impacted all analysis informed by the English translation. Kamakau presented different senses of time to distinguish contemporary practice from discontinued practices of the distant past. These distinctions were mostly edited into past tense only for smooth reading in modern times:

> Some aspects of the older Hawaiian culture were already abandoned or were fast disappearing by Kamakau's day, and some were still very much alive. Kamakau often differentiated in his text by the use of past and present tenses: we have for the sake of conformity used the past tense almost exclusively. (1976:v–vi)

While the following example is drawn from *The Works of the People of Old* (Kamakau 1976), such change was followed regularly in the production of all four

---

[182] Valeri (1985) consulted one of the five pertinent articles (*Ka Nupepa Kuokoa* 1866, Dec. 19), already in translation in the Hawai'i Ethnographic Notes archive at Bishop Museum. Obeyesekere (1992) only acknowledged using *Ruling Chiefs* and *Ka Poʻe Kahiko*, while Sahlins (1995) also used references from *Tales and Traditions*.

[183] The H.E.N. are largely the collected notes of Mary Kawena Pukui (1895–1986), who spent much of her career culling material of cultural or historical interest from the Hawaiian-language newspapers and translating or summarizing them on behalf of the anthropologists at the Bishop Museum. Her collection, a disparate assembly of generally cultural topics with translations by herself and others, is a valuable point of entry into the Hawaiian-language resources she studied.

English publications derived from Kamakau's writings. This excerpt comes from the description of a ritual for deifying an ancestor's spirit:

> I ka wā e pau ai ka umu puaʻa, me ka umu ʻīlio maoli, a ʻo ka ʻawa nō ka mea nui he ʻawa hoʻohāinu no ua poʻe kino lau ʻeʻepa nei, ke mākaukau nei ka umu e huaʻi, aia ke momoe maila nā kino hoʻoweliweli o ua poʻe nei i loko o ka wai, mai ka poʻe nui a ka poʻe liʻiliʻi, aia ka ʻawa ke hoʻohāinu ʻia lā, aia ka ʻīlio ke hānai ʻia lā, aia nā mea a pau ke hānai ʻia lā, ke pule nei ke kahu moʻo, a ke lawe aku nei i kāna ʻope ukana, a hāʻawi aku nei ma ke alo o ka ʻaumakua i manaʻo ʻia e kākūʻai, a ʻo ka lilo akula nō ia, ʻaʻole paha e hala nā lā ʻelua a ʻekolu paha, a laila, ʻo ka hoʻi maila nō ia i luna o kekahi makamaka e noho ai, a e keʻehi paʻa ai paha,… (1870, May 5)

A literal handling of the text clearly reflects the very immediate present tense that Kamakau used:

> [At the time the earth oven for pig and the oven for native dog are finished, *ʻawa* is the most important thing, *ʻawa* to offer as a drink for those aforementioned supernaturals; the oven is becoming ready for opening and the terrifying forms of those beings are lying in the water, from the large beings to the small; *ʻawa* is being offered to drink, the dog is being offered up to eat, all the things [foods] are being offered to eat, the lineage priest is praying and taking his bundle, offering it into the presence of the ancestral spirit considered for this deification, and then it will be borne away; not more than two or perhaps three days might elapse, then [the spirit] will return to temporarily possess an associate, or to reside fixed there,…]

The published English text in *Ka Poʻe Kahiko* re-presents the ritual in the timelessness of the distant past, translated as:

> By the time the pigs and dogs were cooked and the imus ready to be opened, there lay these fearsome beings in the water. All of them, large and small, were given *ʻawa* to drink and fed dog and other foods while the *kahu moʻo* prayed. Then he took the bundle and placed it in front of the *ʻaumakua* to whom it had been decided to offer it, and it was borne away. Not more than

two or three days would pass before the spirit would return and "sit on" (*noho*) or utterly possess (*keʻehi paʻa*) one of the relatives... (Kamakau 1964:86)

It is worth noting that many other articles written around the same time on this topic of ancient worship or religious practice make it a point to describe the particulars in the present tense as activities that were very much ongoing, despite the critical stances of the authors.[184]

Elision

Another editing step distancing the English text from the original is the condensing of seemingly repetitive coverage for inclusion in the English text. While considered to be sound editing practice, minor distinctions are lost in the process. Those relying on the English text seldom consult the Hawaiian text as the actual resource, giving the English translation the status of a primary source. The Hawaiian text, if sought at all, is then utilized only to validate the English presentation, with great potential for missing or misconstruing details in the original.

An example from David Stannard's work in *Before the Horror,* shows the pitfall of such overtly referential use of the Hawaiian to check the "facts" available in the English translation. Stannard deconstructed the references to infanticide presented in *Ruling Chiefs,* using the Hawaiian text to show the English translation had been "willfully misrendered" (1989:138). This allowed him to dismiss Kamakau as a flawed original source and *Ruling Chiefs* as an intentionally misleading translation. Stannard, however, searched the Hawaiian text only enough to check what he found in the English, missing more extensive references that had been elided in the English publication. Such misuse of the translated materials I have referred to as "keyhole scholarship" for the narrow, and potentially misleading, vision it provides. Such application of the canon texts, based on the assumption of parallel meaning, is common.

Kamakau addressed infanticide at two separate points in the same column and the similarity of content led to the elision of the two paragraphs into shorter, yet still split, reference in *Ruling Chiefs,* glossing the original statements. It's worthwhile to present Kamakau's original two paragraphs here with the pertinent text italicized for clarity:

---

[184] For examples, see *Ka Hoku Loa* (1859a), *Ka Hoku Loa* (1859b), *Ka Hae Hawaii* (1860a), and *Ke Au Okoa* (1865b).

9. O ke umi keiki kekahi hana kaumaha loa a keia lahui, a ua hana nui ia i ka wa kahiko pegana, a ua hana nuiia *i keia wa Kristiano*. Ua kinai mau na wahine me ke umi ana i ka lakou mau keiki ma kahi malu; a imua o ke kokua ana o ke kane a me na makua, a *o ke kahuna o-o a me kekahi poe e ae*. O ka hoomake ana i na keiki; he nui wale ke ano o ka imi ana a na wahine e hoomake i na keiki iloko o ka opu, ma ka inu ana i ka apu e hoomake i ke keiki iloko o ka opu, o ka o-o a hoohemo iwaho, o ka pepehi me ka uhai ana i ke keiki iloko o ka opu, o ke kiola iloko o ka wai a me ke kanu maoli iloko o ka lepo ma ka hanau maikai ana mai o ke keiki. O ka luahine, o ka ilihune, o ka lealea o ke kino, o ka moekolohe, o ka lili, o ke kauwa, o ka hookae, o ka hilahila, o ke kanawai. Oia na kumu ino loa o keia hewa imua o ko ke Akua mau maka. Ua ike pinepine ia i keia manawa, ua lehulehu a paapu na wahine a me na kaikamahine opiopio i pau i ka make no ka o-o ana i ka lakou mau keiki. (1867a, Nov. 30)

[9. Infanticide was a very sorrowful act by this race, and it was done often in pagan ancient times, and *is still often done in this Christian era*. The women regularly killed and did away with their children in secret; and in the presence of help from their husband's and parents, *as well as the abortion specialist and others*. The killing of children; there are many ways women seek to terminate a child in the womb, by drinking potions to kill the child in the womb, to pierce and take the child out, to beat and pummel the child in the womb, tossing it into the water or actually burying it in the earth after healthy birth of the child. Age, poverty, physical pleasures, adultery, jealousy, slave status, disdain, shame, the laws. Those are the despicable reasons for this offense in the eyes of God. It has been often seen at this time, numerous and teeming are the women and young girls who have died from aborting their children.]

2. O ke umi keiki kekahi hewa *ma ka wa kahiko*—He mea kupanaha keia hewa nui a me ka hana ino, a he nui na kumu o keia hewa nui o ke umi keiki. O ka moekolohe no ke kumu, a o ka hoohalahala kekahi, o ka hookeekee, ka lili, a o ka

hoohalahala, o ke kauwa, o ka ilihune a me ka uluhua i ka nui o na keiki, a o ka makemake i ka hele kauhale. O ke umi keiki, *ua kokua pu me ke kane a me na makua a me na makamaka i kekahi manawa.* O ka inu ana i apu laau pa e hanau ole ai ka wahine, he mea nui no ia. O ka imi ana i kumu e make ai ke keiki iloko o ka opu, a he lehulehu wale na kumu e pepehi ai i ke keiki iloko o ka opu. He inu apu laau kekahi, a ua hee wale ke keiki iloko o ka opu. O ka o-o ana kekahi mea e pepehi ai i ke keiki, a ua nui ka poe i make pu me na makuahine no ia hana lokoino. O ka omilo, o ka uhai maoli no i ke keiki iloko o ka opu o ka makuahine, a o ke kiola i ka pali, iloko o ka wai, o ke kai, a o ke kanu maoli iloko o ka lepo i na keiki i hanau maikai mai. He hana nui keia i ka wa kahiko, a he oi loa aku keia manawa o ka o-o i na keiki. Ua oleloia no ka makau i ke Kanawai. (1867a, Nov. 30)

[2. Infanticide was another sin *in ancient times*—This great sin and evil is shocking, and this terrible sin of infanticide has many causes. The cause is adultery, and faultfinding is another, shunning, jealousy, and defamation, slave status, poverty, and frustration at the number of children, along with a desire to wander freely. Infanticide *was assisted by husbands, parents, and friends sometimes.* Drinking of potions was frequent for the woman to avoid pregnancy and be unable to give birth. Seeking a reason for the child to die in the womb led to many reasons for killing the fetus. Drinking of potions was one way, and the child became a miscarriage. Piercing was another way to kill the child and many died, along with the mothers, for that evil act. To cause abortion, actually destroying the child in the mother's womb, tossing it over the cliff, into the water, into the sea, and actual burial in the earth of those children born healthy. This was a prevalent practice in ancient times, and at this time abortion of children by piercing is far more prevalent. It is said that this is due to fear of the Law.]

The eliding of the two references resulted in the following translation in *Ruling Chiefs* with the text that Stannard considered to be willfully misrendered marked in italics:

> Infanticide was another evil practiced in pagan days *and still made use of today*. Women dispose of their children in secret places with the help of their husbands, parents, and *of the kahuna ʻōʻō*, and others besides. Women in old days killed the child within the womb by drinking medicine to poison the child, by using a sharp-pointed instrument, by beating on the abdomen, or they would throw a newborn infant into the water or bury it in the earth. Their reasons for killing the child were age, poverty, pleasure-seeking, illicit relations, jealousy, slavery, dislike of children, and shame. (Kamakau 1961:234)

On the next page, another portion of the original reference was tagged onto a listing of reasons for population decline:

> Infanticide was another cause of this decrease...but because of the laws this became more common in late days... (1961:235)

Stannard, no fan of Kamakau, entwined his criticism of both *Ruling Chiefs* and its source articles as "a missionary-edited and translated newspaper article written in 1867 by a Christianized and evangelical Hawaiian chronicler, Samuel M. Kamakau," going on to describe the original as "tainted and secondary source material" (1989:138). In his charge that the translation was "willfully misrendered" he insisted the English translation intentionally imposed an insidious discourse of rampant infanticide among Hawaiians. This imposed discourse was inserted in the English, Stannard explained, by the improper use of the present tense in translating Kamakau's description, and by the addition of the term *kahuna ʻōʻō*, or abortionist, where the original never used it as per his research in the Hawaiian text.

Recognizing most of the English text in one of the two Hawaiian paragraphs shown above, Stannard completely overlooked the remainder of the column, as well as the rest of Kamakau's writings.[185] He missed one of the two paragraphs in Hawaiian that were elided in the English into a lesser, split mention and so he located only the fifteenth paragraph in the Nov. 30, 1867 issue of *Ka Nupepa Kuokoa*, and not the seventh paragraph in the same issue. This earlier paragraph contained both the use of present tense and the mention of *kahuna ʻōʻō*, abortionist, details he charged were imposed into the English. Because he assumed that the

---

[185] Also missed were a number of other writings referring to infanticide by various authors, which today can be located on the Hoʻolaupaʻi website, www.nupepa,org, by searching "umi kamalii" and "umi keiki."

English book contained all of the Hawaiian text in its original sequence, he didn't look for information other than what was presented in English, and subsequently based his critique only on the portion he located and checked. The keyhole scholarship that Stannard applied to the task verified his distrust of Kamakau as a source and his dismissal of the translation as a reliable reference.

Stannard followed the same process of checking only the Hawaiian text most clearly indicated by the elided English gloss in his 1991 article, "Recounting the fables of savagery: Native infanticide and the functions of political myth" (1991). In this case, Stannard assumed the word "pagan days" was imposed into the English translation. The elision and glossing of the Hawaiian text led him to miss the mention of "*ka wa pegana*" in the opening lines of Kamakau's first paragraph quoted above. This misled critique by Stannard was later incorporated into Jeffrey Tobin's article, "Savages, the Poor and the Discourse of Hawaiian Infanticide" (1997:81), and undoubtedly has appeared in subsequent articles, perpetuating a chronic misdirection in contemporary scholarship. While misapplication of Kamakau's portion of the canon leaves a legacy of misdirection and misrepresentation, a focus on Kamakau and other canon texts, to the exclusion of a century of other authors, is its own form of keyhole scholarship.

Another example of elision of original content resulting in loss of data is this note on the uprising against the overthrow of the *kapu* restrictions that occurred following the death of Kamehameha I in 1819:

> …a ulu mai la ka haunaele ma Hamakua, a kipi iho la kekahi kanaka kuaaina o Kainapau ka inoa, a hooulu mai la i ke kaua makaainana, a ke kanaka kuaaina o Kainapau no Hamakua, a ua hoomahui no mahope ona.
>
> A lohe na 'lii ma Kona i ke kaua kipi ma Hamakua; Hoouna ia 'ku la kekahi kaukaualii mai o Liholiho aku, o Kainapaua Lonoàkai e hoomakakiu i ua kaua makaainana la ma Hamakua.
>
> I ko lakou hoomakakiu ana, a ua halawai kino lakou me ke kaua makaainana ma Mahiki, a ua pepehi ia o Kainapau wahi alii e Kainapau kuaaina a make loa, a ua make pu elua kanaka o ke alii, i make i ua kaua makaainana la. (Kamakau 1867a, Nov. 2)

A literal translation would be:

> …then trouble arose at Hāmākua, and a certain country man named Kainapau rebelled and generated a commoners' war,

led by the country person, Kainapau of Hāmākua, and he aligned himself with him [Kekuaokalani].

And the chiefs in Kona heard of the rebellion in Hāmākua; A certain lesser chief, Kainapau[a], son of Lonoakai was sent from the court of Liholiho to spy on that commoners' battle at Hāmākua.

When they did their reconnaissance, they came upon the commoners' battle at Mahiki and the chiefly Kainapau was beaten and slain by the countryside Kainapau, and two men of the chief were also killed, slain in that commoners' battle.

This section appears in the *Ruling Chiefs* text as:

...disorders arose; in Hamakua one man took up arms against the government. A lesser chief named Lono-akahi was sent by Liholiho to see what was going on, and in a scrimmage he and two of his men were killed by the country men of Mahiki. (Kamakau 1961:226)

While this elision has not stirred controversy like the earlier example, important details are lost. For instance, the Hāmākua battle was incited among commoners opposing high chiefs, an event of particular import in historical analysis of Hawaiian society. The opposition was against Liholiho, son and heir of Kamehameha I, and aligned with Kekuaokalani, his cousin and contender for power, and not against the government as an entity. The shared names of the principals involved (Kainapau) are lost in the English; the leader of the commoners' revolt and the court emissary who was killed shared the same name, a point made very clear in Kamakau's report to avoid confusion in other settings, but not included in the English translation. Also, Lonoakai, the name of the chiefly participant's father, is recorded as Lonoakahi and he is mistakenly identified as the one killed.[186]

---

[186] Other historians have made note of this event, such as Ralston (1984), with *Ruling Chiefs of Hawaii* as the source of data. Perkins (1980:70) shows a very similar text in Jules Remy's *Ka Moolelo Hawaii/Histoire de l'Archipel Hawaiien* (Iles Sandwich), published in French and Hawaiian in 1862. Remy's account includes the name Kainapaunoakai, and Perkins discusses the irony of the shared names of the combatants.

John Papa ʻĪʻī

Born in 1800, John Papa ʻĪʻī was raised in the court of Kamehameha I as a playmate of Liholiho, who became Kamehameha II, and was trained in the ways of Hawaiian court life. An obituary following ʻĪʻī's death in 1870 spoke to the depth of cultural knowledge that had been instilled in this very modern political figure of his time:

> Ua piha kona waihona hoomanao i ka paanaau i na mele olioli o na wa kahiko a me na mele a na alii i haku ai, a ua lawe pu akula o ia me ia mau buke mele. Ke hoomanao nei makou i ka make ana o Kamehameha IV, ua olioli mele ia e ia kekahi po holookoa mai ke ahiahi a wehewehe kai ao. (*Ka Nupepa Kuokoa* 1870)
>
> [His repository of remembrances was filled with memorized chants of ancient times and with chants that the chiefs had composed, and he has taken with him those tomes of ancient poetry. We recall at the death of Kamehameha IV that an entire night was spent by him reciting chanted refrains from evening all the way through to daybreak.]

He went on to spend most of his life in government under the subsequent sovereign ruling chiefs until his retirement from service in 1864, at the beginning of Kamehameha V's reign. A founding member of the Privy Council and the House of Nobles, he held a number of government offices in the course of his career, often simultaneously. Beginning in 1866, his narrative accounts described the events he witnessed, the information and insights to which he was privileged, and the oral traditions that were shared among those in court. He never claimed to be either an historian or a journalist, and came upon his writing career almost by accident, encouraged by many peers after having submitted a few initial articles based on his personal remembrances.

The Hawaiian Text

During his many positions with the Hawaiian government, ʻĪʻī was called on to publish announcements, position papers, and official responses on behalf of his offices, but he didn't begin to write serial columns until after his retirement in 1864 at age 64. His first set of seven columns was inspired by the death of his royal ward, Victoria Kamāmalu Kaʻahumanu on May 29, 1866. In the very next issue of

John Papa ʻĪʻī had published a memoir of Victoria Kamāmalu that appeared in 6 issues of Ka Nupepa Kuokoa *in 1866. An 1868 memoir for Mataio Kekūanāoʻa ran for two issues, and then became a serial column on ʻĪʻī's reminiscences of Hawaiian history, "Na Hunahuna o ka Moolelo Hawaii." Photo by David Franzen, Bishop Museum.*

Ka Nupepa Kuokoa, he began a series of recollections about her life and the royal circle into which she had been born. The series, beginning with the June 2, 1866 issue, ended abruptly on August 18th in the midst of an account of his journey by ship to Hawaiʻi island.

Over two years later, Kekūanāoʻa, ʻĪʻī's long-time friend and fellow statesman, passed away and again ʻĪʻī took to writing for the newspaper. Three initial articles were dedicated to the life of Kekūanāoʻa, and then the column became serialized. Topics branched out to include vignettes of court life, biographical accounts of many of the chiefs, historical events that had happened during his long career, stories of ancient chiefs, legends of old, and descriptions of cultural practices, such as surfing, canoeing, and the hula. He wrote bi-weekly and then weekly for the next two years, producing 66 additional columns before the sequence ended following his death on May 2, 1870.[187]

In contrast to Kamakau, John Papa ʻĪʻī wrote about Hawaiian history and culture from a first-person perspective. Whereas Kamakau provided narrative and overview, aiming at presenting ethnography and formal history, ʻĪʻī reminisced and shared personal stories.

---

[187] His last column appeared on May 28, 1870.

Criticism

Unlike Kamakau and many other writers of the decade, it appears that John Papa ʻĪʻī did not generate direct criticism from his contemporaries. Possibly his status as an elder statesman and his first-hand experiences in the courts of the Kamehamehas lent credence to his stories. His humility may have also played a part in the lack of criticism, as ʻĪʻī did not claim to be a historian of the nation, as Kamakau did, but only to be sharing his own memories and personal understandings of the history he saw and heard about. The intricate detail of his accounts, the listing of the persons involved, their actions and their actual words lent great credibility to his authority in recounting the past.

Nonetheless, frequent critical interchanges among other writers of the time undoubtedly made ʻĪʻī cautious in his own work. He printed corrections and subtle criticism about others, including corrections to aspects of the history that Kamakau was presenting during the same period. He did not directly engage with Kamakau as did other critics of the time, like Unauna and Koiʻi, but addressed the readers instead, opening his corrective writings with introductions like "You may have seen in *Ka Moolelo Hawaii*" (the name of Kamakau's column), and then going on to correct or elaborate the point that had been addressed there. Such a style averted the angry response Kamakau gave others. Kamakau never did directly critique ʻĪʻī. However, the intricate interchange between the two obviously helped shape the content of their writing.

Editorial Constraints

No data is available on the editing processes that affected ʻĪʻī's columns, either his own self-editing or that imposed by the newspaper. Little pre-publication material found its way into archival collections, and the Kamakau holographs mentioned earlier appear to be a serendipitous find. It can be assumed that minor editing of phrasing and word choice was a regular process, like that shown in Kamakau's case, but nothing beyond that is known.

The English Text

The publication of John Papa ʻĪʻī's *Fragments of Hawaiian History* in 1959 made his name familiar to a modern audience and introduced researchers and the general public to the value of his personal insights into Hawaiian history and culture. *Fragments* is an invaluable introduction to his work, but the processes of bringing the writings of ʻĪʻī to publication were much the same as those applied to the works of Kamakau. The resulting English texts similarly distance the reader from the Hawaiian-language originals.

Fragments of Hawaiian History contains only a portion of ʻĪʻī's original writings, in altered order and edited form. Examples of the changes imposed on the writings of ʻĪʻī for the English publication highlight the need for consulting the original material. Consideration of the scope of alterations included in the English text is not intended to diminish the value of *Fragments*, but to show that reliance on this and other English texts in lieu of the Hawaiian originals perpetuates a discourse of sufficiency.

Extraction

The material by ʻĪʻī that was identified and extracted from the Hawaiian-language newspapers appears to be the sum of his cultural writings. He was not as prolific as Kamakau, who wrote sporadically for years and kept up a lively written interaction in the newspapers outside of his serial columns. In this way, the extraction of the ʻĪʻī material more completely contains his corpus of writings than the portion drawn from Kamakau's original material, but still decontextualizes this portion of his writings.

Translation

In the introduction to the 1959 printing of *Fragments of Hawaiian History*, Kenneth Emory credits Mary Kawena Pukui with translating the entire set of ʻĪʻī's articles, a very different setting from the translation team who collaborated over the writings of Kamakau. The work of a single translator lent consistency to the translation process that is apparent in the edited translations in *Fragments*.

Although some minor points of contention can be addressed, and are presented below, the scale of inconsistencies in the ʻĪʻī translation is miniscule when compared to the somewhat uneven product of the group effort applied to Kamakau's works. Perceived inconsistencies between ʻĪʻī's columns and the translations appearing in *Fragments* may be Pukui's own interpretation or a result of the editing applied to her translated text. Unfortunately Pukui's original, full translation of the articles seems to have been discarded when the final editing of text for English publication was finished, and no record of her original translation remains with which to check these points.

Overall, the translation of the ʻĪʻī material appears to have been what was described earlier as literal, or formal, in an attempt to fully present the content of the Hawaiian text to an English audience. There are some places where the content seems to have been altered or truncated in the process of translation or possibly in later editing, as the following examples show. The differences, italicized here for emphasis, show a loss of certain detail or a change of meaning in the process.

1. ʻĪʻī's explanation about why he would choose to give his service to Liholiho, rather than to Liholiho's father, Kamehameha Paiʻea:

> O ka hoolohe no hoi paha ka pono o ke alii waiwai ole, i waiwai ai no hoi, a laila, waiwai pu no hoi me ke kanaka. (1869, Nov. 31)

> [It seems necessary for *a chief who is not wealthy to listen and pay heed*, so that he may become wealthy, and then his people will be wealthy as well.]

Published in *Fragments of Hawaiian History*, the statement loses complexity:

> The *chief without wealth should be obeyed*, and when he becomes wealthy, the servant becomes wealthy too. (1959:55)

2. On loss of detail:

> Ua hiki mai kekahi mea mai Waialua mai a wahi e ae paha, he hoa make pu me iala i ka lua hookahi, no ka mea, he mea mau ia i kekahi poe makee alii mai o loa mai, aka no ka maluhia, ua kuu ia oia mai ka make mai me iala. (1869, Nov. 20)

A careful, literal following of the text gives this insight to the event:

> Someone arrived from Waialua or elsewhere, a companion to die in her company and share the same grave, because, from ancient times, it was a regular practice with some who loved their chiefs, *however, to keep the social peace, that person was released from dying along with her*...

Which was published in *Fragments* with a slightly different outcome, as:

> ...someone came from Waialua or thereabouts to die with her and share the same grave, which was another ancient custom with some who loved their chiefs *and sought peace of mind*. (1959:100)

3. Another example of difference between Hawaiian and published English text shows substantial changes in how the writer reflects on Kamehameha I:

> A pehea la ia i hana ai i keia mau ano maikai? Aia paha ma ka maikai o kona poo a me kana liʻa ana, no ka mea he kanaka akamai loa i ke kaua a he haipule no hoi a *ua hoolilo ia kana haipule naauao ana i mea e hiki mai ai ke malamalama oiaio maoli i o kakou nei.* (1870, Jan. 22)

A literal following of the Hawaiian text would give this translation:

> And how is it that he acted in such appropriate ways? It might be a result of the excellence of his mind and his wishes, because he was a very intelligent man in warfare and very religious, and *his wise manner of worship was utilized as a means for the true enlightenment to come here to us.*

The section, however, was published with a puzzling change in *Fragments*, to read as follows:

> Whence came his wisdom and this desire to do good deeds? Perhaps from his skill in warfare and his religious nature. *His unenlightened worship led to the coming of the light of truth.* (1959:106)

    In addition to the examples like those above, the combination of a typographical error in *Fragments* with a possible misunderstanding by the translator or editor about the traditional land division system of *moku, kalana, ahupuaʻa,* and *ʻili*[188] resulted in a set of references that confuse the function and stability of that ancient system of divisions. In the *Fragments* translation of a rarely-documented section on how Kamehameha I distributed the conquered Oʻahu lands among his chiefs, Moanalua is referred to first as a *kalana* and then as an *ahupuaʻa*, two different scales of divisions (ʻĪʻī 1959:71). The first reference, naming Moanalua as a *kalana* or second-level district, is actually a typographical error appearing as

---

[188] These four terms identify divisions of scale: 1st-*moku*, or island; 2nd-*kalana*, or major subdivision of an island (sometimes called *moku o loko*); 3rd-*ahupuaʻa*, interior division of a *kalana*, running mountain to sea; and 4th-*ʻili*, or section within an *ahupuaʻa*.

Waialua in the Hawaiian text ('Ī'ī 1869, Dec. 18) The distinctions of Moanalua as an *ahupua'a* and Waialua as a *kalana* coincide with other references.

Confusion also arises in the same section over use of the term *ahupua'a*, known as a bounded land division within the major district, and usually extending from mountain to sea. Several times in this short description of Kamehameha's land distribution, *ahupua'a* is used in the Hawaiian text with an extended, contextualized meaning of "*ahupua'a*-based lands," rather than a full, individual land division. Such use provides contrast with the smaller, discrete *'ili* lands each chief received within Waikīkī *ahupua'a*, as noted earlier in the same paragraph:

> Pela na iliaina ma Waikiki…O Pahoa ko John Young (Olohana), a o kekahi hapa o Halawa ke ahupuaa. O Kanewai ko Keeaumoku, ke kalana o Waialua kai iaia. O Kapunahou ko Kameeiamoku, o Moanalua ke ahupuaa. ('Ī'ī 1869, Dec. 18)

> [That was the way the 'ili lands in Waikīkī were handled… Pahoa went to John Young ('Olohana) and part of Hālawa made up the ahupua'a-based lands. Kānewai belonged to Ke'eaumoku, the major district of Waialua was his. Kapunahou was Kame'eiamoku's, and Moanalua would be the ahupua'a-based lands.]

In the source narrative, 'Ī'ī makes different references to two separate awards in the *ahupua'a* of Hālawa as "*ke ahupua'a*" and later refers to an award within the two separate *ahupua'a* of Lā'iewai and Lā'iemalo'o again as being "*ke ahupua'a*" ('Ī'ī 1959:70). In each case, the translation follows the dictionary meaning of a single, entire land unit, but such usage would indicate a fluidity in the borders and functions of a land division system that seemingly remained intact for centuries, up until the Māhele of 1845–1848. The context in Hawaiian relies on readers' familiarity with the land division terms, but the English translation of this newly-recontextualized use of the word *ahupua'a* implies that Kamehameha reconfigured the centuries-old *ahupua'a* system of O'ahu, while the context and cultural assumptions of the original narrative clarify this seemingly contradictory reference.

Editing

It appears that the entire set of 73 columns published by 'Ī'ī were originally extracted for translation by Kawena Pukui, but the editing of that translated text resulted in only 65% of those writings being included in the English publication.[189] Seven columns were deleted entirely, and the remaining 66 columns were used in part or in whole. Dorothy Barrère, who was selected to edit the translated manuscript, said she was asked by the Bishop Museum director to leave out legendary material and to select those topics that might be of interest to anthropologists and to the descendents of John Papa ʻĪʻī.[190] The final selections were made by Barrère.

The seven columns deleted in entirety covered a range of topics: one introduced the death of Kekūanāoʻa; four consecutive columns gave a sequential account of ancient chiefs; one column dealt with Kaʻahumanu; and the last deleted column dealt with canoe handling.[191] Only 27 of 55 *mele* in the original columns were included in the English text. Some were dropped as parts of larger deleted blocks of text, while others were simply deleted from the narrative. No *mele* were included in partial form.

ʻĪʻī's prose was often highly descriptive, and the editing that took place made his descriptions more truncated and terse. One example is the description of Kekūhaupiʻo's arrival at Hilo (1869, Feb. 6), which is shortened in *Fragments* (1959: 9–10), resulting in a loss of detail about Kekūhaupiʻo and his nature.

In the text that was selected for *Fragments*, ʻĪʻī's own ordering system is diminished by the absorption of his subtitles. ʻĪʻī included frequent subtitles between sections of his text to make sense of his sometimes disconnected narrative, but in *Fragments* those subtitles are incorporated into the English paragraphs or deleted completely rather than being kept as separate guiding indicators.[192] This process subsumes the organization that the author had included in his writings.

Reordering Text

Deletion of text disarticulated the English publication from its original form, and so did the reordering of text. In *Fragments*, ʻĪʻī's writing is reordered on a massive scale, with sections from different places in his original sequence

---

[189] This figure is based on word counts of a typescript of the original columns, comparing those sections that were included in *Fragments* and those parts that were left out.

[190] Barrère, personal communication, 1998.

[191] These seven columns appeared on the following dates in *Ka Nupepa Kuokoa*: Nov. 28, 1868; Apr. 25, 1869; May 8, 1869; May 15, 1869; May 22, 1869; May 29, 1869; Jun. 26, 1869; and Apr. 16, 1870.

[192] An example is in *Ka Nupepa Kuokoa*, Nov. 13, 1869, where a section about Chiefess Kalaniakua is introduced with the subtitle "Ka Make Ana O Kalaniakua" [The Death of Kalaniakua]; the subtitle is incorporated as the opening sentence of the paragraph of the narrative as, "First, let us speak of the death of the chiefess Kalaniakua." Many subtitles are completely deleted, while others are edited into the narrative.

recombined into a new narrative flow. Less than half of the 147 pages of text included in *Fragments* contain material in ʻĪʻī's original sequence. Even where material from single or consecutive columns is relatively intact, the translated narrative is often reordered within the page or the paragraph. The reordering is thus even more extensive than it appears.

This reordering was a common practice in early 20th-century scholarship, generated here, at least in part, by the sometimes-meandering nature of ʻĪʻī's original text, and by the editor's wish to impose sequential order on the content. Obviously the combining of similar references and a consistent translation style created a smoother flow for an audience of a century later, one unfamiliar with ʻĪʻī's prose and his many references to people and places of the past. Such new order and flow, however, presents a writing style that reflects little of what would have been familiar to ʻĪʻī's contemporaries.

The non-linear processes of narrative common to the oral tradition is exemplified in the writings of ʻĪʻī, who in many ways was representative of an earlier age. The familiar nature of that non-linear form was already changing at the time of his writing, however, it was still evident, at least in the Hawaiian papers, which ran until 1948. There are examples from the 1860s of legends and stories being critiqued for their wandering, seemingly disconnected sequence of narrative, and the following response to such criticism reflects the mindset of one well-published storyteller of the time:

> Mahea ka moolelo o Hawaii nei i aukahi a hiki i kona palena?... Mahea hoi o ua moolelo la kahi i lauwili, a i akaaka ole ai hoi ka heluhelu ana? (Kaulainamoku 1865)
>
> [Where would one find a Hawaiian story that flows in a single current to its conclusion?...Where would one find a story so convoluted as to be unclear?]

Elision

There are some indications of editing where similar, but particular, references have been contracted into a more general translation, although such contraction of text is often obscured by the scale of reordering or the deletion of small sections of the original manuscript. One example of elision leading to loss of detail is as follows:

> ...aka, aole nae kakou i kamailio no kekahi mau hana ana, oia ka oihana lawaia, kalai waa, iako, ama, hoe a oia wale a oia wale. (ʻĪʻī 1869, Dec. 18)

Which would read, in a direct translation, like this:

> ...We haven't, however, discussed other endeavors, those being fishing, carving of canoes, outrigger booms, outrigger floats, paddles, and so on and so forth.

This was condensed into the following in *Fragments,* glossing the reference to booms and floats, a minor loss of detail, but common:

> ...but some not mentioned previously were fishing, canoe-making, paddle-making and the like. ('Ī'ī 1959:69)

Editorial Additions

Beyond changes that diminished 'Ī'ī's original text through deletion or contraction, additions to his work were inserted into the English text in the course of editing. Some of these additions are bracketed, and are clear to readers as editorial additions. Other additions are not marked, and would be mistaken by readers to be part of 'Ī'ī's original text. There are many examples of these unmarked additions, three of which are highlighted below in bold:

1. This entire line, explaining a preceding *mele*, was added in without any acknowledgment:

> Figuratively, this means, "Let that which is unknown become known." (1959:38)

2. The purpose and destination of the sandalwood cargo in the ship *Keoua Lelepali*, data mentioned in separate, deleted sections of 'Ī'ī's narrative, was added here:

> After the king had been in Kailua for two years, the person who had taken the *Keoua Lelepali* laden with sandalwood **to China to be sold** returned. (1959:128)

3. The interpretation of the act of removing one's cloak is included without notice, marked by dashes rather than brackets:

>...he must immediately remove his tapa cloak or cape, bundle it, and cover it with grass–**a sign of humility**–before he entered. (1959:58)[193]

Interestingly, this last example of added material was bracketed in the final edit version on file in the Bishop Museum, but not bracketed in the published book, apparently changed to dashes during editing of the galleys.

Another area of editorial additions was the insertion of dates within the narrative where ʻĪʻī had not included them. Dates were almost always added in without acknowledgment in the English text, although the introduction acknowledges the research that editor Dorothy Barrère had done on ʻĪʻī's writings to "supply dates which he did not include or in which he was in error" (Emory 1959:x). There are many examples: page 157, where December 2, 1829 is added to clarify the time of Boki's departure to the New Hebrides (ʻĪʻī 1869, Jan. 2); page 158, where the date (5th) is added into ʻĪʻī's more general reference of June 1832 (ʻĪʻī 1869, Apr. 10); and page 124, where the year of Kaʻōleiokū's death is edited to be 1818 (ʻĪʻī 1870, Mar. 12).[194] It is sufficient to say that adding dates was a regular practice throughout the book, and one of the stated goals of the project editor, making the text far easier to follow for English readers.

In contrast to some of his contemporaries, ʻĪʻī was more prone to establish time frames in his narrative by reference to events rather than dates, exemplifying the oral tradition in which he was raised. In the whole course of his original narrative, he only refers to specific years 17 times, with only a few of those referencing to specific months or dates. Insertion of dates on the part of the editor was certainly critical for modern English readers who would be unfamiliar with most chronological referents readily known to ʻĪʻī's contemporaries, even if such reference points had not been reordered or deleted in editing.

Intertextuality: Kamakau and ʻĪʻī

Samuel Kamakau and John Papa ʻĪʻī were writing simultaneously in the late 1860s and included many references to each other's work in their respective columns. Their styles of referencing each other were quite different, but the inter-

---

[193] In *Ka Nupepa Kuokoa*, Aug. 7, 1869, the text read "*a laila e wehe koke oia i kona kapa a kihei paha, e popo oia ia mea a uhi ae kahi mauu maluna iho oia mea a pela ia e komo ai i loko*" [then he quickly removed his covering or cloak, bundled it, spread some grass over it, and thus he entered].

[194] ʻĪʻī wrote that 1816 or 1817 was the general timing of this event.

action continued through the 2-year sequence columns by John Papa ʻĪʻī.[195] They were both published in the same newspaper, *Ka Nupepa Kuokoa*, until January of 1869 when Kamakau's serial was taken up by *Ke Au Okoa*. These were the two main Hawaiian-language newspapers of the time, so the interaction would have been apparent to the reading public.[196]

Kamakau's serial column often included correction or re-presentation of material printed earlier by John Papa ʻĪʻī in his columns in *Kuokoa*. He never directly referred to ʻĪʻī or acknowledged his writings, but simply incorporated the material into his own columns, offering corrections, expanding the content or recasting the material in a broader frame. Such a lack of acknowledgment could be seen as an uncharacteristic courtesy on Kamakau's part in not correcting someone of ʻĪʻī's status, or it could be interpreted as simple arrogance; either way, examples of his use of ʻĪʻī's published topics are obvious.

In 1869, ʻĪʻī gave his first-hand observations of a *kauila nui* ritual[197] (1869, Aug. 14), identifying the persons involved and including the pertinent chant texts. Soon after, ʻĪʻī offered a more general description of the *haku ʻōhiʻa* ritual,[198] with some example lines of appropriate chants (1869, Aug. 28). A few months afterwards, in early 1870, Kamakau presented the same topics in reverse order. His description of the *haku ʻōhiʻa* ritual is far more detailed and offers more lines of chant (1870, Feb. 24). Two weeks later, Kamakau gave his coverage of the *kauila nui* ritual, not as a witness' description of a single event, but with a more detailed, ethnographic style of documentation of the ritual process (1870, Mar. 3). He included the three complete chants found in ʻĪʻī's earlier column, in the same order and similar form, but with variations in wording and number of lines. Similar follow-up by Kamakau indicates that far more interaction exists. For instance, he re-presented coverage by ʻĪʻī about the legendary hero Punaʻaikoaʻe[199] as well as the names and order of the Hawaiian months.[200]

---

[195] ʻĪʻī's first identified comment on Kamakau is on Jan. 30, 1869. Other examples include Mar. 6, 1869; Mar. 27, 1869; Apr. 3, 1869; and Jan. 22, 1870.

[196] Newspapers were regularly bound in annual volumes for readers who wished to save them as permanent reference, a regular service offered by the newspaper printers. Readers could either save their own newspapers and have them bound or purchase available bound copies remaining at the end of the year. This book-like maintenance of the Hawaiian newspapers fostered the repository quality of the newspaper content and allowed for easy cross-reference.

[197] A temple ceremony preceding the *haku ʻōhiʻa*, or image-carving ceremony.

[198] This ritual establishes sanctity for the carving of a temple image.

[199] ʻĪʻī (1869, Sept. 4-11; Kamakau (1870, Jan. 6).

[200] ʻĪʻī (1869, Sept. 25; Kamakau (1870, Feb. 10).

While Kamakau didn't overtly acknowledge ʻĪʻī or his writings, John Papa ʻĪʻī often referred directly to what readers had seen in "Ka Moolelo Hawaii" (Kamakau's column), or to *Ka Nupepa Kuokoa* and "*ka mea nona ia moolelo*" [the author of that account]. Most of his references to Kamakau's articles focus on correcting historical details or giving additional information about persons involved in the historical incidents or the sequence of those events.

Some of ʻĪʻī's corrections of Kamakau are introduced by very specific references, giving the date and paragraph of what Kamakau wrote before addressing the subject at hand:

> Ua ike kakou i na hana a Kaahumanu i hai ia ma ke Kuokoa o ka la 26 o Dek. i hiamoe akula, ma ka moolelo Hawaii, a no ka mea ua hahai ia ma laila ka nui o na pauku mai 1-6. (ʻĪʻī 1869, Apr. 3)

> [We have seen the actions of Kaahumanu recounted in the *Kuokoa* on the 26th of Dec. past, in *Ka Moolelo Hawaii*, because most of paragraphs 1-6 followed that topic.]

Others references by ʻĪʻī are introduced in a much more oblique manner, like this aside calling attention to a story about Kaʻahumanu covered in detail by Kamakau over two years earlier, which was brought up again by ʻĪʻī with: "*ua hai mua ia he moolelo*" [an account has been told previously].[201]

ʻĪʻī sometimes stepped beyond direct textual references in his narrative to include some commentary about Kamakau himself. In an example in 1869, he denounced Kamakau's recent column, moving outside of correcting the other's writings and into a personal critique. "*O ka mea nona ka pulima, a nana hoi ka Moolelo Hawaii, ke olelo nei o ia, he ekalesia Karisiano, ua aoao Roma la, aole ka i like me ka aoao pegana*" [The one signing, and writing Moʻolelo Hawaiʻi is saying that the Roman faith is Christian, and dares to say it is not like the pagan religion] (*Ka Nupepa Kuokoa* 1869, Jan. 2). The criticism was initiated by Kamakau's discussion about Catholicism in his column in January of that year in *Ka Nupepa Kuokoa*.[202] ʻĪʻī's inclusion of his personal opinion was rare, and it initiated no response from Kamakau or the readers.

The extent of Kamakau's re-presentation of ʻĪʻī writings, is not documented. Eight clear references by ʻĪʻī to Kamakau's writings have been identified, but only

---

[201] ʻĪʻī (1870, Jan. 22), referring to articles from Kamakau (1867, Jun. 15, Jul. 20, and Aug. 17).
[202] ʻĪʻī (1870, Jan. 22), in reference to Kamakau (1869, Jan. 2)

three of those were included in the English publication. The translation indicated only once that ʻĪʻī was actually addressing Kamakau's work in his comments.[203]

The interchange between these two important authors, which would have been followed closely by readers of their time, is totally obscured in the resulting English texts. Few of ʻĪʻī's comments are incorporated in the published portion of his work, and the reordering makes those references unnoticeable. Kamakau's expounding upon ʻĪʻī's writings is divided up among four English texts, and although nearly all of the material is eventually included in translation, the interaction is lost through reordering, editing, and separate publication.

Kamakau and ʻĪʻī are the only two Hawaiian writers included in the modern canon whose works were published during their lifetimes. That their writings were available for their contemporaries gives special significance to those works, somewhat of a "peer review" quality that is implicitly granted to the English translations. That significance, by association, adds validating power to the translated manuscripts of Davida Malo and Kepelino when the four are referenced as "the" Hawaiian scholars of the past.[204] Together, the four authors' translated works continue to represent the Hawaiian perspective, considered to be foundational references for all fields of study involving Hawaiian culture and history. This reliance, normalized now for decades, has generated and empowered the discourse of sufficiency, and continues to do so. Even as new inroads are made to access the historical cache of resources, curriculum development and scholarship at every level are still based on these "authoritative" canon texts.

The issues discussed in this chapter highlight that even if the canon did not obscure the other historical resources, reliance on these books would still be untenable. The connections between the Hawaiian and English texts are fractured and reconstructed. In regard to Hawaiian history and culture, there is a need for fresh scholarship and study that engages a broader and more reliable level of primary reference. Such scholarship will better inform modern understanding about perspectives of the past, and better document the continuity of those perspectives into the present. The development of appropriate tools, coupled with the initiative to pursue the task, will normalize the use of primary Hawaiian materials.

---

[203] ʻĪʻī (1959:105) added a note to clarify that the reference is regarding Kamakau, and identified which of Kamakau's columns was addressed.

[204] "A translation participates in the 'afterlife' (U'berleben) of the foreign text, enacting an interpretation that is informed by a history of reception ('the age of its fame'). This interpretation does more than transmit message; it recreated the values that accrued to the foreign text over time" (Venuti 2004a:71). The writings of Malo and Kepelino were never published until long after their deaths, but the English books drawn from their works share in the cumulative "afterlife."

5 | New Horizons

The tools necessary to renew the use of Hawaiian-language resources are coming into being. David Kalākaua, the "Editor King," opened his first editorial in *Ka Manawa* using the metaphors of "gold mine" and "vault" to describe the value of English-language resources that his new newspaper would bring to the Hawaiians of 1870, hoping to expand the narrow views being published at the time.[205] Nearly a hundred-forty years later, the situation today is a mirror image, with English language and thought nearly universal in Hawai'i, and historical Hawaiian writings being the *gold mine*, the *vault* to expand the boundaries for writers and thinkers dealing with Hawai'i, past and present. The depth of that mine and extent of that vault is impressive, being, as it is, the product of a small, newly-literate kingdom, and of a people who persisted through, and documented, overwhelming change. The keys to this "mine," whose entrance has been narrow and forbidding for nearly a century, are taking shape through people and projects today.

New efforts initiated in the last few years will provide improved access to the kind of materials addressed here, and hopefully will lead to a growing re-articulation of the historical Hawaiian writings with all other resources pertaining to Hawai'i. These ambitious projects are working to provide powerful tools for locating and accessing Hawaiian materials. They all deal with the Hawaiian-language newspaper repository, but address the corpus from different approaches, as described below.

---

[205] Kalākaua, *He Manao Akea*, in *Ka Manawa*, Jan. 7, 1870, pg. 1.

The Hawaiian Renaissance of the 1970s and '80s both solidified the discourse of sufficiency and initiated forces that may eventually dismantle it. As part of the renaissance, revitalization of Hawaiian language expanded at the university, extended into high schools, and then coalesced as a movement in the mid-1980s with the establishment of Hawaiian-language immersion schools. Widespread efforts fueled, and were fueled by, a growing population of second-language learners in colleges, high schools, immersion schools, families, and the community.

More than ever before, teachers, curriculum planners, researchers, and students tapped into historical writings, including the Hawaiian newspapers, but early efforts were fragmentary, hampered by the need to manually search through microfilms or fragile originals for articles of interest. Though this obstacle has since been partially ameliorated by more recent projects, extracted writings continue to be incorporated haphazardly into a movement that is focused on fluency and future vitality of the language rather than on bridging the historical corpus to the present.

It is not a criticism to say that revitalization has addressed language fluency more than historical continuity, for the dynamic presence of the language renaissance is what has made the restoration of historical Hawaiian knowledge possible. It is important, however, to acknowledge that the expansive goals of the movement have not yet extended to include the entire field. Fortunately, in twenty-some years of foraging for materials, the range of extracted Hawaiian newspaper content for teaching purposes increasingly illuminated new insights about the newspaper resource. Among the observations that crystallized as the work progressed were the inadequacy of existing translations, the unacknowledged extent of the primary sources, and the critical importance of the content.

For myself and those working on the preparation of Samuel Kamakau's newspaper writings for republication in book form, that decade-long project manifested all of these insights, and sparked a wave of fresh directions in research and development.[206] Published in the author's original sequence, *Ke Kumu Aupuni* (1996) and *Ke Aupuni Mōʻī* (2001)[207] revealed the previously undocumented reconstruction of the familiar English versions, *Ruling Chiefs* and its three sequels.[208] Researching Kamakau's writings in the original newspapers also highlighted the

---

[206] Many participated in this project over a ten-year span, most of whom were faculty and students of UH-Mānoa, including myself, Nakila Steele, Lalepa Koga, Sahoa Fukushima, Kaleimakana Saffrey, Tuti Kanahele, Noenoe Silva, Lōkahi Antonio, and others.

[207] A third volume, tentatively titled *Ke Kahua*, is still in process of editing for publication.

[208] *Ruling Chiefs of Hawaiʻi* (1961), *Ka Poʻe Kahiko: The People of Old* (1964), *The Works of the People of Old: Na Hana a ka Poʻe Kahiko* (1976), and *Tales and Traditions of the People of Old: Na Moʻolelo o ka Poʻe Kahiko* (1991).

many other authors and fields of knowledge that contextualized his work. The process changed our group's understanding about the importance of the remaining content, and the resulting publications changed the way Hawaiian-language writings have been published since. Subsequent research branched in multiple directions, connecting with the work of many others in the field who were digitizing, indexing, or researching parts of the whole. All of those efforts continue to encourage and propel scholarship forward.

One product of the Kamakau-related research was the doctoral dissertation from which this book is drawn. Prior to finalizing the dissertation, findings had already provided the impetus to establish Hoʻolaupaʻi to make the archive of Hawaiian newspapers into searchable text files, and as soon as the dissertation was completed, it prompted yet another endeavor—Awaiaulu: Hawaiian Literature Project. These and other current projects are described below.

Hoʻolaupaʻi

Although earlier attempts led to its eventual fruition, Hoʻolaupaʻi: Hawaiian Newspaper Resources was the first dedicated effort to make the whole archive of Hawaiian-language newspapers widely accessible.[209] *Hoʻolaupaʻi* means "to generate abundance, to reproduce." The project makes searchable text files from the Hawaiian newspapers, and is working to place the entire collection, in digital image and searchable text file, on the internet via a single computer database at www.nupepa.org.[210]

Using a recently-expanded optical character recognition (OCR) technology, and based on a production model used with Māori newspapers,[211] microfilm newspaper images are digitized, and the digital images are then rendered by computer into searchable text files. The technical challenges posed by variable-quality microfilms of aged documents require that human operators, fluent in Hawaiian, manually check and correct the computer's reading errors and fill in the sections that the OCR program cannot address.

Initiated in 2001 by Hawaiian-language proponent Dwayne Nakila Steele as a pilot project under Alu Like, Inc., Hoʻolaupaʻi was moved to the Bishop Museum

---

[209] Hoʻolaupaʻi built directly on the seminal efforts at digitizing Hawaiian-language newspapers that were carried out in 1997–2000 at the University of Hawaiʻi's Hamilton Library.

[210] The Hoʻolaupaʻi website is hosted through www.ulukau.org, Alu Like's electronic library project.

[211] On the New Zealand Digital Library site, http://nzdl.sadl.uleth.ca/cgi-bin/library.

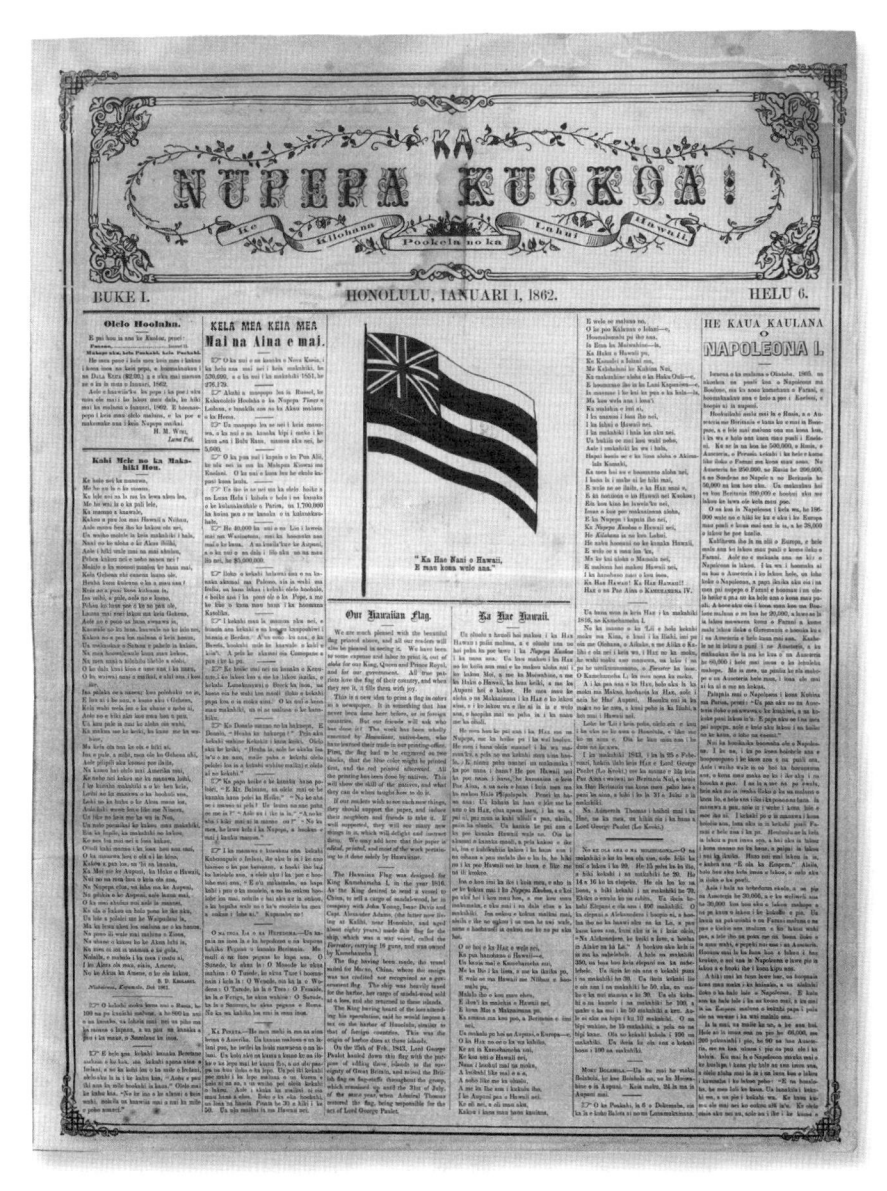

This January 1, 1862, issue of Ka Nupepa Kuokoa *contained the first known color image to be published in a newspaper anywhere. The red and blue inking had to be done separately to each copy after the page was printed. The use of printing space for pictures was debated at the time, and the Kuokoa, in stiff competition with* Ka Hoku o ka Pakipika *made a bold statement with this image, even adding an English explanatory note to expand its readership. Photo by David Franzen, Bishop Museum.*

in 2002 and set up as a formal program of the museum's Library and Archives.[212] Currently run by two full-time staff with contracted operators who can read and correct the OCR-generated text, Hoʻolaupaʻi has rendered nearly 15,000 pages of newspapers—approximately 150,000 searchable typescript pages—during its eight years of operation. The project, launched with the longest-running paper, *Ka Nupepa Kuokoa*, soon began rendering other titles like *Ka Lama*, *Ke Kumu*, and *Ka Hoku o ka Pakipika*, and operators have currently brought 26 newspaper titles into the process.

General awareness about the existence and importance of the Hawaiian newspapers, especially in the Hawaiian community, is critical to the success of the project and to the larger effort of dissembling the overriding existence of the discourse of sufficiency. To inform the public about the availability and importance of the resource, an educational component, Haʻilono, was developed for this project. Along with lectures and presentations, it includes a traveling exhibit, an exhibit catalogue, and a replica of *Ka Nupepa Kuokoa*, January 1, 1862, which had a colorized image, the first of its kind in the world.

The Hoʻolaupaʻi project produces text files in Hawaiian, and although untranslated, does indicate the existence of pertinent texts, their exact locations, and their full content in digital image and rendered typescript form. The ability to mechanically search, by word or phrase, even a portion of the newspaper archive has already greatly increased use of the newspapers as a resource, with three million searches documented to date, originating in Hawaiʻi and around the world.[213] Even those not fluent in Hawaiian can at least locate material, which can then be translated. Methodical, page by page surveys that would have taken years to complete are now possible in minutes, at least in the completed portion, and the eventual impact on Hawaiian scholarship is open-ended. The value of this research tool is worth the estimated ten to twenty years that the rendering may take to complete.[214]

---

[212] Established with a grant from the Dwayne and Marti Steele Fund, the project was given limited federal funding and has received grants from the H. K. Castle Foundation, Kamehameha Publishing, Office of Hawaiian Affairs, State Foundation on Culture and the Arts, and Native Hawaiian Culture and Arts Program.

[213] By late 2009, over two million visits had been made to the site from most U.S. states and over twenty other countries. The majority are initiated in Hawaiʻi, but the impact is already far-reaching.

[214] The actual time frame for completion is dependent on funding and expansion. At the present scale, twenty years is a more reasonable estimate of time, but the work could be done in as little as five years if proposed expansion occurs.

Awaiaulu

Soon after this first analysis was compiled for my dissertation, Nakila Steele established Awaiaulu: Hawaiian Literature Project. This translation initiative was created to open the historical native-language resources for both Hawaiian and English-speaking audiences, fostering Hawaiian language continuity while facilitating dissemination of knowledge in both languages. The goal was to reconnect the archival cache of Hawaiian knowledge to modern audiences by training a cadre of translators who could develop the dormant resources. They could prepare Hawaiian-language texts in a format for contemporary students of the language, and at the same time generate full English translations to serve the broader segment of the population.

The model has been successful. After three years of intensive research, translation, editing of Hawaiian and English manuscripts, design and planning, two books were published in 2007: *Ka Moʻolelo o Hiʻiakaikapoliopele* and *The Epic Tale of Hiʻiakaikapoliopele*.[215] Two new skilled translators and text developers were added to the working circle of resource people in the movement to bridge historical knowledge to the present, and both are currently training others.

Throughout the years of Hawaiian-language revitalization, translation into English has been, and continues to be, a controversial issue. Following the initial translation efforts in the Territorial period that generated the canon texts, few large translations have been generated. While enrollment has grown tenfold or more in Hawaiian-language classes over the last thirty years, Hawaiian translation courses on the books at the University of Hawaiʻi have gone untaught for that whole span.[216] To some, Hawaiian materials are cultural treasures that should be reserved for those who learn the language, functioning as both an attraction and a reward. Others point to the questionable quality of existing published translations and the impossibility of doing justice to the originals in another language. Multiple philosophies exist, but the ambivalence generated by these perspectives has long curbed translation, along with the development of potential translators. Awaiaulu's movement into active translation and training is making every effort to be sensitive to the concerns, and is working to integrate the pressing need for access to this significant repository with the considerations that have been raised.

In 2005, Awaiaulu: Hawaiian Literature Project established a publishing arm, Awaiaulu Press, and is now training a larger group of students, making use of

---

[215] Awaiaulu Press, 2006. Copyrighted in 2006, the books did not reach distribution until 2007.

[216] The exception is one course, HAW 435B, dealing with translation of legal documents, which is taught on a regular basis.

the newly-trained translators' expertise. The project plans to continue expanding the body of available resource people by providing a venue for the experienced translators to mentor upcoming scholars in translation, as well as in the field of text development. The product of this effort is not only expanding access to the historical materials, both in Hawaiian and in English, but is building a generation who can continue to do the work, from inception to completion.[217]

The Hawaiian Language Newspaper Index

Some individuals have pursued "the work" for decades, and some of their personal projects have gained momentum and garnered support in the growing wave of recognition and interest. Noted Hawaiian researcher and genealogist Edith McKinzie is an example, as well as a model of perserverence. Throughout her years of research, she frequently found historical gems in the process of other, unrelated searches, and lamented that such finds would be lost and rediscovered many times before they became documented and known. Mrs. McKinzie's personal experience led her to initiate The Hawaiian Language Newspaper Index.

In 1992, Auntie Edith and a group of supporters set out to manually index and summarize in English all entries in the Hawaiian-language newspapers in chronological sequence.[218] Housed under the Native Hawaiian Culture and Arts Program and funded from multiple sources, The Hawaiian Language Newspaper Index project consists of a variable group of 3 to 10 people who meet once a week under the direction of Mrs. McKinzie. They work with microfilm printouts, preparing data lists or summaries for the project indexer.

In a decade and a half of production, the group has completed detailed indexes or English summaries for ten of the early newspapers, which includes several of the Calvinist mission papers and the first government newspapers, *Ka Elele* and *Ka Hae Hawaii*. Over 2,500 pages of newspaper have been fully indexed or summarized in preparation for indexing, but because many of them are from the smaller papers, this is still less than 2 percent of the whole. In 2003, Mrs. McKinzie estimated that the project would take 20 or more years to complete at the current pace, a time frame which was still considered viable in 2008. Despite funding problems in the last several years, progress is ongoing. Internet

---

[217] This project was initiated through a grant from the Dwayne and Marti Steele Fund, and has also received support from the Kawananakoa Foundation as well as the Kamehameha Publishing. Book sales have also been an important source of ongoing funding.

[218] The project has since moved away from direct chronological sequence and the remaining mission papers will be finished intermittently. Personal communication from E. McKinzie, 2003.

access to the index is provided by Bishop Museum and can be found at www2.bishopmuseum.org/nhcap/hlni/query.asp.

In addition to the large-scale efforts described above, a number of other projects are working to address different portions of the archival repository. Some deal with unpublished, document-based, or audio sections of the archive, while others streamline access to existing published resources. Each effectively builds the level of recognition about historical material while contextualizing and rearticulating these primary sources into modern knowledge. A number of the projects connected to Hawaiian newspaper research are listed in the University of Hawai'i's Hawaiian Language Newspaper website, http://libweb.hawaii.edu/digicoll/newspapers.htm.

OTHER INTERNET RESOURCES

The library at the University of Hawai'i's William S. Richardson School of Law is generating a digital access point for legislative histories, including Privy Council minutes, Executive documents and correspondence, and Legislative Council materials among them, targeting pre-territorial governmental materials that affect law, both then and now. Most of the original material being digitized is housed in the Hawai'i State Archives, and not all is in Hawaiian. Under this project, technicians have also scanned the Land Commission awards and indexes, and plan to do the Patent Awards, Patent Grants, Crown Land materials, Attorneys General opinions, and whatever else is possible under the direction of the State Archives. An eventual goal is to initiate a cooperative effort within the University that involves translation of Hawaiian-language documents by students and faculty to facilitate access. Although this digital collection will eventually become a more public resource, it is currently limited to University faculty and students, and is only available on site.

Audio resources, while perhaps not appearing integral to the historical written sources, link writings of the past to the Hawaiian language of today, fostering use and understanding of the written corpus. The Edwin H. Mo'okini Library at the University of Hawai'i at Hilo has digitized the audio tapes from the first fourteen years of *Ka Leo Hawai'i*, a Hawaiian-language radio program that broadcast live weekly interviews with native speakers of Hawaiian. These first years of the program, from 1972 to 1987, make up part of the largest recorded body of spoken Hawaiian in existence, and document an era when native speakers were far more numerous than today.[219] *Ka Leo Hawai'i* interviews from later years (1989–2001) of the program are also being digitized, as are some of the smaller audio collections at the Bishop Museum and Brigham Young University, Lā'ie campus.[220] These efforts, though not unified, embody the growing interest in access to the knowledge contained in Hawaiian-language sources, and also provide an important linguistic and cognitive bridge between today and the era when Hawaiian newspapers were commonplace.

As an aspect of language revitalization, active publishing by such diverse groups as 'Ahahui 'Ōlelo Hawai'i, Bishop Museum Press, the Hawaiian Historical Society, the Native Hawaiian Culture and Arts Program, Kamehameha Publishing, and UH-Hilo's Hale Kuamo'o has produced at least twenty general-interest or reference books in Hawaiian during the last decade and a half.[221] Some are simple reprint copies of old texts intended to make rare editions more familiar and available.[222] More labor-intensive republication of Hawaiian language texts in modern orthography has generated a number of books,[223] while a few newly-translated texts have been published bilingually, addressing the growing audiences in both English and the original Hawaiian language.[224] These and similar efforts now in production are parts of a dynamic increase in resource development in recent years.

Even those projects that terminated before completion have had a progressive impact. *Ka Ho'oilina: The Legacy,* was an ambitious academic journal established by Alu Like, Inc., and funded by the Administration for Native Amer-

---

[219] After a two-year hiatus, *Ka Leo Hawai'i* was reinstated as a weekly program in 1989 and continued through 2001, operating with different hosts and a diminished pool of native speakers from which to draw interviews. These last years of the program, taped for documentation, are also being digitized for academic, cultural, and historical purposes by the Language and Telecommunications Center of the University of Hawai'i, Mānoa. Access to the digital audio files of both portions of the *Ka Leo Hawai'i* tape collection is currently limited to UH students and faculty.

[220] *Ka Leo Hawai'i* tapes from 1989–2001 are accessible to University of Hawai'i students and faculty; Bishop Museum audio tapes are catalogued at http://bishopmuseumarc.lib.hawaii.edu; and the Joseph Smith Library at BYUH hosts the audio tapes and transcripts of the Clinton Kanahele Collection, accessible through http://library.byuh.edu/library/archives.

[221] This number does not include the hundreds of books, pamphlets, and translated selections that have been generated as curriculum and support materials for the Hawaiian immersion classrooms.

[222] Current projects at the Hawaiian Historical Society (Ke Kupu Hou) and the Bishop Museum (Classical Reprints in Hawaiian Language) have completed eight reprints to date, three through the Hawaiian Historical Society and five through the Bishop Museum.

[223] Examples would include histories by Kamakau (1996, 2001) and biographies by Sheldon (1996), and Desha (1996).

[224] Including the historical narrative *Kekūhaupi'o* (Desha/Frazier 2000), the legend of *Keaomelemele* (Manu/Pukui 2001), the science text, *Anatomia, 1838* (Judd/Mookini 2002), the fishing descriptions of *Ka Oihana Lawai'a* (2006), and the epic legend, *Ka Mo'olelo o Hi'iakaikapoliopele* (2006).

icans and the Kamehameha Schools. Beginning in March 2002, its aim was to reprint Hawaiian materials for community, educational, and scholarly access. Planned as a quarterly publication, and recast as semi-annual the same year, it became an annual journal by 2003, ending publication after the 2005 edition. All issues of *Ka Hoʻoilina* are included in Alu Like's website for Ulukau: The Hawaiian Electronic Library at www.ulukau.org.

Each journal issue drew material from six "legacy" sources, including Hawaiian Ethnographic Notes (H.E.N.) files of the Bishop Museum Archives, government documents, Hawaiian newspapers, humanities pieces, and student materials. Excerpts were presented in columns of original orthography, modern orthography, and English translation, with bilingual annotation of the text as a fourth column on each dual-page. The multiple forms of presentation limited the content of each issue to about forty pages of original Hawaiian text. Though short-lived, *Ka Hoʻolina* did, at least in the academic community, expand a degree of familiarity with the presence of the multi-faceted Hawaiian-language corpus.

The archival holdings in repositories throughout the islands and the staffs of those archives and libraries are the collective foundation and the pillar of support for each of the endeavors described above. While the projects listed here are the initial outcomes of the growing impetus for restoration of Hawaiian-language knowledge, it is the consistent and ongoing support and encouragement of librarians, archivists, collection managers, and administrators that has fueled the awareness and stimulated the progress in each of these efforts. The personal and institutional assistance that is granted on a daily basis, as well as the visionary planning for perceived future needs of researchers, scholars, and practitioners alike is what consistently spurs on the progress.

Contemporary Scholarship

Few people are able to read an old Hawaiian-language newspaper, and those who can rarely do, but the situation is slowly changing. The simple mechanics of access, even for fluent readers, is still daunting. Beyond the 15 percent of the corpus that is searchable, readers must deal with cranky microfilm readers, poor internet images, or crumbling archival originals. For those who delve, the language in those originals is also a barrier, with cultural references and historical contexts that are obscure today, especially for second-language learners. Most people have had to rely on the fortuitous findings of those few readers already working with the materials, or seek out readers and translators to facilitate guided research, but fortunately, in just the last few years, that pool of active or available readers is expanding.

The recent establishment of graduate study programs in Hawaiian Language and Hawaiian Studies at the University of Hawaiʻi Hilo and Mānoa campuses has already had a dynamic impact, and may well be the most powerful "tool" today for use in bridging today's population to Hawaiian knowledge of the past. These academic programs will undoubtedly integrate and multiply existing resources as they flourish, for they combine the impassioned impetus of language revitalization with the broad network of graduate-level scholarship in the language. New resources and an ever-expanding pool of educated readers promises to completely change the field.

A Master of Arts degree in Hawaiian Studies was begun at the University of Hawaiʻi at Hilo in 2000, and was followed by separate M.A. programs for Hawaiian Language and Hawaiian Studies at the flagship Mānoa campus in 2005. A Ph.D. program with a dual focus on Hawaiian and indigenous language revitalization has since been initiated at Ka Haka ʻUla O Keʻelikōlani, the College of Hawaiian Language at UH-Hilo, and will likely be followed by a doctoral program under Hawaiʻinuiākea, the School of Hawaiian Knowledge at Mānoa. The Mānoa Ph.D. now being considered may emerge as separate doctoral degrees in Hawaiian Language and Hawaiian Studies, or be established as a joint effort under the academic umbrella of Hawaiʻinuiākea.

Regardless of how these graduate degree programs are situated academically and administratively, the positive result is already tangible and will continue to develop. Primary Hawaiian sources are now being incorporated into classroom curricula and thesis projects on each of the campuses at an unprecedented pace and level. Almost every graduate course in both Hawaiian language and Hawaiian studies makes use of the new tools for access, and whole new courses have been developed around primary-resource content. The resulting familiarity among both students and faculty is rapidly increasing, and the outcomes are already promising. Only a handful of graduates have completed the programs to date, but their thesis topics have each illuminated new portals into the "vault" of historical knowledge.[225] As a recognizable body of such research and writing becomes established, it will build a new framework for reference and set new standards for a broad range of fields dealing with Hawaiian-related topics.

Multiple lines thread through the fabrics of knowledge in Hawaiʻi today, but it is the written, and especially published, resources that are most accessible to graduate student, researcher, and practitioner alike, and therefore most highly

---

[225] For a listing of theses and dissertations written in Hawaiian or dealing with Hawaiian language, see the updated listing at UH Hamilton Library's website, http://www2.hawaii.edu/~speccoll/hawaiihlangt.html.

regarded and legitimized within the changing arenas of power over knowledge. While more culturally or socially-bounded forms of knowledge may frame personal identity and historical understanding, that identity and understanding is framed in a synthesis with, or in antagonism to, the powerful written discourse of the past, as well as the the written, visual, and electronic production of the present, for it is all of these external forms that are affirmed, legitimized, fostered, and replicated by contemporary discourse.

The impetus to expand the articulation of Hawaiian writings into contemporary awareness does not arise from the assumption that some great truth has been neglected or obscured, and will be restored to its proper place upon reclamation of the documents containing it. The texts themselves are only raw materials, which must be recognized, studied, analyzed, and critiqued to generate understandings of the representation therein and of the potential links between past, present, and future. Philosopher Michel Foucault writes:

> The document is not the fortunate tool of a history that is primarily and fundamentally *memory*; history is one way in which a society recognizes and develops a mass of documentation with which it is inextricably linked. (1972:7)

Historical texts illuminate the past, which affects the present and helps to shape the future, but only to the extent that those texts are incorporated in the processes of knowledge production. Calling attention to the existence of documents neither makes history nor analyzes it, for history entails the recognition and processing of those documents, their incorporation into our understanding, and their articulation with the other ways in which we create knowledge of the past today. Archives and document repositories reflect a level of recognition about historical materials and their importance to us, but do not alone facilitate history, cultural memory, perpetuation, or practice. Rather, it is the forces in place for selecting what is deemed valuable that guide how we weave the fabric of links that we recognize as history in the present. The discourse of sufficiency describes a setting where the documents have been left in their storage boxes and microfilm reels; the cargo which Dening would have successive generations re-inventory has been left in crates on the beach.

The cargo will not be easy to unpack, for there are still institutional barriers. With English as the foundation language for every major historical repository, archivists and librarians have been trained and hired for their skills in handling the largely English-language collections. Facility in Hawaiian has not been required, and only recently has familiarity with the language become a desirable qualification. Local librarians and archivists have learned Hawaiian to facilitate their work through personal motivation rather than institutional intention, and the number of fluent staff remains tiny. Collection specialists are most often who generate the research tools for access to the collections, but limited demand, lack of staff with language skills, funding priorities, and insufficient institutional incentive have generated minimal tools of access. Amy Stillman notes that such a setting is widespread:

> Nor can the Hawaiian case make any particular claim to uniqueness. All over the world, the establishment of museums, libraries, historical societies, and archives marks the institutionalization of knowledge in the form of materials on deposit. While postcolonial critiques are exposing museum practices of collection, preservation, and exhibition as instruments of colonial subjugation by their influence over subsequent construction of knowledge, a comparable critique of library and archival collections and their practices of access is only beginning to reveal equally disturbing insights. The terrain promises to be contentious. (2001:201)

Many practices of the last century may be critiqued for the levels of access they provided, and scholars from many fields have engaged in that process, but the focus of this study is more to recognize critical resources that have become distant over time, and to continue changing the way in which those resources are incorporated into modern discourse. I like Greg Dening's view: "A moralism that stresses that the only thing we can change is the present is less self-indulgent than one that lambastes the past for not having changed itself" (1991:377). The presence of archival repositories of Hawaiian materials shows that value was placed on the maintenance of those resources, if not on their cultivation and dissemination. It provides the chance to change the present.

Contemporary scholarship, within the academy and beyond it, calls for encouragements, cautions, and paradigm shifts. It would be easy to simply critique current work in the field that relies on English sources and laud all new and tentative scholarship that is utilizing historical Hawaiian writings, but the setting is more complex than such simplicity allows. With the cumulative drive assembled through three decades of language and culture revitalization, at least some scholars in every field related to Hawaiʻi are striving to locate and incorporate newly-translated resources, searching out the existing translations and summaries available in archival sources, and seeking the insights of practitioners or knowledgeable elders. Some are even engaging research assistants with the necessary language skills to gain access to untranslated materials or native speakers of the language. These moves will provide both new validations and unforeseen contradictions to the existing bodies of Hawaiian knowledge, expanding the field. Such expansion must be encouraged in all areas, and should become a new standard for evaluation at every level.

Those with Hawaiian language skills and drive are mobilizing to use the historical writings directly, particularly the Hawaiian newspapers. This challenging direction in research is critical, and deserves every possible support. A certain level of caution will be necessary, however, until broad familiarity with the historical corpus is more of a reality. With such a large body of still-uncharted material in which to search, any able researcher can find a wealth of references from multiple periods on a particular topic or perspective. Such discovery is invaluable and will work to reconnect historical knowledge, but with access still limited there is always the possibility that an equivalent amount of complimentary or contradictory references could easily be overlooked in the effort. It could be years before such an oversight or bias would be clarified, considering the extent of the material and the dearth of engaged readers. Until the overall body of historical writings is a more familiar and accessible territory to a general audience, such accidental or intentional misdirection remains a possibility. This gives additional import to the goal of refamiliarization, but attention, care, and integrity will have to guide the interim.

Perhaps the most crippling problem for modern scholarship will be the *discourse of sufficiency*, the mindset itself, assuring, as it does for both scholar and casual reader, that the small amount in hand is enough, and that it is the undisputed foundation of Hawaiian culture and history. This mindset has become a well-established modern myth, as powerful and insidious as what Elizabeth Buck describes: "The ideological work of any dominant myth is to make itself look neutral and innocent and, in the process, to naturalize human relationships of power and domination" (1993:4). In a way that appears neutral, innocent, and natural, the existence of Hawaiian writings has been and continues to be omitted from nearly all reference texts, bibliographies, histories, cultural analyses, and common awareness.[226] The real challenge to current and future scholarship is to step beyond the myth and re-establish a connection with the entire resource.

A new and general familiarity with this long-neglected legacy of historical knowledge is an exciting ideal, and while it is bracing to see the emergence of tangible change, it is daunting to recognize the actual extent of change necessary.

---

[226] The newspaper reference texts of Moʻokini (1974), Johnson (1975, 1976), and Chapin (1984, 1996, 2000) are pioneering exceptions, but the two most recent bibliographies of Hawaiian historical materials, David Forbes' *Hawaiian National Bibliography* (1999–2000) and Richard Lightner's *Hawaiian History: An Annotated Bibliography* (2004), both dismiss the newspaper resources.

Those already engaged in the process are compelled by the importance and the potential for reintegrating a century of dormant information, but the passion of a relative few cannot fuel the obligatory paridigm shift. The imperative to restore connections with the existing, and neglected, part of Hawaiian history must be embraced as a shared ideal, something the entire population seeks to achieve. Nearly two centuries ago, Hawaiʻi embraced a new concept, literacy, as a national endeavor, and within a generation had made it a reality. It will take the same level of engagement and encouragement, in government, business, education, and in public and private spheres, to bring about the restoration of historical literacy and the rejection of sufficiency. Hawaiʻi has achieved it before, and can do it again.

Appendix

S. M. Kamakau Related Articles

☐   Aritcles authored by S. M. Kamakau.

☐   Articles not authored by Kamakau, but generated by or pertaining to his writings.

Newspaper Sources

HH — Hoiliili Havaii

HG — Hawaiian Gazette

HP — Hawaii Ponoi

HL — Hoku Loa

KAO — Ke Au Okoa

KE — Ka Elele

KHH — Ka Hae Hawaii

KKH — Ke Kumu Hawaii

KN — Ka Nonanona

KNH — Ka Nuhou Hawaii

KNK — Ka Nupepa Kuokoa

NKAO — Ka Nupepa Kuokoa me Ke Au Okoa i Huipuia

OKHA/OTHK — O Ta Hae Kiritiano

PCA — Pacific Commercial Advertiser

TI — The Islander

TP — The Polynesian

| 173 |

DATE	NEWS-PAPER	TITLE OF ARTICLE	NOTED BY	ENGLISH ACCESS	OTHER NOTES
2-28-1838	KKH [pp. 78–80]	Halawai No Na Kumuao			This is perhaps Kamakau's first published article. Calls for annual teacher meetings. Kamakau from Waialua, Oahu is listed in KKH 2-15-1837 as student of Lahainaluna.
6-20-1838	KKH [pp. 5–7]	No ka hele ana i ka makaikai mai Lahainaluna aku			Talks of school trip.
11-21-1838	KKH [pp. 49–50]	Ka Pinao Kuhihewa			A story about a confused dragonfly, used as a lesson about how man needs God's guidance.
10-25-1842	KN [pp. 49–52]	Ke kuauhau no na Kupuna kahiko loa mai o Hawaii nei, a hiki mai ia Wakea. Mai ia Wakea mai a hiki mai i keia manawa	Chun		Genealogy "for the people of now and of the future, so that they will know." See Kamakau's later article in KN 11-8-1842 on misprints in this article.
11-8-1842	KN [pp. 63–64]	No ke kuauhau		typescript and translation in KA, 24–25	A. Unauna critique of Kamakau's genealogy in KN 11-8-1842, "Mai hana i ke kuauhau me ka lohe ole."
11-8-1842	KN [p. 64]	Untitled; "Lahaina, Okatoba 31, 1842…"	Chun	typescript and translation in KA, 27	On error in his genealogy in KN 11-8-1842.
2-14-1843	KN [pp. 91–93]	Untitled; "Lahainaluna, Dek. 2, 1842…"	Chun		Response to Unauna's article in KN 11-8-1842; critique of Unauna and his teacher, Auwae.
3-23-1843	KN [pp. 105–106]	No ka hoku welowelo	Chun	typescript and translation in Johnson 28–29	On astronomy.
2-6-1844	KN [p. 95]	Untitled; "Aloha oe ka Nonanona, he wahi ukana kau…"			Leleiohoku on taxes, responded to later by Kamakau in KN 4-2-1844.

Appendix

3-5-1844	KN [p. 109]	Untitled; "Feb. 20, 1844. Aloha oe e Nonanona…"	Chun		Asking for clarification on meanings of words.
4-2-1844	KN [pp. 224–225]	Ke kuhihewa o Leleiohoku	Chun		Critique of Leleiohoku's article in KN 2-6-1844. Calls for clarification on taxes of children.
5-14-1844	KN [pp. 14–16]	Untitled; "Maraki 20, 1844. Auhea oe e Nonanona me ke ahonui a me ka lokomaikai…"	Chun		On children made to work as punishment for breaking law.
8-12-1845	KE [pp. 1–2]	Untitled; "Lahinaluna, Iulai 22, 1845. Aloha maikai Kamehameha III…"			Letter to Kamehameha III concerning haole in government.
8-12-1845	KE [p. 2]	Untitled; "Lahainaluna, Iulai 22, 1845. Aloha maika ka moi…."			Letter to Kamehameha III concerning the country people.
8-12-1845	KE [pp. 2–3]	Untitled; "E S.M. Kamakau…"			Kamehameha III response to Kamakau pertaining to haole in government.
9-23-1845	KE [pp. 3–4]	Untitled			Hoinainau response to Kamakau's letter to Kamehameha III in KE 8-12-1845.
10-7-1845	KE [p. 3]	Untitled			Haumana Hoikehonua response to Kamakau's letter to Kamehameha III in KE 8-12-1845.
9-23-1845	KE [p. 3]	No ka waiwai a me nupepa			On printing of government policy in English, and resulting lack of understanding by the common people.
10-21-1845	KE [p. 2]	No ke aloha			Regarding proper etiquette when greeting royalty.
11-4-1845	KE [p. 1]	He mau olelo kahiko i ka manawa i holo mai ai o Lono (Kapena Kuke)	Chun		On arrival of Capt. Cook. Later incorporated into Kamakau's written history.

2-10-1846	KE [pp. 5–6]	He mau mea kahiko loa no Hawaii nei	Chun	Typescript and translation, "Some very ancient things of Hawaii," in BMA–HEN: Thrum 279.	On formation of Islands, division of lands, first humans, and arrival of Cook.
2-4-1847	KE [p. 1]	He mele no ke akua, no Iehova	Chun		Religious mele.
10-24-1848	KE [p. 37]	Untitled; "Kipahulu, Papalahoomau, 25 Sepatemaba, 1848…"			Signed "L. M. Kamakau," but presumably by S. M. Kamakau. On government policy, like taxation on cats and dogs.
3-12-1849	KE [p. 61]	Untitled; "Honolulu, Feberuari, 1849…"			On taxing of cats.
6-1854		Report on the Committee on the Olona		Translated from Hawaiian, available in BML.	Report on olona, appearing in Transactions of the Royal Hawaiian Agricultural Society at its Fourth Annual Meeting in June 1854, pp. 142–144. Authored by S. M. Kamakau, J. Kekaulahao, and J. W. E. Maikai.
5-17-1855	KE [pp. 11–12]	He moolelo no ka Moi Kamehameha III			History of Kamehameha III.
9-15-1855	KE [p. 2]	No ka make ana a me ka moolelo o A. Paki			On death and story of Abner Paki.
9-15-1855	KE [pp. 3–4]	He kanikau no A. Paki			Dirge for Abner Paki.
2-21-1855	KE	Mookuauhau no Kamehameha III			Genealogy of Kamehameha III. Continuation could not be located.
5-10-1856	TP [p. 2]	Address to the Polynesian		Original in English.	Calling for removal of the Editor of the *Polynesian*.
6-10-1857	KHH [p. 3]	Untitled; "Waihee, Maui, Mei 26, 1857…"			On fencing of lands at Waihee and Waiehu, Maui.
1860	HH	He mele no ke aloha	Chun		Mele for unnamed Kauai soldier.

APPENDIX

1860	HH	He mele koihonua	Chun		Genealogy chant.
1860	HH	He mele koihonua	Chun		Genealogy chant.
1860	HH	He vahi mele	Chun		Mele for "kai"; word play; kinds of seas as well as particular places.
1860	HH	Untitled	Chun		On Catholic Church finances.
3-21-1860	KHH [p. 4]	He mele i Kilauea			Mele by Kaleipaoa, aikane of Lohiau, submitted by Kamakau. (Printed previously in *Nu Hou* 1854.)
3-28-1860	KHH [p. 3]	Ka lua o Kaleiopaoa mau mele	Chun		Second mele by Kaleipaoa. (Printed previously in *Nu Hou* 6-24-1854.) Copy in BMA HI.M.45, p.80: "He Mele na Kaleiopaoa Kilauea." See note with 5-4-1865.
4-11-1860	KHH [p. 4]	He mele	Chun		Mele for chiefs and their kaai. First of three. BMA HI.M.45, p. 49: "He Mele Kumuhonua." See note with 5-4-1865.
4-18-1860	KHH [p. 4]	He mele			Second mele of three starting on 4-11-1860. BMA HI.M.45, p. 50: "He Mele Kumuhonua." See note with 5-4-1865.
5-2-1860	KHH [p. 4]	He mele			Third mele of three starting on 4-11-1860. BMA HI.M.45, p. 54: "He Mele." See note with 5-4-1865.
6-1860	OTHK [pp. 41–44]	Aloha oe me ka maikai	Chun	Partial typescript and translation: "Greetings to You with Blessings," in Chun 1988, pp. 29–31.	Halavai 11. First of two parts of support for Catholic Church.
6-1860	OTHK [pp. 45–46]	Aloha oe me ka maikai			Halavai 12. Second of two parts beginning with Halavai 11.
6-1860	OTHK [p. 47]	He mele no ke aloha			Seems to be same as HH 1860.
6-1860	OTHK [pp. 47–48]	He mele koihonua			Seems to be generally same as HH 1860, but incomplete.

10-1860	HL [p. 14]	O ke kapekepeke iwaena o na manao elua			P. Kanemahuka says that Kamakau became Catholic just to irritate Alexander and the other hoa hanau.
2-1862	OKHK [p. 1]	He mele no ka Hae-Kiritiano			Mele honoring the newspaper.
5-1862	OKHK [p. 2]	Untitled; "E ka hae Kiritano, e aloha oe…"			Urging people to turn to Catholicism.
7-1862	OKHK [p. 4]	No ke aloha ia kakou e na lahuihavaii			Proselytizing.
1-21-1864	PCA [p. 2]	Andrews' Hawaiian Dictionary		Announcement of forthcoming Andrews dictionary, printed by PCA in 1865. For indepth discussion on development of the Hawaiian dictionary, see Marguerite K. Ashford in *Bishop Museum Occasional Papers* 27, Feb 1987, pp. 1–24.	"Judge Andrews has carefully revised the work [the dictionary] with aid of S. M. Kamakau, who is probably the best Hawaiian scholar living, and with his help has added over one thousand words." In Preface, "Vocabulary of S. M. Kamakau" acknowledged as a source. Unpublished Hawaiian dictionary is located in BMA, Case 5 La31 is thought to be Kamakau's vocabulary book, although listed as a work of Andrews.
6-25-1864	KNK [p. 1]	He ku auhau no na 'lii kahiko			S. W. B. Kaulainamoku gives genealogy from Haloa and Hinamanouluae.
7-30-1864	KNK [p. 4]	Moolelo kuauhau o ka hanauna o na 'lii mai ka po mai			P. S. Pakele critiques Kaulainamoku of KNK 6-25-1864. He does his own genealogy.
4-20-1865	KNK [p. 3]	Ka moolelo o Kamehameha I			S. N. Haleole announces that he and two other people will put out a history of Kamehameha I. (Note that Kamakau starts his Moolelo o Kamehameha I on 10-22-1866.)

5-4-1865	KNK [p. 2]	Ka hoonohonoho ana i ka mookuauhau o Kamehameha, Helu 1	Chun		S. N. Haleole seeks clarity between Kamakau and Unauna. The follow up article could not be found. See other articles by Haleole in KNK of 4-10-1865, 6-1-1865, and 6-15-1865 (latter two translated in BMA). Kamehameha's genealogy, said to be from the genealogy book of Kamakau, which apparently did not survive the fire at his house in 1865; HI.M.45 at BMA according to Thrum is not Kamakau's genealogy book, but just mele copied from the newspapers.
5-22-1865	KAO [p. 4]	Ka mookuauhau, a he papa hoomanao hoi			Historical dates compiled by Rev. A. Forbes, published in the Andrews Dictionary. Supplemented with more dates by Wm. H. Pease. Continued on 5-29.
5-29-1865	KAO [p. 4]	Ka mookuauhau, a he papa hoomanao hoi			Second part of historical dates compiled by Forbes. First part on 5-22.
5-29-1865	KAO [p. 3]	Hookae i ke kuauhau alii			Kauinui of Hamakualoa, Maui, critiques genealogy in Haleole of KNK 5-4-1865
6-1-1865	KNK [p. 3]	Na manao o S. N. Haleole			Haleole responds to Kauinui of KAO 5-29-1865. Part one of series of articles.
6-12-1865	KAO [p. 4]	Hookae i ke kuauhau alii			Mateo Makauole reponse to Kauinui of KAO 5-29-1865. Admonishment, advising Kauinui to write what he does know of genealogy instead of faulting others.
6-15-1865	KNK [p. 3]	Na manao o S. N. Haleole			Continuation of Haleole of KNK 6-1-1865. Also says that in the following week, he will start a history starting with Oahu, and then on to Molokai and the other islands. There seems to be no followup.

6-15-1865	KNK [p. 1]	No ke kaapuni makaikai i na wahi kaulana a me na kupua, a me na ʻlii kahiko mai Hawaii a Niihau; Helu 1	Chun, Thrum	*Na moolelo a ka poe kahiko*, pp. 2–5 (The Story of Paao). Nearly complete translation of chapters 1-15, "Ancient Hawaiian History," which ran from 6-13-1865 to 10-7-1865 in KNK, is in BMA–HEN: Thrum 246.	This 16-part series runs from 6-15 to 10-7-1865. 100 page manuscript of the Hawaiian text of chapters 1-15, "No ke kaapuni maikai i na wahi kaulana, a me na ʻlii kahiko mai Hawaii a Niihau" (A successful journey to famous places and chiefs from Hawaii to Niihau), dated 8-5-1964, and funded by the UH Committee for the Preservation and Study of Hawaiian Language, Art and Culture, is located in BMA–Case 4, K47; it has never been published.
6-22-1865	KNK [p. 1]	Ka moolelo o Hawaii nei; Helu 2 (No ke kaapuni makaikai i na wahi kaulana a me na kupua, a me na ʻlii kahiko mai Hawaii a Niihau	Chun, Thrum	*Na moolelo a ka poe kahiko*, pp. 6–9 (Oahu; story of Kuhooneenuu; concerning Kahuoi). Nearly complete translation of chapters 1-15, "Ancient Hawaiian History," which ran from 6-13-1865 to 10-7-1865 in KNK, is in BMA–HEN: Thrum 246.	See notes with 6-15-1865 entry.
6-26-1865	KAO [p. 4]	Untitled; "Honolulu, Mei 8, 1865."			Comments on and inserts corrections into chronology of events collected by Rev. A. Forbes, and published in KAO of 5-22 and 5-29-1865.
6-29-1865	KNK [p. 1]	Ka moolelo o Hawaii nei; Helu 3	Chun, Thrum	*Na moolelo a ka poe kahiko*, pp. 9–13 (concerning Kahuoi; concerning Kahaoi; of Kamehaikana becoming a goddess).	See notes with 6-15-1865 entry.
7-6-1865	KNK [pp. 1–2]	Ka moolelo o Hawaii nei; Helu 4	Chun, Thrum	*Na moolelo a ka poe kahiko*, pp. 14–18 (obtaining of kapa; Kalana; famous places of Nuuanu; Pu o Poiake).	See notes with 6-15-1865 entry.
7-6-1865	KNK [p. 4]	He papa kuhikuhi			Z. Poli's chronology of events, running until 9-16-1865.

7-13-1865	KNK [p. 1]	Ka moolelo o Hawaii nei; Helu 5	Chun, Thrum	*Na moolelo a ka poe kahiko*, pp. 18–22 (Pu o Poiake; story of Kihapu; Puapualenalena).	See notes with 6-15-1865 entry.
7-13-1865	KNK [p. 4]	Ke akamai o kekahi poe kanaka i ke aohoku			Dealing with astronomy and navigation.
7-22-1865	KNK [p. 1]	Ka moolelo o Hawaii nei; Helu 6	Chun, Thrum	*Na moolelo a ka poe kahiko*, pp. 23–30 (story of Kapoi; Huanuikalalailai; Puowaina; story of Kaupe; Kawaaokekupu; concerning Luanuu).	See notes with 6-15-1865 entry.
7-22-1865	KNK [p. 2]	He Haiao			Rev. Mr. Holo commenting on religion.
7-29-1865	KNK [p. 1]	Ka moolelo o Hawaii nei; Helu 7	Chun, Thrum	*Na moolelo a ka poe kahiko*, pp. 30–35 (Waolani; story of creation).	See notes with 6-15-1865 entry.
7-29-1865	KNK [p. 3]	Ka la hoihoi ea	Chun	Typescript and translation, "Restoration Day" in BMA–HEN: Thrum 249.	Telling of taking of islands by Paulet, commander of the Carysfort, in February 1843 and the eventual return of the islands on July 31, 1843.
7-31-1865	KAO [p. 3]	He ninau			W. P. K. disagreement with Holo of KNK 7-22-1865.
8-5-1865	KNK [p. 1]	Ka moolelo o Hawaii nei; Helu 8	Chun, Thrum	*Na moolelo a ka poe kahiko*, pp. 35–40 (divisions of the ancient chiefs; Kukaniloko; Iao; ranks of chiefs).	See notes with 6-15-1865 entry.
8-5-1865	KNK [p. 4]	No ke ao hoku	Chun		First of series that continues on 8-12-1865. Deals with traditional navigation.
8-5-1865	KNK [p. 4]	No ke kula holomoku a me ka wehewehe i ke ano	Chun		On modern navigation schools.

8-12-1865	KNK [pp. 1–2]	Ka moolelo o Hawaii nei; Helu 9	Chun, Thrum	*Na hana a ka poe kahiko*, pp. 129–132 (heiau; heiau of human sacrifice; heiau of the people). *Na moolelo a ka poe kahiko*, pp. 40–42 (the populace).	See notes with 6-15-1865 entry.
8-12-1865	KNK [p. 4]	No ke ao hoku	Chun		Second part of series that began on 8-5-1865. Indicates that it is to be continued, but no continuation found. On traditional navigation.
8-19-1865	KNK [pp. 1–2]	Ka moolelo o Hawaii nei; Helu 10	Chun, Thrum	*Na moolelo a ka poe kahiko*, pp. 42–48 (chiefly signs; Waikiki; Kalamakua; Keleanuinohoanaapiapi).	See notes with 6-15-1865 entry.
8-19-1865	KNK [p. 3]	Untitled; "Honolulu, Oahu, Augate 2, 1865..."			Response to W. P. K. of KAO [7-31-1865]. Preceded by commentary by editor. On religion.
8-26-1865	KNK [pp. 1–2]	Ka moolelo o Hawaii nei; Helu 11	Chun, Thrum	*Na moolelo a ka poe kahiko*, pp. 48–54 (Keleanuinohoanaapiapi; Laielohelohe; Lo Kaholialale; Mailikukahi).	See notes with 6-15-1865 entry.
9-2-1865	KNK [pp. 1–2]	Ka moolelo o Hawaii nei; Helu 12	Chun, Thrum	*Na moolelo a ka poe kahiko*, pp. 54–61 (Mailikukahi; Kalanimanuia).	See notes with 6-15-1865 entry.
9-4-1865	KAO [p. 3]	He hana naauao me ke akamai, ka ninau me ka hooponopono iho i na wahi hemahema			Reply to Z. Poli's chronology of events of KNK 7-6 to 9-16-1865.
9-9-1865	KNK [p. 1]	Ka moolelo o Hawaii nei; Helu 13	Chun, Thrum	*Na moolelo a ka poe kahiko*, pp. 61–67 (Kaihikapuamanuia).	See notes with 6-15-1865 entry.
9-9-1865	KNK [p. 1]	Ahahui imi i na mea kahiko o Hawaii nei	Chun	Typescript and holograph translation, "Hawaiian Historical Society" in BMA–HEN: Thrum 35a.	Discussion of the first Hawaiian Historical Society formed in 1841.

9-11-1865	KAO [p. 4]	Untitled; "Waialua, Oahu, Augate 28, 1865…"			Response to Kaulainamoku's genealogy of KNK 6-25-1864.
9-11-1865	KAO [p. 2]	Untitled; "E Ke Au Okoa; Aloha oe…"			WPK response to Kamakau's critique of Z. Poli in KAO 9-4-1865.
9-16-1865	KNK [p. 3]	Makuahine keiki nui	Chun		
9-16-1865	KNK [p. 3]	Untitled; "Pihanakalani Home, Augate 23, A.D. 1865…"		Typescript and translation in BMA–HEN: Thrum 254 and 258.	J. Palapalapoi questions S. H. P. Kalawaiaopuna on various historical points.
9-23-1865	KNK [p. 1]	Ka moolelo o Hawaii nei; Helu 13 [14]	Chun, Thrum	Na moolelo a ka poe kahiko, pp. 67–72 (Kaihikapuamanuia; Kakuhihewa; Maui genealogies).	See notes with 6-15-1865 entry.
9-23-1865	KNK [p. 3]	No ka pepehi ana o ke alii i ke keiki a ke kahuna	Chun	Typescript and translation, "On the killing of a priest's child by the king," in BMA–HEN: Thrum 255.	
9-25-1865	KAO [p. 2]	Untitled; "Apana o Waialae, Oahu, Sept. 15, 1865…"			Z. Poli's two-part response (continuing on 10-2) to Kamakau's critique in KAO 9-4-1865.
9-25-1865	KAO [p. 1]	Olelo pane ia S. M. Kamakau			S. W. B. Kaulainamoku's response to Kamakau critique of KAO 9-11-1865.
9-30-1865	KNK [p. 1]	Ka moolelo o Hawaii nei; Helu 14 [15]	Chun, Thrum	Na moolelo a ka poe kahiko, pp. 72–79 (Maui genealogies; Nanaulu genealogy).	See notes with 6-15-1865 entry.
10-7-1865	KNK [p. 1]	Ka moolelo o Hawaii nei; Helu 15 [16]	Chun, Thrum	Na moolelo a ka poe kahiko, pp. 79–81 (Nanaulu genealogy).	See notes with 6-15-1865 entry.
10-7-1865	KNK [p. 1]	Na mea kaulana o ka wa kahiko i hala aku	Chun		

10-7-1865	KNK [p. 1]	Mea hanohano i na moi ka hookupu o na makaainana	Chun	Typescript and translation, "Honoring the kings, the tribute of the people," in Chun 1988, pp. 39–43.	On tribute paid to chiefs.
10-9-1865	KAO [p. 2]	Kanalua i ka moolelo Hawaii			J. K. Unauna, opio critique of Kamakau's moolelo.
10-14-1865	KNK [p. 1]	Lononuiakea, Lonoikaoualii, a me Lonoikamakahiki	Chun	Typescript and translation, "Story of the three Lonos," in BMA–HEN: Thrum 257.	Response to legends recently told in the newspapers of the time. Gives genealogy of the three Lono figures.
10-16-1865	KAO [p. 1]	Hooheihei ka nukahalale			Critique of Poli's chronology of KAO (9-25 and) 10-2-1865.
10-23-1865	KAO [p. 2]	Ka hakui me ka hauoli			Says he will not respond to childish questions.
10-23-1865	KAO [p. 2]	He kahiko oe no Peleioholani			On man still living, born in time of Peleioholani...
10-28-1865	KNK [p. 1]	Kumumanao; he mea maikai loa ka imi ana i na mea i haule a nalowale o na mea kahiko o Hawaii nei	Chun	Typescript and translation, "Thought source," in BMA–HEN: Thrum 254 and 258.	Reply to Palapalapoi of KNK 9-16-1865. It is here that we learn that all of Kamakau's papers were lost in a fire at his house in Waihee, Maui, around 12-16-1856.
11-6-1865	KAO [p. 4]	No ka hoakea ana a me ka hoomolaelae ana, e pau ai ka pohihihi o ka mooolelo Hawaii			Response to J. K. Unauna's critique in KAO 10-9-1865. Says Malo's moolelo appearing in Pogue is not reliable.
11-18-1865	KNK [p. 1]	He puu kaulana o Kauwiki ma Maui Hikina	Chun	Typescript of English translation, "The famous hill of Kauwiki at East Maui" in BMA–HEN: Thrum 45. Typescript and translation, "Kauwiki is a famous hill in East Maui," in Chun pp. 45–55.	Description of Kauiki and its history.
12-4-1865	KAO [p. 2]	Untitled; "Kalakaiamanu, Waialua, 28 Novemaba 1865…"			Response to Unauna article. Also mentions Helu 27 of Hoomana kahiko (J. Waiamau of 11-11-1865).

12-4-1865	KAO [p. 4]	Makee i ke kupa alii			J. K. Unauna response to Kamakau of KAO 10-23 and 11-6-1865.
12-9-1865	KNK [pp. 1–2]	He moolelo no Waipio i Hawaii a me kekahi mau alii i noho aupuni	Chun	Typescript of English translation, "Legends of Waipio in Hawaii" in BMA–HEN: Thrum 691–96. Typescript and translation, "History of Waipio, Hawaii," in BMA–HEN: Thrum 264. Typescript and translation, "Story of Waipio at Hawaii," in Chun 1988, pp. 56–64.	Description of Waipio Valley and its history.
12-11-1865	KAO [p. 4]	Makee i ke kupa alii			J. K. Unauna response to Kamakau article of KE 5-17-1855.
12-25-1865	KAO [p. 4]	Untitled; "Ka-lakaiamanu, Waialua, 12 Dekemaba 1865…"			First of two articles (part two on 1-1-1866), responding to J. K. Unauna of KAO 12-4-1865.
1-1-1866	KAO [p. 1]	Untitled; "Ka-lakaiamanu, Waialua, 12 Dekemaba 1865…"			Second part of two articles starting on 12-25-1865.
1-29-1866	KAO [p. 1]	Ka lama-ku e pau ai ka hualu o S. M. Kamakau			J. K. Unauna two-part (following in KAO 2-5) response to Kamakau of KAO 12-4-1865.
2-5-1866	KAO [p. 3]	Ka lama-ku e pau ai ka hualu o S. M. Kamakau			J. K. Unauna two-part (previous in KAO 1-29) response to Kamakau of KAO 12-4-1865.
3-31-1866	PCA [p. 2]	Untitled; "Saturday, March 31. There was a report…"			Short description on the ailing Kamakau. "In ancient traditional knowledge of the Hawaiians, the late David Malo alone excelled him."
4-2-1866	KAO [p. 4]	He aloha! He aloha!! He aloha!!!			Response to Unauna. First part of two (followed by KAO 4-10).

4-9-1866	KAO [p. 4]	Untitled; "Kalakaiamanu M, Waialua, Feb. 24, A.D. 1866…"			Second part of two, responding to Unauna. Previous article in KAO 4-3.
5-28-1866	KAO [p. 4]	Ua ola au, ua makai kuu noho, ua pale hoi kana, ua ono ka ai.			J. K. Unauna three-part response to Kamakau (KAO 4-3 and 4-10-1866). Followed by KAO 6-18 and 6-25.
6-2-1866	KNK [p. 4]	No ka minamina i ka moolelo Hawaii no ka nalowale	Chun	Typescript of English translation, "Because of the regret of the loss of Hawaiian Folklore" in BMA–HEN: Newsp 6-2-1866.	Lists people still alive at the time that know history. Seems that there is no ending to this article.
6-18-1866	KAO [p. 3]	Ua ola au, ua makai kuu noho			J. K. Unauna response to Kamakau, part two of three. Previous on 5-28, and following on 6-25.
6-25-1866	KAO [p. 4]	Ua ola au, ua makai kuu noho			J. K. Unauna response to Kamakau, part three of three. Previous on 5-28 and 6-18.
7-23-1866	KAO [p. 3]	O J. Koii, kau i Kapua	Chun	Partial typescript and translation, "O J. Koii, kau i ka pua," in McKinzie, Vol. 2, pp. 52–53.	Three-part response to Unauna (KAO 5-28, 6-18 and 6-25-1866). Followed by 7-30 and 8-6.
7-30-1866	KAO [p. 3]	O J. Koii, kau i Kapua	Chun		Second of three part response to Unauna. Preceded by 7-23 and followed by 8-6.
8-6-1866	KAO [p. 4]	O J. Koii, kau i Kapua	Chun		Third of three part response to Unauna. Preceded by 7-23 and 7-30.
8-11-1866	KNK [p. 3]	La hoihoi ea	Chun		Discusses taking of islands by Paulet, commander of the *Carysfort* in February 1843 and the return on July 31, 1843.
8-13-1866	KAO [p. 4]	E S.M. Kamakau e			J. Kauiomanoa chastising Kamakau and Unauna. They should not publicize genealogies of alii.
8-20-1866	KAO [p. 2]	Ia S.M. Kamakau			J. Kauiomanoa response to Kamakau of KAO 7-30-1866.

APPENDIX

8-25-1866	KNK [p. 4]	Untitled; "Kolikowailehua, Manua, Kahehuna, Aug. 14, 1866…"	Chun, Thrum		
10-20-1866	KNK [p. 1]	Ka moolelo o Kamehameha I; [Helu 1]	Thrum	*Ruling Chiefs*, pp. 66–69 (Ch. VI: Hawaii under Alapainui).	Thrum's title: "Relates the time and birth of Kamehameha; of reign of Kekaulike."
10-27-1866	KNK [p. 1]	Ka moolelo o Kamehameha I; [Helu 2]	Thrum	*Ruling Chiefs*, pp. 69–72 (Ch. VI: Hawaii under Alapainui).	Thrum's title: "Movements of Alapai and Peleioholani."
11-3-1866	KNK [p. 1]	Ka moolelo o Kamehameha I; [Helu 3]	Thrum	*Ruling Chiefs*, pp. 72–74 (Ch. VI: Hawaii under Alapainui).	Thrum's title: "Alapai and Peleioholani meet; Alapai returns to Hawaii."
11-10-1866	KNK [p. 1]	Ka moolelo o Kamehameha I; Helu 4	Thrum	*Ruling Chiefs*, pp. 74–78 (Ch. VI: Hawaii under Alapainui).	Thrum's title: "Relates to Alapai's movements on Hawaii"
12-1-1866	KNK [p. 1]	Ka moolelo o Kamehameha I; Helu 5	Thrum	*Ruling Chiefs*, pp. 78–82 (Ch. VII: Hawaii under Kalaniopuu's time).	Thrum's title: "Relates to the time of Kalaniopuu of Hawaii."
12-1-1866	KNK [p. 2]	Untitled; "Puakoliko, Manua, Kahehuna, Nov. 27, 1866…"	Chun		
12-8-1866	KNK [p. 1]	Ka moolelo o Kamehameha I; Helu 5 [6]	Thrum	*Ruling Chiefs*, pp. 82–85 (Ch. VII: Hawaii under Kalaniopuu's time).	Thrum's title: "Contests of Kahekili, Keeaumoku, and Kalaniopuu."
12-15-1866	KNK [p. 1]	Ka moolelo o Kamehameha I; Helu 6 [7]	Thrum	*Ruling Chiefs*, pp. 85–89 (Ch. VII: Hawaii under Kalaniopuu's time). Partial typescript of English translation, "Notes on tattooing" in BMA-HEN: vol. 1, pp. 1289–91.	Thrum's title: "Movements of Kalaniopuu and Kahekili."
12-22-1866	KNK [p. 1]	Ka moolelo o Kamehameha I; Helu 7 [8]	Thrum	*Ruling Chiefs*, pp. 89–91 (Ch. VII: Hawaii under Kalaniopuu's time). *Na moolelo a ka poe kahiko*, pp. 90–97 (The lands of Kahiki; Some travelers to Kahiki).	Thrum's title: "Kalaniopuu cont'd; Advent of foreigners."

12-29-1866	KNK [p. 1]	Ka moolelo o Kamehameha I; Helu 8 [9]	Thrum	*Na moolelo a ka poe kahiko*, pp. 97–100 (The story of Paao).	Thrum's title: "Traditional accounts of Paao and other voyagers."
1-5-1867	KNK [p. 1]	Ka moolelo o Kamehameha I; Helu 9 [10]	Thrum	*Na moolelo a ka poe kahiko*, pp. 100–106 (The story of Paao; Ancient chiefs of Hawaii nei; More travelers).	Thrum's title: "Introduction of priest and rulers from Kahiki; First heiaus constructed—Wahaula and Mookini." Beginning in 1867, Kamakau appears as an official part of the newspaper staff; he is listed as "Poe haku manao no ke Kuokoa."
1-5-1867	KNK [p. 3]	He wahi manao paipai	Chun		Encourages readership of his history. Asks for contributions by experts.
1-12-1867	KNK [p. 1]	Ka moolelo o Kamehameha I; Helu 10 [11]	Thrum	*Na moolelo a ka poe kahiko*, pp. 106–112 (More travelers; The coming of the gods).	Thrum's title: "Advent of Laamaikahiki and others; Advent of the gods (images)."
1-19-1867	KNK [p. 1]	Ka moolelo o Kamehameha I; Helu 11 [12]	Thrum	*Ruling Chiefs*, pp. 92–94 (Ch. VII: Captain Cook's visit to Hawaii). *Na moolelo a ka poe kahiko*, pp. 113–118 (Na haole; Kualii; Kahiki).	Thrum's title: "Traditional accounts of prior visitors and arrival of Captain Cook at Kauai."
1-19-1867	KNK [pp. 1–2]	Nu hou o na mea kahiko	Chun	Typescript and translation, "New light on things ancient" in BMA–HEN; Thrum 57.	Comparison of Hawaiian and Maori words and place names.
1-21-1867	KAO [p. 3]	Untitled; "Puakoliko, Manua, Kahehuna, Ian. 8, 1867…"			Matthew, on the dwindling number of the Hawaiian race.
1-26-1867	KNK [p. 3]	Untitled; "Puakoliko, Manua, Kahehuna, Ianuari 9, 1867…"		Typescript of English translation, "Lament for loss of records" in BMA–HEN; Nwsp KNK 1-26-1867.	View of himself and his role in the clarification of Hawaiian antiquities. Tells of the condensing of his history by the editors.
1-26-1867	KNK [p. 1]	Ka moolelo o Kamehameha I; Helu 12 [13]	Thrum	*Ruling Chiefs*, pp. 94–98 (Ch. VIII: Captain Cook's visit to Hawaii).	Thrum's title: "Relates to Captain Cook's visit at Kauai and at Maui."

2-2-1867	KNK [p. 1]	Ka moolelo o Kamehameha I; Helu 13 [14]	Thrum	*Ruling Chiefs*, pp. 98–102 (Ch. VIII: Captain Cook's visit to Hawaii).	Thrum's title: "Cook's arrival at Hawaii."
2-2-1867	KNK [p. 4]	Untitled; "Puakoliko, Manua, Kahehuna, Ianuari 23, 1867…"	Chun		Comparison of Hawaiian and Tahitian place names…
2-9-1867	KNK [p. 1]	Ka moolelo o Kamehameha I; Helu 14 [15]	Thrum	*Ruling Chiefs*, pp. 102–103 (Ch. VIII: Captain Cook's visit to Hawaii); pp. 105–107 (Events of Kalaniopuu's time).	Thrum's title: "Death of Captain Cook and departure of ships; Kalaniopuu reign."
2-16-1867	KNK [p. 1]	Ka moolelo o Kamehameha I; Helu 15 [16]	Thrum	*Ruling Chiefs*, pp. 103–105 (Ch. VIII: Captain Cook's visit to Hawaii); pp. 107–111 (Events of Kalaniopuu's time).	Thrum's title: "Kalaniopuu and summary of his principal deeds; Kamehameha sacrificed Imakakoloa at heiau, Pakini."
2-16-1867	KNK [p. 3]	No ke Kuokoa			Luna Auhau comments that the name of Kamakau's history should be more inclusive. It is not only the history of Kamehameha I.
2-23-1867	KNK [p. 1]	Ka moolelo o Kamehameha I; Helu 16 [17]	Thrum	*Ruling Chiefs*, pp. 92–94 (Ch. VIII: Captain Cook's visit to Hawaii).	Thrum's title: "Celebrities in the time of Kalaniopuu; Kahekili of Maui."
3-2-1867	KNK [p. 1]	Ka moolelo o Kamehameha I; Helu 17 [18]	Thrum	*Ruling Chiefs*, pp. 117–121 (Ch. X: Kamehameha wins half Hawaii).	Thrum's title: "Conflict between Kiwalao and Kamehameha in Kona."
3-9-1867	KNK [p.1]	Ka moolelo o Kamehameha I; Helu 18 [19]	Thrum	*Ruling Chiefs*, pp. 121–126 (Ch. X: Kamehameha wins half Hawaii).	Thrum's title: "Kamehameha moi of Hawaii; The times of Kamehameha; His relatives."
3-9-1867	KNK [p. 4]	No William Hoapili Kaauwai ma	Chun		On lineage of William Hoapili Kaauwai of New Zealand
3-16-1867	KNK [p. 1]	Ka moolelo o Kamehameha I; Helu 19 [20]	Thrum	*Ruling Chiefs*, pp. 126–131 (Ch. X: Kamehameha wins half Hawaii; Ch. XI: Kahahana loses Oahu).	Thrum's title: "History of Kahahana of Oahu."

3-16-1867	KNK [p. 4]	Untitled; "Puakoliko, Manua, Kahehuna…"	Chun		On his publication of genealogies for all to see…
3-18-1867	KAO [p. 1]	S. M. Kamakau			J. Kaimiloa response to Helu 16 (KNK 2-23-1867). Disagrees with Kamakau's assesment of Cook.
3-23-1867	KNK [p. 1]	Ka moolelo o Kamehameha I; Helu 20 [21]	Thrum	Ruling Chiefs, pp. 131–135 (Ch. XI: Kahahana Loses Oahu). Typescript of partial English translation, "Notes on tattooing" in BMA–HEN: vol. 1, pp. 1289–1291.	Thrum's title: "History of Kahahana continued."
3-30-1867	KNK [p. 1]	Ka moolelo o Kamehameha I; Helu 21 [22]	Thrum	Ruling Chiefs, pp. 135–138 (Ch. XI: Kahahana loses Oahu).	Thrum's title: "Conflict between Kahahana and Kahekili; Oahu conquered 1772–1773."
4-6-1867	KNK [p. 1]	Ka moolelo o Kamehameha I; Helu 22 [23]	Thrum	Ruling Chiefs, pp. 138–143 (Ch. XI: Kahahana loses Oahu; Ch. XII: Kamehameha wins all Hawaii).	Thrum's title: "Transactions on Oahu; Rebellion on Maui."
4-6-1867	KNK [p. 4]	Ia Ioane Kaimiloa	Chun		Response to Kaimiloa of KAO 3-18-1867. Uses Malo, Dibble, and Pogue as support.
4-13-1867	KNK [p. 1]	Ka moolelo o Kamehameha I; Helu 23 [24]	Thrum	Ruling Chiefs, pp. 147–151 (Ch. XII: Kamehameha wins all Hawaii).	Thrum's title: "Maui incidents; Foreteller of Kamehameha as sole moi; Battle of Keoua."
4-20-1867	KNK [p. 1]	Ka moolelo o Kamehameha I; Helu 24 [25]	Thrum	Ruling Chiefs, pp. 143–147, 151 (Ch. XII: Kamehameha wins all Hawaii).	Thrum's title: "Kamehameha pursues Keoua; Foreigners after Cook; the Eleanor-Olowalu tragedy."
4-27-1867	KNK [p. 1]	Ka moolelo o Kamehameha I; Helu 24 [26]	Thrum	Ruling Chiefs, pp. 151–153 (Ch. XII: Kamehameha wins all Hawaii).	Thrum's title: "John Young and Isaac Davis; Sloop captured; Kamehameha wars against Maui."
5-4-1867	KNK [p. 1]	Ka moolelo o Kamehameha I; Helu 25 [27]	Thrum	Ruling Chiefs, pp. 153–157 (Ch. XII: Kamehameha wins all Hawaii).	Thrum's title: "Heiau at Kawaihae built; Plans to overcome Keoua."

Appendix

5-11-1867	KNK [p. 1]	Ka moolelo o Kamehameha I; Helu 26 [28]	Thrum	*Ruling Chiefs*, pp. 157–162 (Ch. XII: Kamehameha wins all Hawaii; Ch. XIII: Last days of Kahekili).	Thrum's title: "Death of Keoua; Kamehameha wars against kings of Maui and Kauai."
5-18-1867	KNK [p.1]	Ka moolelo o Kamehameha I; Helu 27 [29]	Thrum	*Ruling Chiefs*, pp. 162–164 (Ch. XIII: Last days of Kahekili).	Thrum's title: "Arrival of Vancouver, 1792."
5-25-1867	KNK [p. 1]	Ka moolelo o Kamehameha I; Helu 28 [30]	Thrum	*Ruling Chiefs*, pp. 165–168 (Ch. XIII: Last days of Kahekili).	Thrum's title: "Vancouver continued; Kaeokulani succeeds Kahekili of Maui, 1793."
6-1-1867	KNK [p. 1]	Ka moolelo o Kamehameha I; Helu 29 [31]	Thrum	*Ruling Chiefs*, pp. 168–171 (Ch. XIV: Kamehameha's conquest of Maui and Oahu).	Thrum's title: "Kaeokulani starts for Kauai; Returns and battles at Ewa; Murder of Captain Brown; *Jackall* and *Prince Leeboo* sail for Hawaii."
6-8-1867	KNK [p. 1]	Ka moolelo o Kamehameha I; Helu 30 [32]	Thrum	*Ruling Chiefs*, pp. 171–173 (Ch. XIV: Kamehameha's conquest of Maui and Oahu).	Thrum's title: "War between Kamehameha and Kalanikupule, 1795, and Namakeha, 1796."
6-15-1867	KNK [p. 1]	Ka moolelo o Kamehameha I; Helu 31 [33]	Thrum	*Ruling Chiefs*, pp. 173–179 (Ch. XIV: Kamehameha's conquest of Maui and Oahu; Ch. XV: Reminiscences of Kamehameha).	Thrum's title: "Namakeha's rebellion; Times of Kamehameha, 1797–1811; Battle of Nuuanu—Oahu conquered; Kamehameha returns to Hawaii; Various callings assigned."
7-6-1867	KNK [p. 1]	Ka moolelo o Kamehameha I; Helu 32 [34]	Thrum	*Ruling Chiefs*, pp. 179–182 (Ch. XV: Reminiscences of Kamehameha).	Thrum's title: "Kamehameha erecting heiaus; Various idols and their powers; Kamehameha a devout worshiper; A considerate king; Marks the place of sedition plotters."
7-13-1867	KNK [p. 1]	Ka moolelo o Kamehameha I; Helu 33 [35]	Thrum	*Ruling Chiefs*, pp. 182–185 (Ch. XV: Reminiscences of Kamehameha).	Thrum's title: "Kamehameha adjusting affairs on Hawaii; John Young governor; Lava flows to Kiholo."

7-20-1867	KNK [p. 1]	Ka moolelo o Kamehameha I; Helu 34 [36]	Thrum	*Ruling Chiefs*, pp. 185–189 (Ch. XV: Reminiscences of Kamehameha; Ch. XVI: The peaceful transfer of Kauai to Kamehameha).	Thrum's title: "Kamehameha sends for the prophet of Pele to stay the flow; Peleleu fleet begun; Liholiho at age of five empowered to consecrate heiaus; Peleleu fleet sails to Lahaina and Oahu; Royal family a year on Oahu when the okuu scourge decimates his army, chiefs and people."
7-27-1867	KNK [p. 1]	Ka moolelo o Kamehameha I; Helu 35 [37]	Thrum	*Ruling Chiefs*, pp. 189–192 (Ch. XVI: The peaceful transfer of Kauai to Kamehameha).	Thrum's title: "Death of Keeaumoku; Kamehameha resides on Oahu; Revenues of Hawaii and Maui sent him; Ancient criminal laws."
7-27-1867	KNK [p. 6]	Untitled; "Puakoliko, Manua, Kahehuna…"		Typescript of text and translation, "Relative to Kamehameha" in BMA–HEN; Thrum 61	Deals with different aspects of life of Kamehameha, and calls into question Pogue's historical facts surrounding place of Kamehameha's birth.
7-27-1867	KNK [p. 3]	Na S. M. Kamakau, Esq.	Chun		He talks of going to the newspapers to do the history of Kamehameha, but they show no interest…
8-3-1867	KNK [p. 1]	Ka moolelo o Kamehameha I; Helu 35 [38]	Thrum	*Ruling Chiefs*, pp. 192–194 (Ch. XVI: The peaceful transfer of Kauai to Kamehameha).	Thrum's title: "Kamehameha encourages industry; Introduction of rum, 1791; Kanihonui put to death; Kamehameha gives up plan to invade Kauai."
8-3-1867	KNK [p. 3]	Untitled; "Puakoliko, Manua, Kahehuna, Iulai 30, 1867…"	Chun		Reply to Mose Nahora of California, dated 5-20-1867
8-3-1867	KNK [p. 3]	He mea kupanaha ka aikanaka ana o ka haole			
8-10-1867	KNK [p. 1]	Ka moolelo o Kamehameha I; Helu 36 [39]	Thrum	*Ruling Chiefs*, pp. 194–197 (Ch. XVI: The peaceful transfer of Kauai to Kamehameha).	Thrum's title: "Kamehameha invites Kaumualii to Oahu; Kaumualii cedes Kauai to Kamehameha."

APPENDIX

8-10-1867	KNK [p. 3]	Untitled; "Puakoliko, Manua, Kahehuna…"	Chun		Dialogue between Kahuake of Oahu and Pukeke of Hawaii.
8-17-1867	KNK [p. 1]	Ka moolelo o Kamehameha I; Helu 37 [40]	Thrum	*Ruling Chiefs*, pp. 197–201 (Ch. XVI: The peaceful transfer of Kauai to Kamehameha; Ch. XVII: Death of Kamehameha).	Thrum's title: "Return of Kamehameha to Hawaii; Ancient religion and kinds of heiaus."
8-24-1867	KNK [p. 1]	Ka moolelo o Kamehameha I; Helu 38 [41]	Thrum	*Ruling Chiefs*, pp. 201–205 (Ch. XVII: Death of Kamehameha).	Thrum's title: "Idolatry; Sandalwood; Kamehameha's cultivation."
8-31-1867	KNK [p. 1]	Ka moolelo o Kamehameha I; Helu 39 [42]	Thrum	*Ruling Chiefs*, pp. 205–208 (Ch. XVII: Death of Kamehameha).	Thrum's title: "Attempt well digging at kalae; Russians arrive; Death of Kaoleioku; Erection of fort at Honolulu."
8-31-1867	KNK [p. 4]	He iwi haiao Hawaii	Chun		Asks for historical information, for the good of the nation.
9-7-1867	KNK [p. 1]	Ka moolelo o Kamehameha I; Helu 40 [43]	Thrum	*Ruling Chiefs*, pp. 208–209 (Ch. XVII: Death of Kamehameha).	Thrum's title: "Heirs of Kamehameha; his admonitions."
9-14-1867	KNK [p. 4]	Ka moolelo o Kamehameha I; Helu 41 [44]	Thrum	*Ruling Chiefs*, pp. 209–212 (Ch. XVII: Death of Kamehameha).	Thrum's title: "Death of Kamehameha at Kailua, Hawaii, 1819."
9-21-1867	KNK [p. 1]	Ka moolelo o Kamehameha I; Helu 42 [45]	Thrum	*Ruling Chiefs*, pp. 212–214 (Ch. XVII: Death of Kamehameha). pp. 219–220 (Ch. XVIII: Abolition of the Tabus under Liholiho).	Thrum's title: "Succeeded by Liholiho as Kamehameha II."
9-28-1867	KNK [p. 1]	Ka moolelo o Kamehameha I; Helu 43 [46]	Thrum	*Ruling Chiefs*, pp. 214–216 (Ch. XVII: Death of Kamehameha). pp. 220–222 (Ch. XVIII: Abolition of the Tabus under Liholiho).	Thrum's title: "Liholiho and chiefs of his time; Obsequies of Kamehameha I."
10-5-1867	KNK [p. 1]	Ka moolelo o Kamehameha I; Helu 44 [47]	Thrum	*Ruling Chiefs*, pp. 216–218 (Ch. XVII: Death of Kamehameha). pp. 222–223 (Ch. XVIII: Abolition of the Tabus under Liholiho).	Thrum's title: "Reign of Liholiho; Overthrow of the kapus."

10-5-1867	KNK [p. 4]	No ka papa alii Hawaii	Chun	Typescript of translation, "The hereditary chiefs of Hawaii" in BMA–HEN: vol. 1, pp. 3127–3129	On chiefly lines.
10-12-1867	KNK [p. 1]	Ka moolelo o Kamehameha I; Helu 45 [48]	Thrum	*Ruling Chiefs*, pp. 223–224 (Ch. XVIII: Abolition of the Tabus under Liholiho).	Thrum's title: "Reign of Liholiho; Overthrow of the kapus, cont'd."
10-26-1867	KNK [p. 3]	Untitled; "E ke Kuokoa e - Aloha oe…"			Lahui Hawaii response to article by Kamakau on chiefly lines of KNK 10-5-1867.
11-2-1867	KNK [p. 1]	Ka moolelo o na Kamehameha; Helu 46 [49]	Thrum	*Ruling Chiefs*, pp. 225–227 (Ch. XVIII: Abolition of the Tabus under Liholiho).	Overall title of series changes with this number. Thrum's title: "Proceedings following overthrow of the kapus."
11-2-1867	KNK [p. 1]	He wahine i hanau i na keiki 7	Chun		Concerning multiple birth of children to woman in Waihee, Maui.
11-2-1867	KNK [p. 4]	Ka moolelo o na alii a me na makaainana I loaa mai loko mai o na Alii o keia pae aina, he wahi ninau naʻe			J. H. K. Punimoolelo response to Kamakau's article on chiefly lines of KNK 10-5-1867.
11-9-1867	KNK [p. 1]	Ka moolelo o na Kamehameha; Helu 47 [50]	Thrum	*Ruling Chiefs*, pp. 227–229 (Ch. XVIII: Abolition of the Tabus under Liholiho).	Thrum's title: "Battle of Kuamoo; Conditions prior to advent of missionaries."
11-9-1867	KNK [p. 3]	Untitled; "Puakoliko, Manua, Kahehuna…"	Chun		Response to Lahui Hawaii of KNK 10-26-1867, and to Punimoolelo of KNK 11-9-1867.
11-16-1867	KNK [p. 1]	Ka moolelo o na Kamehameha; Helu 47 [51]	Thrum	*Ruling Chiefs*, pp. 229–231 (Ch. XIX: Hawaii before foreign innovations).	Thrum's title: "Conditions, etc., cont'd; Genealogy of chiefs."
11-23-1867	KNK [p. 1]	Ka moolelo o na Kamehameha; 48 [52]	Thrum	*Ruling Chiefs*, pp. 231–233 (Ch. XIX: Hawaii before foreign innovations).	Thrum's title: "Conditions, etc., cont'd—under the kapu system."
11-23-1867	KNK [p. 3]	He waiwai nui makamae	Chun		Response to letter from Levi Kalani of California, which follows the article.

Appendix

11-30-1867	KNK [p. 1]	Ka moolelo o na Kamehameha; 49 [53]	Thrum	*Ruling Chiefs*, pp. 233–236 (Ch. XIX: Hawaii before foreign innovations).	Thrum's title: "Treatment of prisoners of war; Decrease of population—causes of."
11-30-1867	KNK [p. 4]	Sila! Sila!! Sila!!! Sila!!!!	Chun		On land issues.
12-7-1867	KNK [p. 1]	Ka moolelo o na Kamehameha; 50 [54]	Thrum	*Ruling Chiefs*, pp. 236–237 (Ch. XIX: Hawaii before foreign innovations).	Thrum's title: "Population on arrival of foreigners and missionaries."
12-14-1867	KNK [p. 1]	Ka moolelo o na Kamehameha; 51 [55]	Thrum	*Ruling Chiefs*, pp. 237–239 (Ch. XIX: Hawaii before foreign innovations).	Thrum's title: "Conditions and employment of the people under Kamehameha."
12-21-1867	KNK [p. 1]	Ka moolelo o na Kamehameha; 52 [56]	Thrum	*Ruling Chiefs*, pp. 239–242 (Ch. XIX: Hawaii before foreign innovations).	Thrum's title: "Conditions and employment of the people under Kamehameha."
12-28-1867	KNK [p. 1]	Ka moolelo o na Kamehameha; 53 [57]	Thrum	*Ruling Chiefs*, pp. 242–244 (Ch. XIX: Hawaii before foreign innovations).	Thrum's title: "Sundry professions; Hale Nauwa."
1-4-1868	KNK [p. 1]	Ka moolelo o na Kamehameha; 54 [58]	Thrum	*Ruling Chiefs*, pp. 244–246 (Ch. XIX: Hawaii before foreign innovations).	Thrum's title: "Remarks on changing conditions."
1-11-1868	KNK [p. 1]	Ka moolelo o na Kamehameha; 55 [59]	Thrum	*Ruling Chiefs*, pp. 246–248 (Ch. XX: Rule and Death of Liholiho).	Thrum's title: "Liholiho consents to residence of missionaries; John Reves."
1-18-1868	KNK [p. 1]	Ka moolelo o na Kamehameha; 56 [60]	Thrum	*Ruling Chiefs*, pp. 248–249 (Ch. XX: Rule and Death of Liholiho).	Thrum's title: "The people accept Christianity; Schools established; Printing."
1-25-1868	KNK [p. 1]	Ka moolelo o na Kamehameha; 57 [61]	Thrum	*Ruling Chiefs*, pp. 249–251 (Ch. XX: Rule and Death of Liholiho).	Thrum's title: "Proceedings under Kamehameha II."
2-1-1868	KNK [p. 1]	Ka moolelo o na Kamehameha; 58 [62]	Thrum	*Ruling Chiefs*, pp. 251–253 (Ch. XX: Rule and Death of Liholiho).	Thrum's title: "The king's dissipations; He tours Oahu and visits Kauai."
2-8-1868	KNK [p. 1]	Ka moolelo o na Kamehameha; 59 [63]	Thrum	*Ruling Chiefs*, pp. 253–255 (Ch. XX: Rule and Death of Liholiho).	Thrum's title: "Kaahumanu returns from Kauai with Kaumualii; Keeaumoku's death."

2-15-1868	KNK [p. 1]	Ka moolelo o na Kamehameha; 60 [64]	Thrum	*Ruling Chiefs*, pp. 255–257 (Ch. XX: Rule and Death of Liholiho).	Thrum's title: "Liholiho and party sail for England; Death of the king and queen."
2-15-1868	KNK [p. 3]	He mau mea i hoohalahala ia no na mea iloko o na kaao Hawaii	Chun		Criticism of the content of Hawaiian legends being printed in the newspapers.
2-22-1868	KNK [p. 1]	Ka moolelo o na Kamehameha; Helu 61 [65]	Thrum	*Ruling Chiefs*, pp. 257–259 (Ch. XX: Rule and Death of Liholiho).	Thrum's title: "Return of royal remains; Regency of Kauikeaouli; His genealogy."
2-29-1868	KNK [p. 1]	Ka moolelo o na Kamehameha; Helu 62 [66]	Thrum	*Ruling Chiefs*, p. 259 (Ch. XXI: The childhood of Kauikeaouli, Kamehameha III).	Thrum's title: "Genealogy of chiefs, etc., cont'd; Plan to exchange Keopuolani in childhood failed."
2-29-1868	KNK [p. 3]	He mau wahi ninau ia S. M. Kamakau			S. B. Hoaʻloha asks for clarification from Kamakau of his history, "i mea hoi e kekee ole ai imua o ka poe o ka hanauna hou e ku mai ana."
3-7-1868	KNK [p. 3]	He mau kuluhio ia S. B. Hoaaloha			Response to critique by S. B. Hoaaloha of KNK 2-29-1868.
3-14-1868	KNK [p. 1]	Ka moolelo o na Kamehameha; Helu 63 [67]	Thrum	*Ruling Chiefs*, pp. 259'–261 (Ch. XXI: The childhood of Kauikeaouli, Kamehameha III).	Thrum's title: "History of Keopuolani; Her husband and children."
3-21-1868	KNK [p. 1]	Ka moolelo o na Kamehameha; Helu 64 [68]	Thrum	*Ruling Chiefs*, pp. 261–266 (Ch. XXI: The childhood of Kauikeaouli, Kamehameha III).	Thrum's title: "History of Keopuolani cont'd; Her death."
3-21-1868	KNK [p. 4]	Untitled; "Puakoliko, Manua, Kahehuna…"	Chun		Says that Lorrin Andrews told him that the history of Hawaii should be translated into English… He asked KNK for a column to fill with mele kahiko.
3-28-1868	KNK [p. 1]	Ka moolelo o na Kamehameha; Helu 65 [69]	Thrum	*Ruling Chiefs*, pp. 263–264 (Ch. XXI: The childhood of Kauikeaouli, Kamehameha III).	Thrum's title: "Keopuolani; Birth and early years of Kauikeaouli."

3-28-1868	KNK [p. 1]	He mele no Kaumualii				Begins a series of chants collected by Kamakau which ran weekly until 11-7-1868. This is first of two-part mele for Kaumualii by Kumuhelei.
4-4-1868	KNK [p. 1]	Ka moolelo o na Kamehameha; Helu 66 [70]	Thrum	*Ruling Chiefs*, pp. 264–266 (Ch. XXI: The childhood of Kauikeaouli, Kamehameha III). Partial translation in notes on "tattooing" in BMA–HEN: vol. 1, pp. 1289–1291.		Thrum's title: "His youth; Death of Kaumualii; Kauai rebellion."
4-4-1868	KNK [p. 1]	He mele no Kaumualii				Second of two-part mele for Kaumualii submitted by Kamakau. First part in KNK 3-28-1868
4-11-1868	KNK [p. 1]	Ka moolelo o na Kamehameha; Helu 67 [71]	Thrum	*Ruling Chiefs*, pp. 263–264 (Ch. XXI: The childhood of Kauikeaouli, Kamehameha III).		Thrum's title: "Eclipse noted; Progress of Kauai war."
4-11-1868	KNK [p. 1]	He mele no Kualii				First of seven-part mele by Kumahukia and Kaiwiokaekaha for Kualii...
4-18-1868	KNK [p. 1]	Ka moolelo o na Kamehameha; Helu 68 [72]	Thrum	*Ruling Chiefs*, pp. 263–264 (Ch. XXI: The childhood of Kauikeaouli, Kamehameha III).		Thrum's title: "Rebellion ends; Arrival of the Blonde with bodies of the king and queen."
4-18-1868	KNK [p. 1]	He mele no Kualii				Second of seven-part mele starting on 4-11.
4-25-1868	KNK [p. 1]	Ka moolelo o na Kamehameha; Helu 69 [73]	Thrum	*Ruling Chiefs*, pp. 270–271 (The career of Boki).		Thrum's title: "Kauikeaouli becomes Kamehameha III; Schools established."
4-25-1868	KNK [p. 1]	He mele no Kualii				Third of seven-part mele starting on 4-11.
5-2-1868	KNK [p. 1]	Ka moolelo o na Kamehameha; Helu 70 [74]	Thrum	*Ruling Chiefs*, pp. 271–273 (The career of Boki).		Thrum's title: "Rulers accept Christianity; Course of government under Kamehameha III."
5-2-1868	KNK [p. 1]	He mele no Kualii				Fourth of seven-part mele starting on 4-11.

5-9-1868	KNK [p. 1]	Ka moolelo o na Kamehameha; Helu 71 [75]	Thrum	*Ruling Chiefs*, pp. 273–275 (The career of Boki).	Thrum's title: "Boki as Kuhina nui; Serious epidemic and death of many chiefs."
5-9-1868	KNK [p. 4]	He mele no Kualii	Chun		Fifth of seven-part mele starting on 4-11.
5-16-1868	KNK [p. 1]	Ka moolelo o na Kamehameha; Helu 72 [76]	Thrum	*Ruling Chiefs*, pp. 275–280 (The career of Boki).	Thrum's title: "Revolt of Boki; He runs into debt and opens grog shops."
5-16-1868	KNK [p. 4]	He mele no Kualii	Chun		Sixth of seven-part mele starting on 4-11.
5-23-1868	KNK [p. 1]	Ka moolelo o na Kamehameha; Helu 72 [77]	Thrum	*Ruling Chiefs*, pp. 275–280 (The career of Boki).	Thrum's title: "Kamehameha III directs sandalwood gathering at Waialua; Kinau and Kekuanaoa married; New royal house."
5-23-1868	KNK [p. 4]	He mele no Kualii	Chun		Seventh of seven-part mele starting on 4-11.
5-30-1868	KNK [p. 1]	Ka moolelo o na Kamehameha; Helu 73 [78]	Thrum	*Ruling Chiefs*, pp. 280–281 (The career of Boki).	Thrum's title: "Attack on Mr. Richards by Captain Black at Lahaina."
5-30-1868	KNK [p. 4]	He mele kanikau no Walia Kahahana			First of three-part dirge by Kulawela for the chief, Walia Kahahana. See note with 3-28-1868 entry.
6-6-1868	KNK [p. 1]	Ka moolelo o na Kamehameha; Helu 74 [79]	Thrum	*Ruling Chiefs*, pp. 281–283 (The career of Boki).	Thrum's title: "Kaahumanu, David Malo and chiefs defend Richards."
6-6-1868	KNK [p. 4]	He mele kanikau no Walia Kahahana			Second of three-part dirge by Kulawela for the chief, Walia Kahahana.
6-13-1868	KNK [p. 1]	Ka moolelo o na Kamehameha; Helu 75 [80]	Thrum	*Ruling Chiefs*, pp. 283–286 (The career of Boki).	Thrum's title: "The king visits Hawaii; Government and Boki debt troubles; Kaahumanu visits Hawaii, 1828."
6-13-1868	KNK [p. 4]	He mele kanikau no Walia Kahahana			Third of three-part dirge by Kulawela for the chief, Walia Kahahana.

APPENDIX

6-20-1868	KNK [p. 1]	Ka moolelo o na Kamehameha; Helu 76 [81]	Thrum	*Ruling Chiefs*, pp. 286–288 (The career of Boki).	Thrum's title: "Kaahumanu annuls French's Kewalo land transaction; Boki's advice to Kamehameha III respecting Nahienaena; He threatens Kaahumanu with the aid of foreigners."
6-20-1868	KNK [p. 4]	He mele koihonua no Ahukai Kauukualii			First of two-part genealogy chant by Kahekiliwahine and Kailinaoa for Ahukai Kauukualii. See note with 3-28-1868 entry.
6-27-1868	KNK [p. 1]	Ka moolelo o na Kamehameha; Helu 77 [82]	Thrum	*Ruling Chiefs*, pp. 288–291 (The career of Boki).	Thrum's title: "Boki gathers his forces at Waikiki; Kekuanaoa alone dissuades Boki in his course."
6-27-1868	KNK [p. 4]	He mele koihonua no Ahukai Kauukualii			Second of two-part genealogy chant by Kahekiliwahine and Kailinaoa for Ahukai Kauukualii.
7-4-1868	KNK [p. 1]	Ka moolelo o na Kamehameha; Helu 78 [83]	Thrum	*Ruling Chiefs*, pp. 291–293 (The career of Boki).	Thrum's title: "Street work in Honolulu begun; Arrival of Vincennes; Chiefs concentrated; Regal procession to service at Kawaiahao."
7-4-1868	KNK [p. 4]	He mele koihonua no Kalua i Konahale Kuakini			First of six-part genealogy chant by Kukupuohi and other chiefs for Kaluaikonahale Kuakini. See note with 3-28-1868.
7-11-1868	KNK [p. 1]	Ka moolelo o na Kamehameha; Helu 79 [84]	Thrum	*Ruling Chiefs*, pp. 293–294 (The career of Boki).	Thrum's title: "Boki plans for his sandalwood expedition."
7-11-1868	KNK [p. 4]	He mele koihonua no Kalua i Konahale Kuakini			Second of six-part genealogy chant by Kukupuohi and other chiefs for Kaluaikonahale Kuakini.
7-16-1868	KAO				R. Kapihe to Kamakau.
7-18-1868	KNK [p. 1]	Ka moolelo o na Kamehameha; Helu 80 [85]	Thrum	*Ruling Chiefs*, pp. 294–296 (The career of Boki).	Thrum's title: "Attempts to dissuade him fruitless."

7-18-1868	KNK [p. 1]	He mele koihonua no Kalua i Konahale Kuakini			Third of six-part genealogy chant by Kukupuohi and other chiefs for Kaluaikonahale Kuakini.
7-23-1868	KAO [p. 3]	He papa hulikoa; he alukakoa			Response to Kapihe of KAO 7-16-1868, concerning birth of Kaoleioku.
7-25-1868	KNK [p. 1]	Ka moolelo o na Kamehameha; Helu 81 [86]		Ruling Chiefs, pp. 297–298 (Kuini Liliha, 1830–1831).	Thrum's title: "Liliha appointed to Boki's position; Paki-Kaahumanu dispute."
7-25-1868	KNK [p. 1]	He mele koihonua no Kalua i Konahale Kuakini			Fourth of six-part genealogy chant by Kukupuohi and other chiefs for Kaluaikonahale Kuakini.
8-1-1868	KNK [p. 1]	Ka moolelo o na Kamehameha; Helu 82 [87]		Ruling Chiefs, pp. 298–300 (Kuini Liliha, 1830–1831).	Thrum's title: "Liliha revolts at Kaahumanu's acts and laws."
8-1-1868	KNK [p. 1]	He mele koihonua no Kalua i Konahale Kuakini			Fifth of six-part genealogy chant by Kukupuohi and other chiefs for Kaluaikonahale Kuakini.
8-8-1868	KNK [p. 1]	Ka moolelo o na Kamehameha; Helu 83 [88]	Thrum	Ruling Chiefs, pp. 301–302 (Kuini Liliha, 1830–1831).	Thrum's title: "Liliha after much persuasion submits to rightful authority."
8-8-1868	KNK [p. 1]	He mele koihonua no Kalua i Konahale Kuakini			Sixth of six-part genealogy chant by Kukupuohi and other chiefs for Kaluaikonahale Kuakini.
8-8-1868	KNK [p. 4]	O ke ano o kekahi mau mea o ka lahui Hawaii	Chun	Partial translation in notes on, "Tattooing" in BMA–HEN: vol. 1, pp. 1289–1291. Translation, "Some of the practices of the Hawaiians" in BMA–HEN: vol. 1, pp. 2723–2729.	On the nature of Hawaiians in ancient times as well as in his own time.
8-8-1868	KNK [p. 4]	Palapala mai ka Haku Moolelo o Hawaii nei	Chun		Talks of his history, and how it is difficult to do without help.

Appendix

8-15-1868	KNK [p. 1]	Ka moolelo o na Kamehameha; Helu 84 [89]	Thrum	*Ruling Chiefs*, pp. 302–304 (Kuini Liliha 1830–1831).	Thrum's title: "Chief Ulumahiehie arrives; Liliha dispossessed of all power."
8-15-1868	KNK [p. 1]	He mele koihonua no Kekauluohi			First of seven-part genealogy chant by Keaweheulu Kalanimamahu and other chiefs for Kekauluohi. See note with 3-28-1868.
8-22-1868	KNK [p. 1]	Ka moolelo o na Kamehameha; Helu 85 [90]	Thrum	*Ruling Chiefs*, pp. 304–306 (Kuini Liliha 1830–1831).	Thrum's title: "Sundry changes; Kaahumanu visits Maui, urging attention to instruction."
8-22-1868	KNK [p. 1]	He mele koihonua no Kekauluohi			Second of seven-part genealogy chant by Keaweheulu Kalanimamahu and other chiefs for Kekauluohi.
8-26-1868	HG [p. 2]	Hawaiian history by Hawaiians			Mentions Lorrin Andrews translating mele assisted by Kamakau. Talks about the commencement of the translation of Kamakau's history of Kamehameha taken from KNK
8-26-1868	HG [p. 1]	History of the Kamehamehas; Translated from the Hawaiian of S. M. Kamakau			First of five installments of "unauthorized" English translation of Kamakau's history.
8-29-1868	KNK [p. 1]	Ka moolelo o na Kamehameha; Helu 86 [91]	Thrum	*Ruling Chiefs*, pp. 306–308 (Hawaii under Kaahumanu).	Thrum's title: "Return of Kaahumanu; Her death at Manoa, aged 64."
8-29-1868	KNK [p. 1]	He mele koihonua no Kekauluohi			Third of seven-part genealogy chant by Keaweheulu Kalanimamahu and other chiefs for Kekauluohi.
9-2-1868	HG [p. 1]	History of the Kamehamehas; Ch. II			Second of five installments of "unauthorized" English translation of Kamakau's history.

9-2-1868	HG [p. 3]	History of Kamehameha			A Hawaiian writes, criticizing Kamakau's facts. "This is evident by the controversy lately entered into by the native newspapers." He is not in the class of the "kuauhaus, such as Kepookulou, David Malo, Auwae, Kaoo, Unauna, Kamokuiki..."
9-5-1868	KNK [p. 1]	Ka moolelo o na Kamehameha; Helu 87 [92]	Thrum	*Ruling Chiefs*, pp. 308–310 (Hawaii under Kaahumanu).	Thrum's title: "Life of Kaahumanu; Her high rank."
9-5-1868	KNK [p. 1]	He mele koihonua no Kekauluohi			Fourth of seven-part genealogy chant by Keaweheulu Kalanimamahu and other chiefs for Kekauluohi.
9-9-1868	HG [p. 1]	History of the Kamehamehas; Ch. III			Third of five installments of "unauthorized" English translation of Kamakau's history.
9-12-1868	KNK [p. 1]	Ka moolelo o na Kamehameha; Helu 88 [93]	Thrum	*Ruling Chiefs*, pp. 311–312 (Hawaii under Kaahumanu).	
9-12-1868	KNK [p. 1]	He mele koihonua no Kekauluohi			Fifth of seven-part genealogy chant by Keaweheulu Kalanimamahu and other chiefs for Kekauluohi.
9-12-1868	KNK [p. 3]	Palapala mai a S. M. Kamakau mai		Translation, "Reply from S. M. Kamakau" in BMA–HEN: vol. 1, pp. 3067–3069.	Reply to a critique from "A Hawaiian," whom he presumes to be R. Kapihe of HG 9-2-1868.
9-16-1868	HG [p. 1]	History of the Kamehamehas; Ch. IV			Fourth of five installments of "unauthorized" English translation of Kamakau's history.
9-19-1868	PCA [p. 2]	Letter from Mr. Kamakau			Reply to a critique from "A Hawaiian," whom he presumes to be R. Kapihe of HG 9-2-1868. Similar to his response in KNK 9-12.

APPENDIX

9-19-1868	PCA [p. 3]	History of Kamehameha			States that Kamakau wrote his history with the intent that it would be translated by Andrews, and that the HG was translating it without permission.
9-19-1868	KNK [p. 1]	Ka moolelo o na Kamehameha; Helu 89 [94]	Thrum	*Ruling Chiefs*, pp. 312–314 (Hawaii under Kaahumanu).	Thrum's title: "Life of Kaahumanu cnt'd."
9-19-1868	KNK [p. 1]	He mele koihonua no Kekauluohi			Sixth of seven-part genealogy chant by Keaweheulu Kalanimamahu and other chiefs for Kekauluohi.
9-23-1868	HG [p. 1]	History of the Kamehamehas; Ch. IV [V]			Last of five installments of "unauthorized" English translation of Kamakau's history.
9-23-1868	HG [p. 2]	Copyright			Translator of History of the Kamehameha responds to plagiarism claims in PCA 9-19, saying that he did in fact ask Kamakau for permission, and that he gave it whole-heartedly.
9-26-1868	KNK [p. 1]	Ka moolelo o na Kamehameha; Helu 90 [95]	Thrum	*Ruling Chiefs*, pp. 314–318 (Hawaii under Kaahumanu).	Thrum's title: "Life of Kaahumanu cnt'd."
9-26-1868	KNK [p. 1]	He mele koihonua no Kekauluohi			Last of seven-part genealogy chant by Keaweheulu Kalanimamahu and other chiefs for Kekauluohi.
10-1-1868	KAO				R. Kapihe to Kamakau.
10-3-1868	KNK [p. 1]	Ka moolelo o na Kamehameha; Helu 91 [95]	Thrum	*Ruling Chiefs*, pp. 318–319 (Hawaii under Kaahumanu).	Thrum's title: "Life of Kaahumanu cnt'd; Views of Kauikeaouli."
10-3-1868	KNK [p. 1]	He mau mele koihonua a me na mele no Kauilanui-makehaikalani Kamaialii			First of six-part genealogy chant by S. M. Kamakau for Kauilanuimakehaikalani Kamaialii. See note with 3-28-1868 entry.

Date	Source	Title			Notes
10-8-1868	KAO [p. 2]	Ka moolelo a S. M. Kamakau			A. L. response to article in PCA 9-19-1868. Says that translation of Kamakau in HG is not plagiarism.
10-8-1868	KAO [p. 4]	Pane ia Hapaimemeue, S. M. Kamakau			Kapihe critique of Kamakau's article of KNK 9-12. He asks where the history done by the Historical Society is.
10-8-1868	KAO [p. 3]	He pili no			Kapihe response to Kamakau of HG 9-2. He corrects Kamakau's genealogy.
10-10-1868	KNK [p. 1]	Ka moolelo o na Kamehameha; Helu 92 [97]	Thrum	*Ruling Chiefs*, pp. 320–321 (Hawaii under Kaahumanu).	Thrum's title: "Views of Nahienaena and Kalanimoku."
10-10-1868	KNK [p. 1]	He mau mele koihonua a me na mele no Kauilanui-makehaikalani Kamaialii			Second of six-part genealogy chant by S. M. Kamakau for Kauilanuimakehaikalani Kamaialii.
10-17-1868	KNK [p. 1]	Ka moolelo o na Kamehameha; Helu 93 [98]	Thrum	*Ruling Chiefs*, pp. 321–323 (Hawaii under Kaahumanu).	Thrum's title: "Views of Kaahumanu."
10-17-1868	KNK [p. 1]	He mau mele koihonua a me na mele no Kauilanui-makehaikalani Kamaialii			Third of six-part genealogy chant by S. M. Kamakau for Kauilanuimakehaikalani Kamaialii.
10-17-1868	KNK [p. 4]	Na olelo pane a S. M. Kamakau	Chun, Thrum		First of three-part attack of his critics, namely Kapihe.
10-24-1868	KNK [p. 1]	Ka moolelo o na Kamehameha; Helu 94 [99]	Thrum	*Ruling Chiefs*, pp. 324–326 (Roman Catholicism in Hawaii).	Thrum's title: "Arrival of Roman Catholics."
10-24-1868	KNK [p. 3]	Na olelo pane a S. M. Kamakau	Chun, Thrum		Second of three-part attack of his critics, namely Kapihe.
10-24-1868	KNK [p. 1]	He mau mele koihonua a me na mele no Kauilanui-makehaikalani Kamaialii			Fourth of six-part genealogy chant by S. M. Kamakau for Kauilanuimakehaikalani Kamaialii.

10-31-1868	KNK [p. 4]	Na olelo pane a S. M. Kamakau	Chun, Thrum		Third of three-part attack of his critics, namely Kapihe.
10-31-1868	KNK [p. 1]	He mau mele koihonua a me na mele no Kauilanui-makehaikalani Kamaialii			Fifth of six-part genealogy chant by S. M. Kamakau for Kauilanuimakehaikalani Kamaialii.
11-7-1868	KNK [p. 1]	He mau mele koihonua a me na mele no Kauilanui-makehaikalani Kamaialii			Last of six-part genealogy chant by S. M. Kamakau for Kauilanuimakehaikalani Kamaialii.
11-12-1868	KAO [p. 3]	No na hanene, me na haualaoa	Chun		First of two-part on uprising at South Kona and characters responsible.
12-10-1868	KAO [p. 4]	He olelo pane ia S. M. Kamakau			Konakaiopua's response to Kamakau of KAO 11-12. Part one of three.
12-17-1868	KAO [p. 4]	He olelo pane ia S. M. Kamakau			Konakaiopua's response to Kamakau of KAO 11-12. Part two of three.
12-19-1868	KNK [p. 1]	Ka moolelo o Hawaii; Helu 95 [100]	Thrum	Ruling Chiefs, pp. 326–328 (Roman Catholicism in Hawaii).	Thrum's title: "Arrival of Roman Catholics, cont'd."
12-24-1868	KAO [p. 3]	He olelo pane ia S. M. Kamakau			Konakaiopua's response to Kamakau of KAO 11-12. Part three of three.
12-26-1868	KNK [p. 1]	Ka moolelo o Hawaii; Helu 96 [101]	Thrum	Ruling Chiefs, pp. 328–329 (Roman Catholicism in Hawaii).	Thrum's title: "Arrival of Roman Catholics, cont'd."
12-31-1868	KAO [p. 1]	No na hanene, me na haualaoa	Chun		Second of two-part on uprising at South Kona and characters responsible.
1-2-1869	KNK [p. 1]	Ka moolelo o Hawaii; Helu 97 [102]	Thrum	Ruling Chiefs, pp. 329–332 (Roman Catholicism in Hawaii).	Thrum's title: "Views of John Reves; Arrival of French frigate l'Artemese."
1-7-1869	KAO [p. 2]	Ka moolelo Hawaii			Announcing its continuation of Moolelo Hawaii which was printed in KNK.

1-7-1869	KAO [p. 1]	Ka moolelo o Hawaii; Helu 94 [103]	Thrum	*Ruling Chiefs*, pp. 334–339 (Premiership of Kinau).	Kamakau's history series moves to KAO with numbering discrepancies. One installment remains in KNK. Thrum's title: "The king under evil influences of Kaomi; Kinau becomes Premier; Removal of Kaomi."
1-7-1869	KAO [p. 3]	Ua kaawale ke kanawai mare	Chun		
1-9-1869	KNK [p. 1]	Ka moolelo o Hawaii; Helu 98 [104]	Thrum	*Ruling Chiefs*, p. 332 (Roman Catholicism in Hawaii).	Thrum's title: "Laplace secures $20,000 indemnity; Actions of the Protestant Mission."
1-14-1869	KAO [p. 1]	Ka moolelo Hawaii; Helu 99 [105]	Thrum	*Ruling Chiefs*, pp. 339–342 (Premiership of Kinau).	Thrum's title: "Kaomi removal cont'd; Death of Nahienaena; Body taken to Lahaina; The king on Maui."
1-21-1869	KAO [p. 1]	Ka moolelo Hawaii; Helu 100 [106]	Thrum	*Ruling Chiefs*, pp. 342–346 (Premiership of Kinau).	Thrum's title: "Appointment of Richards as king's tutor; Kinau's death and history."
1-28-1869	KAO [p. 1]	Ka moolelo Hawaii; Helu 101 [107]	Thrum	*Ruling Chiefs*, pp. 346–352 (Premiership of Kinau; Troubles under the premiership of Miriam Kekauluohi, 1839–1845).	Thrum's title: "Kinau and Kekuanaoa troubles of 1839."
2-4-1869	KAO [p. 1]	Ka moolelo Hawaii; Helu 102 [108]	Thrum	*Ruling Chiefs*, pp. 352–356 (Troubles under the premiership of Miriam Kekauluohi, 1839–1845).	Thrum's title: "Hoapili's death and history; His conversion to Christianity; Succession of Kekauluohi I to Kinau as Kuhinanui."
2-11-1869	KAO [p. 1]	Ka moolelo Hawaii; Helu 103 [109]	Thrum	*Ruling Chiefs*, pp. 356–359 (Troubles under the premiership of Miriam Kekauluohi, 1839–1845).	Thrum's title: "Kekauluohi, Kuhinanui; Catholic priests and the l'Artemise; Forcible cession of islands to Great Britain, and restoration by Thomas."
2-11-1869	KAO [p. 4]	He olelo hou keia a S. M. Kamakau			Kapihe critique of Kamakau.
2-18-1869	KAO [p. 1]	Ka moolelo Hawaii; Helu 104 [110]	Thrum	*Ruling Chiefs*, pp. 342–346 (Premiership of Kinau).	Thrum's title: "Proceedings with Paulet."

Appendix

2-18-1869	KAO [p. 4]	He olelo hou keia a S. M. Kamakau			Kapihe critque continuation of KAO 2-11.
2-25-1869	KAO	Ka moolelo Hawaii; Helu 105	Thrum		MISSING ISSUE. Also acknowledged as missing by Thrum.
3-4-1869	KAO	Ka moolelo Hawaii; Helu 106	Thrum		MISSING ISSUE. Also acknowledged as missing by Thrum.
3-11-1869	KAO	Ka moolelo Hawaii; Helu 107	Thrum		MISSING ISSUE. Also acknowledged as missing by Thrum.
3-18-1869	KAO [p. 1]	Ka moolelo Hawaii; Helu 108 [111]	Thrum	*Ruling Chiefs*, pp. 332–333 (Roman Catholics in Hawaii).	Thrum's title: "Proceedings with Mallet of French sloop, Embuscade, concerning Catholic priests."
3-25-1869	KAO	Ka moolelo Hawaii; Helu 109	Thrum		MISSING ISSUE. Also acknowledged as missing by Thrum.
4-1-1869	KAO [p. 1]	Ka moolelo Hawaii; Helu 110 [112]	Thrum	*Ruling Chiefs*, pp. 366–368 (A constitutional monarchy, 1839–1845).	Thrum's title: "Departure of the embassy to America and Europe."
4-8-1869	KAO [p. 1]	Ka moolelo Hawaii; Helu 110 [113]	Thrum	*Ruling Chiefs*, pp. 368–369 (A constitutional monarchy, 1839–1845).	Thrum's title: "Negotiations of the ambassadors."
4-15-1869	KAO	Ka moolelo Hawaii; Helu 111	Thrum		MISSING ISSUE. Also acknowledged as missing by Thrum.
4-22-1869	KAO [p. 1]	Ka moolelo Hawaii; Helu 112 [114]	Thrum	*Ruling Chiefs*, pp. 369–370 (A constitutional monarchy, 1839–1845).	Thrum's title: "Hawaiian constitution; Ancient laws and customs; Forming the new laws under constitutional government."
4-29-1869	KAO [p. 1]	Ka moolelo Hawaii; Helu 113 [115]	Thrum	*Ruling Chiefs*, pp. 370–371 (A constitutional monarchy, 1839–1845).	Thrum's title: "Relates to formation of constitutional government of Kamehameha III, 1840."
5-6-1869	KAO [p. 1]	Ka moolelo Hawaii; Helu 114 [116]	Thrum	*Ruling Chiefs*, pp. 371–373 (A constitutional monarchy, 1839–1845).	Thrum's title: "Ancient and modern laws, and methods thereunder compared."

5-13-1869	KAO [p. 1]	Ka moolelo Hawaii; Helu 115 [117]	Thrum	*Ruling Chiefs*, pp. 373–376 (A constitutional monarchy, 1839–1845).	Thrum's title: "Ancient and modern laws, knowledge and customs compared."
5-20-1869	KAO [p. 1]	Ka moolelo Hawaii; Helu 116 [118]	Thrum	*Ruling Chiefs*, pp. 376–378 (A constitutional monarchy, 1839–1845); p. 396 (Legislative Problems, 1845–1852).	Thrum's title: "Changes under constitutional government; Foundation of Legislatures at Lahaina, 1840."
5-27-1869	KAO [p. 1]	Ka moolelo Hawaii; Helu 117 [119]	Thrum	*Ruling Chiefs*, pp. 396–398 (Legislative Problems, 1845–1852).	Thrum's title: "Work of the legislature of 1842."
6-3-1869	KAO [p. 1]	Ka moolelo Hawaii; Helu 118 [120]	Thrum	*Ruling Chiefs*, pp. 379–383 (Passing of the chiefs). Translation, "The story of Kapiolani" in BMA–HEN: Thrum, 171c.	Thrum's title: "Kekauluohi kuhinanui; History of Kapiolani and her works."
6-10-1869	KAO [p. 1]	Ka moolelo Hawaii; Helu 118 [121]	Thrum	*Ruling Chiefs*, pp. 383–386 (Passing of the chiefs). Translation, "The story of Kapiolani" in BMA–HEN: Thrum, 171c.	Thrum's title: "Exemplary works of Kapiolani; Her death; Death of Hoapiliwahine; Her history."
6-17-1869	KAO [p. 1]	Ka moolelo Hawaii; Helu 119 [122]	Thrum	*Ruling Chiefs*, pp. 386–389 (Passing of the chiefs).	Thrum's title: "Biographical sketch of Hoapiliwahine; Death and sketch of Kalua Kuakini."
6-24-1869	KAO [p. 1]	Ka moolelo Hawaii; Helu 120 [123]	Thrum	*Ruling Chiefs*, pp. 389–394 (Passing of the chiefs).	Thrum's title: "Kuakini's chant to Christianity; Death and sketch of Kekauluohi."
7-1-1869	KAO [p. 1]	Ka moolelo Hawaii; Helu 121 [124]	Thrum	*Ruling Chiefs*, pp. 394–395 (Passing of the chiefs); pp. 398–400 (Legislative Problems, 1845–1852).	Thrum's title: "Kamakau's letter to the king continued; Government situation following her death; Kamakau letter to the king."
7-8-1869	KAO [p. 1]	Ka moolelo Hawaii; Helu 122 [125]	Thrum	*Ruling Chiefs*, pp. 400–403 (Legislative Problems, 1845–1852).	Thrum's title: "The government of Kamehameha III; Ministerial reports; W. Richards as minister of public instruction."

APPENDIX

Date	Source	Title	Translator	Reference	Notes
7-15-1869	KAO [p. 1]	Ka moolelo Hawaii; Helu 122 [126]	Thrum	*Ruling Chiefs*, pp. 403–406 (Legislative Problems, 1845–1852).	Thrum's title: "Appointment of Richards as king's tutor; Kinau's death and history."
7-22-1869	KAO [p. 1]	Ka moolelo Hawaii; Helu 123 [127]	Thrum	*Ruling Chiefs*, pp. 406–407 (Legislative Problems, 1845–1852).	Thrum's title: "Progress of education; Sundry schools established; Sketch of W. Richards, first minister of public instruction."
7-29-1869	KAO [p. 1]	Ka moolelo Hawaii; Helu 123 [128]	Thrum	*Ruling Chiefs*, pp. 407–409 (Legislative Problems, 1845–1852); this appears to be only a partial translation of these events which includes the following two installments as well, but which were not acknowledged in the footnoting of the book.	Thrum's title: "Legislature of 1847; Report of John Ricord, attorney-general."
7-29-1869	KAO [p. 2]	Ka aha kiekie			Kamakau sworn in at court to explain practice of hanai of old times.
8-5-1869	KAO [p. 1]	Ka moolelo Hawaii; Helu 124 [129]	Thrum	*Ruling Chiefs*, pp. 407–409 (Legislative Problems, 1845–1852).	Thrum's title: "Legislature of 1847; Report of Keoni Ana, minister of the interior."
8-12-1869	KAO [p. 1]	Ka moolelo Hawaii; Helu 125 [130]	Thrum	*Ruling Chiefs*, pp. 407–409 (Legislative Problems, 1845–1852).	Thrum's title: "Keoni Ana's report continued; Comparative considerations of ancient knowledge and ability."
8-19-1869	KAO [p. 1]	Ka moolelo Hawaii; Helu 126 [131]	Thrum	*Ruling Chiefs*, pp. 409–411 (Legislative Problems, 1845–1852).	Thrum's title: "Considerations, continued; Laws established; The cabinet; Government acts, 1848–1850."
8-26-1869	KAO [p. 1]	Ka moolelo Hawaii; Helu 127 [132]	Thrum	*Ruling Chiefs*, pp. 411–412 (Legislative Problems, 1845–1852).	Thrum's title: "Catholic troubles considered; Hawaii losing her good qualities; Progress of the government."
9-2-1869	KAO [p. 1]	Ka moolelo Hawaii; Helu 128 [133]	Thrum	*Ruling Chiefs*, pp. 412–414 (Legislative Problems, 1845–1852).	Thrum's title: "Progress of the government, continued; Agricultural effort establishing; Legislative proceedings."

9-9-1869	KAO [p. 1]	Ka moolelo Hawaii; Helu 129 [134]	Thrum	*Ruling Chiefs*, pp. 414–417 (Legislative problems, 1845–1852; Death of Kamehameha III). *Ka poe kahiko*, pp. 105–106 (The medical profession, class 2: kahuna paaoao and kahuna ea).	Thrum's title: "The new constitution of 1852; Introduction of the smallpox, 1853; Scarcity of doctors; Hawaiians' treatment successful."
9-16-1869	KAO [p. 1]	Ka moolelo Hawaii; Helu 130 [135]	Thrum	*Ruling Chiefs*, pp. 417–420 (Death of Kamehameha III).	Thrum's title: "Important events of 1854; Closing days of Kamehameha III."
9-23-1869	KAO [p. 1]	Ka moolelo Hawaii; Helu 131 [136]	Thrum	*Ruling Chiefs*, pp. 420–424 (Death of Kamehameha III).	Thrum's title: "Some contrasts considered; The king at Koolau; Returns to Honolulu: His illness and death; Progress of Hawaii under his reign."
9-30-1869	KAO [p. 1]	Ka moolelo Hawaii; Helu 131 [137]	Thrum	*Ruling Chiefs*, pp. 424–427 (Death of Kamehameha III).	Thrum's title: "Progress of Hawaii under Kamehameha III, continued."
10-7-1869	KAO [p. 1]	Ka moolelo Hawaii; Helu 132 [138]	Thrum	*Ruling Chiefs*, pp. 427–428 (Death of Kamehameha III).	Thrum's title: "Benefits under constitutional government; Seven granted under Kamehameha III."
10-14-1869	KAO [p. 1]	Ka moolelo Hawaii; Helu 133 [139]	Thrum	*Ruling Chiefs*, pp. 428–430 (Death of Kamehameha III).	Thrum's title: "Benefits under ancient mois, and how Kamehameha III came to the throne." This is the last of Kamakau's series concerning the chiefs.
10-14-1869	KAO [p. 1]	Ka moolelo Hawaii; Mokuna 1	Thrum	*Na moolelo o ka poe kahiko*, pp. 124–129 (The origin of Hawaii nei; Origin of the Hawaiian people). Typescript and holograph translation, "On the formation of the Hawaiian Islands" in BMA-HEN: Thrum 171a.	This new series follows the ending of the other, with a brief explanation separating the two. Thrum's title: "Origin of the islands and their people." There is a collection of the original articles of this series in BMA Case 4, L16.

10-21-1869	KAO [p. 1]	Ka moolelo Hawaii; Helu 2	Thrum	*Na moolelo a ka poe kahiko*, pp. 129–140 (The origin of Hawaiian people; The first man mentioned in Hawaii; Of the generations after Wakea; The Ulu genealogy; Kapawa; Heleipawa; Aikanaka; Ulu-Hema Genealogy). Typescript and holograph translation, "On the formation of the Hawaiian Islands" in BMA–HEN: Thrum 171a.	Thrum's title: "Original name of different islands; First man created by Kane, Ku and Lono tradition."
10-28-1869	KAO [p. 1]	Ka moolelo Hawaii; Helu 3	Thrum	*Na moolelo a ka poe kahiko*, pp. 140–154 (Hema; Kahainuiahema; Wahieloa; Laka; Luanuu; Huaapohukaina; Pauahua; Huaapau; Paumakua; The Hema line; The original chiefs; Signs of chieftainship).	Thrum's title: "Hema; Kahai; Wahieloa; Laka; Luanuu; Hua (2) Paumakua; Hanalaanui and iki; Circumcision and Aha ili introduced."
11-4-1869	KAO [p. 1]	Ka moolelo Hawaii; Helu 4	Thrum	*Na hana a ka poe kahiko*, pp. 3–6 (The cardinal points; The horizons; Space). *Na moolelo a ka poe kahiko*, pp. 154–159 (Signs of chieftainship; Aha kapu alii).	Thrum's title: "Signs by the elements on birth of royalty; Instances named; Their establishment and kind."
11-11-1869	KAO [p. 1]	Ka moolelo Hawaii; Helu 5	Thrum	*Na hana a ka poe kahiko*, pp. 6–13 (Land divisions; The mountains; Mountain zones; Hills and cliffs; Roadways; The waters; The seas; The waves; The tides). Partial translation, "The short digging tool" in BMA–HEN: Nwsp-KAO 11-11-1869.	Thrum's title: "Divisions of the lands; shore portions; cultivable sections."

11-18-1869	KAO [p. 1]	Ka moolelo Hawaii; Helu 6	Thrum	*Na hana a ka poe kahiko*, pp. 23–32 (Mahiai ana: Cultivation of sweet potatoes, cultivation of taro).	Thrum's title: "Potato culture descibed; Prayers to the gods; Kanepuaa; Other cultures."
11-25-1869	KAO [p. 1]	Ka moolelo Hawaii; Helu 7	Thrum	*Na hana a ka poe kahiko*, pp. 32–40 (Mahiai ana: Cultivation of taro; pond field: Loi, Prayers and rituals; Cultivation of bananas; Cultivation of sugar cane; Cultivation of fish).	Thrum's title: "Wet taro culture; preparation of the loi; Bananas; Sugar cane and wauke."
12-2-1869	KAO [p. 1]	Ka moolelo Hawaii; Helu 8	Thrum	*Na hana a ka poe kahiko*, pp. 40–45 (Mahiai ana: Cultivation of wauke; Cutlivation of Awa; Cultivation of olona); pp. 47–48 (Mahiai ana: Cultivation of fish).	Thrum's title: "Cultivating awa and olona; Fish pond construction; Noted ponds."
12-9-1869	KAO [p. 1]	Ka moolelo Hawaii; Helu 9	Thrum	*Na hana a ka poe kahiko*, pp. 46–50 (The cultivation of bitter gourds; Cultivation of fish); pp. 117–122 (Making of Fishnets; Canoe making).	Thrum's title: "Fish pond construction, continued; Canoe building."
12-16-1869	KAO [p. 1]	Ka moolelo Hawaii; Helu 10	Thrum	*Na hana a ka poe kahiko*, pp. 59–66 (Methods of fishing: Bag nets; Bag net fishing with melomelo stick; Kaka uhu fishing).	Thrum's title: "Fishing with nets and seines; Ancient kaka uhu fishing."
12-23-1869	KAO [p. 1]	Ka moolelo Hawaii; Helu 11	Thrum	*Na hana a ka poe kahiko*, pp. 66–72 (Methods of fishing: Kaka uhu fishing; Upena Kaka uhu; Fishing with lures; Okilo hee; O hee; Aku fishing).	Thrum's title: "Catching squid of various kinds; Hiaku."
12-30-1869	KAO [p. 1]	Ka moolelo Hawaii; Helu 12	Thrum	*Na hana a ka poe kahiko*, pp. 72–79 (Methods of fishing: Aku fishing; Aku lure; Deep sea fishing).	Thrum's title: "Various kinds of fishing and implements."

Appendix

1-6-1870	KAO [p. 1]	Ka moolelo Hawaii; Helu 13	Thrum	*Na hana a ka poe kahiko*, pp. 79–86 (Methods of fishing: Baits and traps; Hinai hinalea; Hinai puhi; Hinai palani; Hinai kala; Unusual ways of fishing).	Thrum's title: "Basket fishing; Seizing with the hand."
1-13-1870	KAO [p. 1]	Ka moolelo Hawaii; Helu 14	Thrum	*Na hana a ka poe kahiko*, pp. 79–86 (Methods of fishing…); pp. 95–99 (House building: The framework).	Thrum's title: "Catching eels and sharks; House building; Affixing the ahos."
1-20-1870	KAO [p. 1]	Ka moolelo Hawaii; Helu 15	Thrum	*Na hana a ka poe kahiko*, pp. 99–108 (House building…).	Thrum's title: "Thatching; The openings; Trimming the doorway and its ceremony."
1-27-1870	KAO [p. 1]	Ka moolelo Hawaii; Helu 16	Thrum	*Na hana a ka poe kahiko*, pp. 108–116 (House building; Making tapa…); pp. 122–123 (The skills of yesterday gone today).	Thrum's title: "Plaited Hawaiian cloth originally; Kapa making from wauke bark."
2-3-1870	KAO [p. 1]	Ka moolelo Hawaii; Helu 17	Thrum	*Ka poe kahiko*, pp. 25–27 (Marriage; Rearing of children). *Na hana a ka poe kahiko*, pp. 116–117 (Tapa making; Aumakua of the tapa maker; How fire was obtained).	Thrum's title: "Kapa making, continued; Net and twine making; Procuring fire; Care of children."
2-10-1870	KAO [p. 1]	Ka moolelo Hawaii; Helu 18	Thrum	*Ka poe kahiko*, p. 27 (Rearing of children). *Na hana a ka poe kahiko*, pp. 13–18 (The reckoning of time; The seasons; The months; The days; The kapu periods).	Thrum's title: "Birth and consecration of children; Divisions of the year; Names of the months."
2-17-1870	KAO [p. 1]	Ka moolelo Hawaii; Helu 19	Thrum	*Ka poe kahiko*, pp. 19–21 (The makahiki festival). *Na hana a ka poe kahiko*, pp. 17–18 (The days); pp. 132–135 (Heiaus).	Thrum's title: "Annual festivals; Of heiaus; Koas, ipu olono; Pookanaka; Their construction."
2-24-1870	KAO [p. 1]	Ka moolelo Hawaii; Helu 20	Thrum	*Na hana a ka poe kahiko*, pp. 135–141 (Heiaus; Haku ohia rites; Aha kai rituals).	Thrum's title: "Heiaus, continued; The hakuohia; His functions in heiau building; Ceremonies."

3-3-1870	KAO [p. 1]	Ka moolelo Hawaii; Helu 21	Thrum	*Ka poe kahiko*, pp. 32–33 (Pohaku o Kane). *Na hana a ka poe kahiko*, pp. 141–144 (Aha kai rituals; Hono ritual; Heiaus of Hawaii).	Thrum's title: "Heiau ceremonies, continued; Closing day of sacrifice; Pohakuokane; Places of refuge."
3-10-1870	KAO [p. 1]	Ka moolelo Hawaii; Helu 22	Thrum	*Ka poe kahiko*, p. 11 (Kanawai; Laws and edicts); pp. 17–19 (Puuhonua). *Na hana a ka poe kahiko*, p. 145 (Heiaus of Hawaii).	Thrum's title: "List of heiaus; Places of refuge; Laws relating thereto."
3-17-1870	KAO [p. 1]	Ka moolelo Hawaii; Helu 23	Thrum	*Ka poe kahiko*, pp. 11–15 (Kanawai; Laws and edicts; Some kanawai of gods and chiefs).	Thrum's title: "Human sacrifices; Ancient laws; Kapus; Penalties, etc.; The niaupio kalowalo of Kualii; A beneficent law; Kualii's death at Kailua, Oahu, aged 175."
3-24-1870	KAO [p. 1]	Ka moolelo Hawaii; Helu 24	Thrum	*Ka poe kahiko*, pp. 15–17 (Kanawai; Laws and edicts; Some kanawai of gods and chiefs); pp. 63–66 (Hosts of heaven and earth; Volcanic manifestations–Pele).	Thrum's title: "The Mamalahoa law; The gods and worshiping the host of heaven."
3-31-1870	KAO [p. 1]	Ka moolelo Hawaii; Helu 25	Thrum	*Ka poe kahiko*, pp. 60–70 (Volcanic manifestations–Pele; Thunder and lightning forms). Partial typescript of translation in notes on, "Tattooing" in BMA-HEN: vol. 1, pp. 1289–1291.	Thrum's title: "Deities of Pele and traditions thereof; Of thunder and lightning; Kanehekili."
4-7-1870	KAO [p. 1]	Ka moolelo Hawaii; Helu 26	Thrum	*Ka poe kahiko*, pp. 70–74 (Thunder and lightning forms; Shark forms).	Thrum's title: "Kanehekili traditions; Spirits of deceased persons to assume electrical powers; Traditions thereof; Humans changing to shark deities."
4-14-1870	KAO [p. 1]	Ka moolelo Hawaii; Helu 27	Thrum	*Ka poe kahiko*, pp. 74–77 (Shark forms).	Thrum's title: "Sundry shark traditions; Worshiping sharks."
4-21-1870	KAO [p. 1]	Ka moolelo Hawaii; Helu 28	Thrum	*Ka poe kahiko*, pp. 77–81. Not acknowledged in the footnotes of this book.	Thrum's title: "Shark worship, continued; Their diefication; Traditions thereof."

4-28-1870	KAO [p. 1]	Ka moolelo Hawaii; Helu 29	Thrum	*Ka poe kahiko*, pp. 81–86 (Shark forms; Moo forms). Incorrectly acknowledged in this book.	Thrum's title: "Relating to lizard deities and worship and assuming lizard form."
5-5-1870	KAO [p. 1]	Ka moolelo Hawaii; Helu 30	Thrum	*Ka poe kahiko*, pp. 86–89 (Moo forms).	Thrum's title: "Ceremonies and traditions of lizard superstitions, etc."
5-12-1870	KAO [p. 1]	Ka moolelo Hawaii; Helu 31	Thrum	*Ka poe kahiko*, pp. 89–90 (Kapus of consecration); pp. 128–130 (Sorcery gods of Molokai; Coming of the Kalaipahoa gods).	Thrum's title: "Divisions of minor kapus; Of Kalaipahoa and Kapo."
5-19-1870	KAO [p. 1]	Ka moolelo Hawaii; Helu 32	Thrum	*Ka poe kahiko*, pp. 130–132 (Sorcery gods of Molokai; Coming of the Kalaipahoa gods).	Thrum's title: "Kalaipahoa continued; Molokai's fame for evil doing and sorcery."
7-14-1870	KAO [p. 1]	Ka moolelo Hawaii; Helu 33	Thrum	*Ka poe kahiko*, pp. 132–135 (Pua ma; Akua kumuhaka); pp. 137–138 (Kamehameha's care of the Kalaipahoa and Pua gods).	Thrum's title: "Molokai matters, continued; Kamehameha's care of Kalaipahoa and Pua gods."
7-21-1870	KAO [p. 1]	Ka moolelo Hawaii; Helu 34	Thrum	*Ka poe kahiko*, pp. 119–120 (Anaana magic); pp. 135–138 (Kamehameha's care of the Kalaipahoa and Pua gods).	Thrum's title: "Kamehameha worships Kalaipahoa and crowns it; Praying to death."
8-4-1870	KAO [p. 1]	Ka moolelo Hawaii; Helu 35	Thrum	*Ka poe kahiko*, pp. 120–124 (Anaana magic; Divisions of anaana); p. 133 (Pua ma).	Thrum's title: "Ceremonies of the pule anaana; Divisions therein; Sundry kahuna."
8-11-1870	KAO [p. 1]	Ka moolelo Hawaii; Helu 36	Thrum	*Ka poe kahiko*, pp. 98–99 (The medical profession, class 1: Kahuna hoohapai keiki and hoohanau keiki); pp. 124–128 (The divisions of anaana).	Thrum's title: "Sundry prayers; Medical kahunas."

8-18-1870	KAO [p. 1]	Ka moolelo Hawaii; Helu 37	Thrum	*Ka poe kahiko*, pp. 99–104 (The medical profession, class 1: Kahuna hoohapai keiki and hoohanau keiki; Class 2: Kahuna paaoao and kahuna ea).	Thrum's title: "Medical kahunas, continued."
8-25-1870	KAO [p. 1]	Ka moolelo Hawaii; Helu 38	Thrum	*Ka poe kahiko*, pp. 101–105 (The medical profession, class 2: Kahuna paaoao and kahuna ea).	Thrum's title: "List of remedies for ailments; Instances in aid of offspring; Haha kahunas."
9-1-1870	KAO [p. 1]	Ka moolelo Hawaii; Helu 39	Thrum	*Ka poe kahiko*, pp. 107–109 (The medical profession, class 4: Kahuna haha).	Thrum's title: "Lonopuha and other kahuna schools."
9-15-1870	KAO [p. 1]	Ka moolelo Hawaii; Helu 40	Thrum	*Ka poe kahiko*, pp. 95–97 (Kahuna aumakua); pp. 102–103, 105 (The medical profession, Class 2: Kahuna Paaoao and Kahuna ea); p. 109 (Class 4: Kahuna haha); pp. 138–140 (Remedies for illness sent by Pua ma; Remedies of the kahuna anaana).	Thrum's title: "Various medical schools and remedies."
9-22-1870	KAO [p. 1]	Ka moolelo Hawaii; Helu 41	Thrum	*Ka poe kahiko*, pp. 28–29 (Aumakua ancestral dieties); p. 97 (Kahuna aumakua); pp. 109–114 (Class 4: Kahuna haha). Translation, in "Of ancestral spirits—their true source" in BMA–HEN: Thrum 132–199; continued on 9-29-1870; 171b.	Thrum's title: "Sundry remedies; Ancient medicines; Aumakuas and kumupaa."

9-29-1870	KAO [p. 1]	Ka moolelo Hawaii; Helu 42	Thrum	*Ka poe kahiko*, pp. 28–29 (Aumakua ancestral dieties); pp. 33–34 (Customs at death); pp. 36–38 (Kuni rituals); pp. 97–98 (Kahuna aumakua). Partial translation, in "Tattooing" in BMA–HEN: vol. 1, 1289–1291. Typescript of translation, 9-29-1870; 171b. "Of ancestral spirits—their true source" in BMA–HEN: Thrum 132–199; 171b.	Thrum's title: "Aumakuas, etc., continued; Approaching death; Sorcery and provisioning the dead; Treatment thereof."
10-6-1870	KAO [p. 1]	Ka moolelo Hawaii; Helu 43	Thrum	*Ka poe kahiko*, pp. 34–35 (Customs at death); pp. 38–44 (Disposal of corpses; Death); pp. 47–50 (The three spirit realms). Typescript of Hawaiian and translation, "Customs at death" in BMA–HEN: Thrum 171b.	Thrum's title: "Treatment of the dead, continued; The nupa or deep pit; Dr. John Pelham of Waimea, Hawaii; The spirit after death; Superstitions."
10-13-1870	KAO [p. 1]	Ka moolelo Hawaii; Helu 44	Thrum	*Ka poe kahiko*, pp. 50–55 (The three spirit realms). Typescript of Hawaiian and translation, "Beliefs and customs at death" in BMA–HEN: Thrum 171b.	Thrum's title: "The realm of Milu; Myths of Mokulehua; Maluae and Kawelu; Spirits resting on the living; Instances narrated."
10-20-1870	KAO [p. 1]	Ka moolelo Hawaii; Helu 45	Thrum	*Ka poe kahiko*, pp. 29–32 (The aumakua: ancestral dieties; Hoaumakua: the acquiring and contacting aumakua); pp. 55–59 (Noho ana: Medium possession; Visions and dreams). Typescript of Hawaiian and translation, "Ancestral spirits, dreams, sacrificing to ancestral gods" in BMA–HEN: Thrum 171b.	Thrum's title: "Trance, visions, and dreams; Ancestral spirits (aumakuas); The depression thereunder."

10-27-1870	KAO [p. 1]	Ka moolelo Hawaii; Helu 46	Thrum	*Ka poe kahiko*, pp. 3–6 (Ka poe kahiko: degrees of chiefs); pp. 59–60 (Akua aumakua: the aumakua gods). Typescript of Hawaiian and translation, "Ancestral spirits" in BMA–HEN: Thrum 171b.	Thrum's title: "Of ancient chiefs; Their several ranks."
11-3-1870	KAO [p. 1]	Ka moolelo Hawaii; Helu 47	Thrum	*Ruling Chiefs*, pp. 1–2 (Story of Umi); *Ka poe kahiko*, pp. 7–10 (Kahuna orders; Classes of people; Kapus of the chiefs).	Thrum's title: "Boards of priests, prophets; Grades of the people; Kapus of aliis and the gods; History of certain kings, notably Liloa; His heiau construction in various places."
11-10-1870	KAO [p. 1]	Ka moolelo Hawaii; Helu 48	Thrum	*Ruling Chiefs*, pp. 3–7 (Story of Umi).	Thrum's title: "Liloa meets Akahiakuleana who becomes mother of Umi; Her history; Umi visits Waipio and makes himself known to Liloa...."
11-17-1870	KAO [p. 1]	Ka moolelo Hawaii; Helu 49	Thrum	*Ruling Chiefs*, pp. 8–12 (Story of Umi).	Thrum's title: "Hakau shows disapproval; History of Umialiloa."
11-24-1870	KAO [p. 1]	Ka moolelo Hawaii; Helu 50	Thrum	*Ruling Chiefs*, pp. 12–17 (Story of Umi).	Thrum's title: "History of Umi, continued; Battles with and defeats Hakau; He wars against Hilo chiefs and conquers that district."
12-1-1870	KAO [p. 1]	Ka moolelo Hawaii; Helu 51	Thrum	*Ruling Chiefs*, pp. 17–23 (Story of Umi; Story of Kihaapiilani).	Thrum's title: "He overcomes Huaa and annexes Puna; Imaikalani the blind king of Kau; Ehunuikaimalina, king of Kona; Kihaapiilani joins forces with Umi and wages war on Maui."

APPENDIX

12-8-1870	KAO [p. 1]	Ka moolelo Hawaii; Helu 52	Thrum	*Ruling Chiefs*, pp. 23–27 (Story of Kihaapiilani).	Thrum's title: "Kihaapiilani in Makawao incognito; Scarcity of food; He settles at Hana; Surf-riding contest; Wins the affianced of Lonaapiilani; Her father disowns her; Division of land sought; Is promised subject to fealty to Lono; Kihaapiilani seeks aid on Hawaii and falls in with Piikea of Umi's household."
12-15-1870	KAO [p. 1]	Ka moolelo Hawaii; Helu 53	Thrum	*Ruling Chiefs*, pp. 27–33 (Story of Kihaapiilani).	Thrum's title: "Kihaapiilani visits Piikea; Declines Umi's offer to settle on Hawaii; Fights for his rights on Maui against Lonoapiilani; Holoae defender of Kauiki escapes; His reported death of some doubt; Death and secret burial of Lonoapiilani; Kihaapiilani divides land; Umi returns to Hawaii; Stones hewn for his tomb; Dies at Kailua; Koi set out to conceal his body; Kills a man resembling the king and substitutes the body."
12-15-1870	KAO [p. 3]	Pane ia S. M. Kamakau			Critique of Kamakau by Haule.
12-22-1870	KAO [p. 1]	Ka moolelo Hawaii; Helu 54	Thrum	*Ruling Chiefs*, pp. 33–38 (Story of Kihaapiilani; Story of Keawenuiaumi).	Thrum's title: "Koi secretes the bones of Umi; Chief of Hawaii after Umi's time; War between Hilo and Kona; Death of Kealiiokaloa; History of Pakaa, famous canoeist; Through intrigue Keawenuiaumi disrates him, so he secretly departs and dwells on Molokai; Keawenuiaumi searches for Pakaa."
12-29-1870	KAO [p. 1]	Ka moolelo Hawaii; Helu 55	Thrum	*Ruling Chiefs*, pp. 38–43 (Story of Keawenuiaumi).	Thrum's title: "Canoes built to search for him; Diviners sought to locate him; Keawenuiaumi sets out in search; Visits Maui and Molokai; Kuapakaa is introduced; One having knowledge of all winds."

1-5-1871	KAO [p. 1]	Ka moolelo Hawaii; Helu 56	Thrum	*Ruling Chiefs*, pp. 43–45 (Story of Keawenuiaumi).	Thrum's title: "Canoe fleet of Keawenuiaumi meets disaster; Pakaa and son follow their chief to Molokai; Takes charge of all food, clothing, etc.; Food given out; Ku directs lunas to secure supply; After three months they set out for a long voyage and are lost; The chief returns and sees Pakaa; Death of Keawenuiaumi and division of land."
1-12-1871	KAO [p. 1]	Ka moolelo Hawaii; Helu 57	Thrum	*Ruling Chiefs*, pp. 45–48 (Story of Keawenuiaumi; Story of Lonoikamakahiki).	Thrum's title: "Chiefs of Kona; Kanaloakuaana, Lonoikamakahiki; Lonoikamakahiki and Kaikilani; Tradition of Lonoikamakahiki's tour; Domestic troubles; In his demented state, he is cared for by Kapaihiahilina."
1-19-1871	KAO [p. 1]	Ka moolelo Hawaii; Helu 58	Thrum	*Ruling Chiefs*, pp. 48–54 (Story of Lonoikamakahiki).	Thrum's title: "Returning to Hawaii Kapaihiahilina is made chamberlain; He chants the king's experiences; Lonoikamakahiki starts on regal tour of the islands; Is entertained on Maui; His insignia a mammoth kahili called Hawaiiloa."
1-26-1871	KAO [p. 1]	Ka moolelo Hawaii; Helu 59	Thrum	*Ruling Chiefs*, pp. 54–59 (Story of Lonoikamakahiki). Partial translation in notes on "Tattooing" in BMA–HEN: vol. 1, pp. 1289–1291.	Thrum's title: "Lonoikamakahiki visits Molokai; Becoming jealous he strikes Kaikilani, his wife, and sails for Oahu; Meets a princess of Kauai and learns the latest name chant which in a contest he repeats; Visits Kauai, etc., then returns to Kona and enjoys friendship treaty made with all the aliis; Treaty broken by Kamalalawalu of Maui, who invades and wars on Hawaii."

Appendix

Date	Source	Title		Reference	Notes
2-2-1871	KAO [p. 1]	Ka moolelo Hawaii; Helu 60	Thrum	*Ruling Chiefs*, pp. 59–65 (Story of Lonoikamakahiki; Keawe's Reign).	Thrum's title: "Engagement between Puapuakea and Makahukilani; The latter killed in battle between Hawaii and Maui forces; Kamalalawalu is killed and Kauhiakama reigns in his stead; Kings of Hawaii after Lonoikamakahiki's death; Internal wars on Hawaii; Keawe comes to the throne."
3-1-1873	KNK [pp. 1–2]	Ke kulana o ke aupuni Hawaii i ke au ia Kamehameha I	Chun	Translation, "The kingdom of Hawaii in the reign of Kamehameha I" in BMA-HEN: vol. 1, pp. 2683–2686. Typescript and translation, "The politics of the Hawaiian government during the time of Kamehameha I" in Chun 1988, pp. 33–38.	Discusses role of Kaahumanu in the building of the kingdom of Hawaii.
4-5-1873	KNK [pp. 2–3]	Ka hooululauai kanaka a me ka hoopiha hou ana i ka lahui Hawaii	Chun		First of two ending on 4-12.
4-12-1873	KNK [p. 1]	Ka hooululauai kanaka a me ka hoopiha hou ana i ka lahui Hawaii	Chun		Second of two, starting on 4-5.
8-20-1873	HP [p. 3]	Huikau, pohihihi ke kuikahi panai like me ka uku kaulele o Puuloa			Decrying possible sale of lands of Puuloa.
11-25-1873	KNH [p. 3]	Na papa alii kiekie			On ranks and genealogy.
12-23-1873	KNH [p. 3]	Ka papa alii o Hawaii i hoonoho pono ia			Unauna (probably) critique of Kamakau's genealogy of KNH 11-25-1873. Bolstering Kalakaua's position. First part of four?

| 221 |

12-30-1873	KNH [p. 3]	Ka papa alii o Hawaii i hoonoho pono ia				Unauna (probably) critique of Kamakau's genealogy of KNH 11-25-1873. Second part of four?
1-6-1874	KNH [p. 3]	Ka papa alii o Hawaii i hoonoho pono ia				Unauna (probably) critique of Kamakau's genealogy of KNH 11-25-1873. Third part of four? Continuation not found.
1-31-1874	NKAO [p. 3]	Ka mookuauhau alii o ka moiwahine Kaleleonalani	Chun	Translation, "Royal genealogy of Queen Kaleleonalani, showing her relationship to Kamehameha I" in BMA–HEN: vol. 1, pp. 2993–2995.		Genealogy of Queen Emma.
2-3-1874	KNH [p. 5]	Untitled; "E ka Nuhou Hawaii; Aloha oe…"				Unauna denies Kamakau's Emma genealogy in KAO 1-31.
2-7-1874	NKAO [p. 3]	Hopuhopualulu maoli				Political article.
2-10-1874	KNH [p. 6]	Untitled; "E ka Nuhou Hawaii; Aloha oe…"				Unauna's denial of Kamakau of KNH 2-3 is reprinted in full.
9-17-1875	TI [pp. 194–195]	Mele; composed in honor of Kualii		Mele in English and Hawaiian; Explanatory notes in English; Another copy of this mele in Journal of the Polynesian Society, Volume 2, pp. 160–178; Also Vol. 5, p. 70 of the 1896 Journal contains another explanatory note.		First of seven parts of a 600-line chant for Kualii. According to article in Journal of the Polynesian Society, Curtis J. Lyons undertook the task of translating this piece with the assistance of Kamakau.
9-24-1875	TI [pp. 202–203]	A song for Kualii				Second of seven parts of a 600-line chant for Kualii.
10-1-1875	TI [pp. 210–211]	A song for Kualii				Third of seven parts of a 600-line chant for Kualii.
10-8-1875	TI [pp. 217–218]	A song for Kualii				Fourth of seven parts of a 600-line chant for Kualii.

10-15-1875	TI [pp. 225–227]	A song for Kualii			Fifth of seven parts of a 600-line chant for Kualii.
10-22-1875	TI [pp. 230–233]	A song for Kualii			Sixth of seven parts of a 600-line chant for Kualii.
10-29-1875	TI [pp. 239–241]	A song for Kualii			Last of seven parts of a 600-line chant for Kualii.
10-30-1875	NKAO [p. 4]	He manawa haowale anei keia?			Responds to letter from Kamehameha also appearing in this issue.
12-25-1880	NKAO [p. 1]	Ka moolelo o Kaahumanu			First of three parts on Kaahumanu. Released long after his death.
1-1-1881	NKAO [p. 5]	Ka moolelo o Kaahumanu			Second of three parts on Kaahumanu. Released long after his death.
1-15-1881	NKAO [p. 1]	Ka moolelo o Kaahumanu			Last of three parts on Kaahumanu. Released long after his death.

References

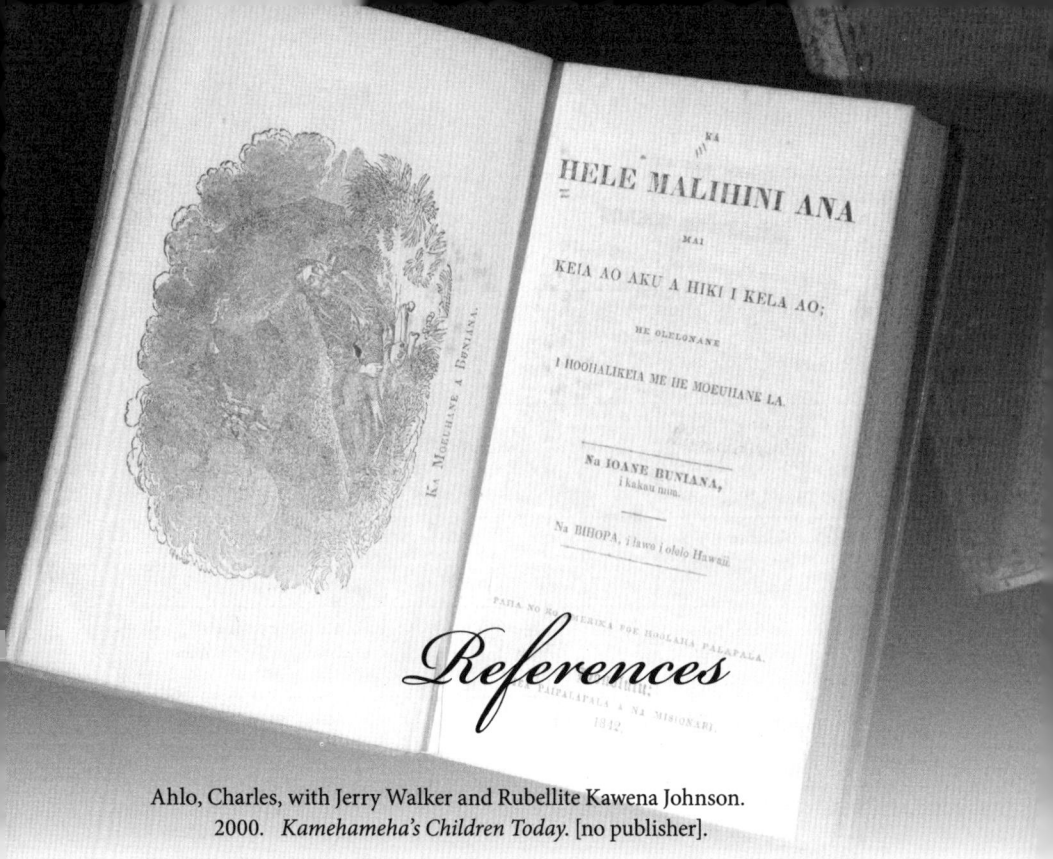

Ahlo, Charles, with Jerry Walker and Rubellite Kawena Johnson.
    2000. *Kamehameha's Children Today*. [no publisher].

Akana, Collette Leimomi.
    2002. Kahuna Hoʻopunipuni Letters of 1863. *The Hawaiian Journal of History* 36:1–39.

Aldrich, Robert.
    1990. *The French Presence in the South Pacific: 1842–1940*. Honolulu: University of Hawaiʻi Press. Quoted in Paul Deschanel, *La Politique Française En Océanie: A Propos du Canal de Panama* (Paris: Berger-Levrault Et Cie, 1884), 1.

Andrews, Lorrin.
    1835. ABCFM Report. Quoted in Albert J. Schütz, *The Voices of Eden* (Honolulu: University of Hawaiʻi Press, 1994), 171.

    2003 [1865]. *A Dictionary of the Hawaiian Language*. Honolulu: Island Heritage Publishing.

Andrews, Lorrin, and Henry H. Parker.
    1922. *A Dictionary of the Hawaiian Language*. Honolulu: The Board of Commissioners of Public Archives of the Territory of Hawaii.

Ashford, Marguerite K.
    1987. The Evolution of the Hawaiian Dictionary and Notes on the Early Compilers, with Particular Attention to Manuscript Resources of the Bishop Museum Library. *Bishop Museum Occasional Papers* 27:1–24.

Bacchilega, Cristina.
    2007. *Legendary Hawai'i and the Politics of Place: Tradition, Translation, and Tourism*. Philadelphia: University of Pennsylvania Press.

Barrère, Dorothy B.
    1964. Foreword. In *Ka Po'e Kahiko: The People of Old*, Samuel M. Kamakau, trans. Mary Kawena Pukui, ed. Dorothy B. Barrère, vii–viii. Honolulu: Bishop Museum Press.

    1987 [1976]. Preface. In *The Works of the People of Old: Na Hana a ka Po'e Kahiko*, Samuel M. Kamakau, trans. Mary Kawena Pukui, ed. Dorothy B. Barrère, v–vi. Honolulu: Bishop Museum Press.

    1991. Preface. In *Tales and Traditions of the People of Old: Na Mo'olelo a ka Po'e Kahiko*, Samuel M. Kamakau, trans. Mary Kawena Pukui, ed. Dorothy B. Barrère, ix–x. Honolulu: Bishop Museum Press.

Barieant-Schiller, R.
    1993. Review of *Anahulu: The Anthropology of History in the Kingdom of Hawai'i, Volume 1*, by Patrick V. Kirch and Marshall Sahlins. *Choice: Current Reviews for Academic Libraries* 30(10):1169.

Barker, John.
    1987. Review of *Kingship and Sacrifice: Ritual and Society in Ancient Hawai'i*, by Valerio Valeri, trans. Paula Wissing. *Pacific Affairs* 60(1):157–159.

    1996. Review of *How "Natives" Think: About Captain Cook, For Example*, by Marshall Sahlins. *Pacific Affairs* 69(2):297–299.

Bassnett, Susan.
    1997. Intricate Pathways: Observations on Translation and Literature. In *Essays and Studies*, ed. Susan Bassnett, 1–13. Cambridge: D. S. Brewer.

Beckwith, Martha Warren.
    1978 [1932]. Introduction. In *Kepelino's Traditions of Hawaii*, Zephryn Kepelino Kahoali'ikūmai'eiwakamoku Keauokalani, trans. Martha Warren Beckwith, 3–7. Milwood, NY: Kraus Reprint Co.

    1939. Proposed Introduction to History of Hawaii, Part 2: Traditional Beliefs and Customs (ultimately divided into the three texts). MS SC Kamakau, Box 8.1. Bishop Museum Archives, Bernice Pauahi Bishop Museum, Honolulu, HI.

    1949a. Letter to Caroline Curtis of July 18. MS SC Kamakau, Box 11.3. Bishop Museum Archives, Bernice Pauahi Bishop Museum, Honolulu, HI.

    1949b. Letter to Caroline Curtis of Aug. 14. MS SC Kamakau, Box 11.3. Bishop Museum Archives, Bernice Pauahi Bishop Museum, Honolulu, HI.

Bickerton, Derek, and William H. Wilson.
    1987. Pidgin Hawaiian. In *Pidgin and Creole Languages: Essays in Memory of John E. Reinecke*, ed. Glenn G. Gilbert, 61–76. Honolulu: University of Hawai'i Press.

Biersack, Aletta.
    1991. Introduction: History and Theory in Anthropology. In *Clio in Oceania: Toward a Historical Anthropology*, ed. Aletta Biersack, 1–35. Washington: Smithsonian Institution.

Bingham, Hiram (Binamu).
    1835. Ke Kuauhau no na Alii o Hawaii. *Ke Kumu Hawaii*, Aug. 19.

Bishop Museum.
    1936. Letter to A. F. Judd on May 1. Institutional Records, BPBM Letters in Book II, 1897–1898. Bishop Museum Archives, Bernice Pauahi Bishop Museum, Honolulu, HI.

Booklist and Subscription Books Bulletin.
    1969. Review of *A Shoal of Time: A History of the Hawaiian Islands*, by Gavan Daws. *The Booklist and Subscription Books Bulletin* 65(11):569–570.

Brown, Giles T.
    1969. Review of *A Shoal of Time: A History of the Hawaiian Islands*, by Gavan Daws. *The Journal of American History* 56(1):156–157.

Buck, Elizabeth.
    1993. *Paradise Remade: The Politics of Culture and History in Hawai'i*. Philadelphia: Temple University Press.

Burns, Eugene.
    1939. He Recalls Princess Ruth. *Honolulu Star-Bulletin*, May 20: Saturday Magazine, 1, 3.

Bushnell, O. A.
    1993. *The Gifts of Civilization: Germs and Genocide in Hawai'i*. Honolulu: University of Hawai'i Press.

Cachola-Abad, Kēhau.
    1993. Evaluating the Orthodox Dual Settlement Model for the Hawaiian Islands: An Analysis of Artifact Distribution and Hawaiian Oral Traditions. In *The Evolution and Organization of Prehistoric Society in Polynesia*, eds. M. Graves and Roger Green, 13-32. Auckland: New Zealand Archaeological Association.

    2000. The Evolution of Hawaiian Socio-Political Complexity: An Analysis of Hawaiian Oral Traditions. Ph.D. dissertation, Department of Anthropology, University of Hawai'i.

    2001. Review of *Exalted Sits the Chief: The Ancient History of Hawai'i Island*, by Ross Cordy. *Asian Perspectives* 40(2):315–317.

Chapin, Helen Gracimos.
    1984. Newspapers of Hawai'i 1834 to 1903: From He Liona to the Pacific Cable. *The Hawaiian Journal of History* 18:47–86.

1996. *Shaping History: The Role of Newspapers in Hawai'i*. Honolulu: University of Hawai'i Press.

2000. *Guide to Newspapers of Hawai'i: 1834–2000*. Honolulu: Hawaiian Historical Society.

Charlot, John P.
    1983. *Chanting the Universe: Hawaiian Religious Culture*. Honolulu: Emphasis International.

    N.d. Classical Hawaiian Education: Generations of Hawaiian Culture. Unpublished MS.

Chun, Malcolm Nāea.
    1994. *Must We Wait in Despair: The 1867 Report of the Ahahui Laau Lapaau of Wailuku, Maui on Native Hawaiian Health*. Honolulu: First People's Productions.

    1993. *Nā Kukui Pio 'Ole: The Inextinguishable Torches*. Honolulu: First People's Productions.

Clark, Rev. E. W.
    2001 [1872]. *He Buke Wehewehe Hua'ōlelo Baibala me Nā Palapala 'āina me nā Ki'i*. Reprint with foreword by M. Puakea Nogelmeier. Honolulu: Bishop Museum Press.

Coffman, Tom.
    1998. *Nation Within: The Story of America's Annexation of the Nation of Hawai'i*. Kāne'ohe, Hawai'i: EPICenter.

Cordy, Ross H.
    2000. *Exalted Sits the Chief: The Ancient History of Hawai'i Island*. Honolulu: Mutual Publishing.

Cruz, Lynette.
    2003. Sovereignty, Process and the "Sacred Community." Ph.D. dissertation, Department of Anthropology, University of Hawai'i.

Curnow, Jenifer.
    2002. A Brief History of Maori-Language Newspapers. In *Rere Atu, Taku Manu! Discovering History, Language & Politics in the Maori-Language Newspapers*, eds. Jenifer Curnow, Ngapare Hopa and Jane McRae, 17–41. Auckland: Auckland University Press.

Davenport, William.
    1987. Review of *Kingship and Sacrifice: Ritual and Society in Ancient Hawai'i*, by Valerio Valeri, trans. Paula Wissing. *American Anthropologist* 89(1):177–178.

Daws, Gavan.
    1968a. *Shoal of Time: A History of the Hawaiian Islands*. New York: Macmillan.

1968b. Writing Local History in Hawaii—A Personal Note. *Hawaii Historical Review* 2(10):417–418.

Daws, Gavan, and Ed Sheehan.
    1970. *The Hawaiians*. Norfolk Island, Australia: Island Heritage, Ltd.

Day, A. Grove, and Albertine Loomis.
    1997. *Ka Paʻi Palapala: Early Printing in Hawaiʻi*. Honolulu: Mission Houses Museum.

Deloria, Jr., Vine
    1995. *Red Earth, White Lies: Native Americans and the Myth of Scientific Fact*. New York: Scribner.

Dening, Greg.
    1989. History "in" the Pacific. *The Contemporary Pacific* 1(1&2):134–139.

    1991. A Poetic for Histories: Transformations that Present the Past. In *Clio in Oceania: Toward a Historical Anthropology*, ed. Aletta Biersack, 347–380. Washington: Smithsonian Institution.

    1995. *The Death of William Gooch: A History's Anthropology*. Honolulu: University of Hawaiʻi Press.

Desha, Stephen Langhern.
    1996. *He Moʻolelo Kaʻao no Kekūhaupiʻo: Ke Koa Kaulana o ke Au o Kamehameha ka Nui*. Vols. 1 and 2. Eds. William H. Wilson and Larry Kimura. Hilo: Hale Kuamoʻo.

    2000. *Kamehameha and His Warrior Kekūhaupiʻo*. Trans. Frances N. Frazier. Honolulu: Kamehameha Schools Press.

Dibble, Sheldon.
    1836–1837. Mooolelo Hawaii. *Ke Kumu Hawaii*. Jul. 20, 1836–Mar. 29, 1837.

    1838. *Ka Mooolelo Hawaii*. Lahainaluna: Mea Pai Palapala no ke Kulanui.

    1843. *The History of the Sandwich Islands*. Lahainaluna: Press of the Mission Seminary.

Dickerson, Donna G.
    1977. Review of *The Works of the People of Old: Ka Hana a ka Poʻe Kahiko*, by Samuel M. Kamakau. *American Anthropologist* 79(1):187.

Emerson, Nathaniel B.
    1898. Letter to C. R. Bishop on Mar. 30. Institutional Records, BPBM Letters in Book II, 1897–1898. Bishop Museum Archives, Bernice Pauahi Bishop Museum, Honolulu, HI.

Emory, Kenneth P.
    1995 [1959]. Foreword. In *Fragments of Hawaiian History*, John Papa Īʻī, trans. Mary Kawena Pukui, ed. Dorothy B. Barrère, ix–x. Honolulu: Bishop Museum Press.

Finney, Ben.
    1999. The Sin at Awarua. *The Contemporary Pacific* 11(1):1–33.

Forbes, David W.
    1999–2002. *Hawaiian National Bibliography, 1780–1900, Vols. 1–4.* Honolulu: University of Hawai'i Press.

Fornander, Abraham.
    1980 [1878–1885]. *An Account of the Polynesian Race: Its Origins and Migrations, and the Ancient History of the Hawaiian People to the Times of Kamehameha I.* Rutland, VT: Charles E. Tuttle.

    1916–1920. *The Fornander Collection of Hawaiian Antiquities and Folk-lore.* Ed. Thomas G. Thrum. Memoirs of the Bernice P. Bishop Museum, Vols. 4–6. Honolulu: Bishop Museum Press.

Foucault, Michel.
    1971. *The Order of Things: An Archaeology of the Human Sciences.* New York: Pantheon Books.

    1972. *The Archaeology of Knowledge.* Trans. Alan M. Sheridan Smith. New York: Pantheon Books.

    1977. *Discipline and Punish: The Birth of the Prison.* Trans. Alan M. Sheridan Smith. New York: Pantheon Books.

Friedman, Jonathan.
    1997. Review of *How "Natives" Think: About Captain Cook, For Example,* by Marshall Sahlins. *American Ethnologist* 24(1):261–262.

Friend, The.
    1856. The Hawaiian Flag. Apr. 1.

Gegeo, David Welchman.
    2001. Cultural Rupture and Indigeneity: The Challenge of (Re)visioning "Place" in the Pacific. *The Contemporary Pacific* 13(2):491–507.

Hale'ole, S. N.
    1863. *Ke Kaao o Laieikawai.* Honolulu: H. M. Whitney, pub.

    1865. Ua Kina ka Moolelo o Lonoikamakahiki. *Ke Au Okoa*, Oct. 23.

    1997 [1919]. *Laieikawai.* Trans. Martha Warren Beckwith. Reprint. Honolulu: First People's Productions.

Handler, Richard, and Jocelyn Linnekin.
    1984. Tradition, Genuine or Spurious. *Journal of American Folklore* 97(385):273–290.

Hanlon, David, and Geoffrey M. White, eds.
    2000. *Voyaging Through The Contemporary Pacific.* Lanham, Maryland: Rowman & Littlefield Publishers.

Hanson, E. Allen.
    1993. Review of *The Apotheosis of Captain Cook: European Mythmaking in the Pacific*, by Gananath Obeyesekere. *American Anthropologist* 95(3):762–763.

Hauʻofa, Epeli.
    2000. Epilogue: Pasts to Remember. In *Remembrances of Pacific Pasts*, ed. Robert Borofsky. Honolulu: University of Hawaiʻi Press.

Hapuku, Rev. J.
    N.d. Unpublished Journal. Societé de Études Océaniens Archives, Papeete, Tahiti.

Hawaii Holomua.
    1912. Ka Olelo Makuahine a ka Lahui Hawaii. Apr. 12.

Hawaiian Gazette, The.
    1868a. History of the Kamehamehas. Aug. 26–Sept. 23.

    1868b. Copyright. Sept. 23.

    1900. Mass Meeting of the Native Independents: Saturday's Speeches at the Drill Shed. Wise Speaks in English. Kalauokalani, "Bob" Wilcox and Kaulia Address the Crowd in Hawaiian. Jun. 12.

Hawaii Legislature, Committee on Public Education.
    1882. Report of the Committee on Public Education. Honolulu.

Hawaii Library Association.
    1968. *Index to the Honolulu Advertiser and Honolulu Star-Bulletin, 1929–1967*. Honolulu: State of Hawaii Department of Education.

    1975. *Index to Periodicals of Hawaii, Vol. 1 and 2*. Honolulu: State of Hawaii Department of Education.

Helekunihi, E.
    1893. Letter to Kahu O. Emerson on Feb. 25. Bishop Museum Archives, Bernice Pauahi Bishop Museum, Honolulu, HI.

Hilliard, David.
    1970. Review of *Shoal of Time: A History of the Hawaiian Islands*, by Gavan Daws. *The Journal of Pacific History* 5:232–233.

Hilt, Douglas.
    1993. Review of *The Apotheosis of Captain Cook: European Mythmaking in the Pacific*, by Gananath Obeyesekere. *Biography* 16(3):285–289.

Historical Commission of the Territory of Hawaii.
    1925. *Report of the Historical Commission of the Territory of Hawaii for Two Years: Ending December 31, 1924*. Honolulu: Star-Bulletin Publishing Company.

Hobsbawm, Eric.
    1999 [1983]. Introduction: Inventing Tradition. In *The Invention of Tradition*, eds. Eric Hobsbawm and Terence Ranger, 1–14. Cambridge: Cambridge University Press.

Hori, Joan.
    N.d.   Background and Historical Significance of Ka Nupepa Kuokoa. http://libweb.hawaii.edu/digicell/nupepa_kuokoa_/kuokoa_htm/kuokoa.html.

Hukilani, S. K.
    1864.   Na Akua o ko Onei Poe i ka Wa Kahiko. *Ka Nupepa Kuokoa*, Nov. 19.

Hunter, Charles H.
    1969.   Review of *Shoal of Time: A History of the Hawaiian Islands*, by Gavan Daws. *Pacific Historical Review* 38(2):241–242.

ʻĪʻī, John Papa.
    1866.   Ke Ola a me ka Make ana iho nei o Victoria K. Kaahumanu. *Ka Nupepa Kuokoa*, Jun. 2–Aug. 18.

    1868.   Ka Make ana o Mataio Kekuanaoa. *Ka Nupepa Kuokoa*, Nov. 28–Dec. 19.

    1869–1870. [Beginning with...*Kanaenae*...then becoming] Ka Hunahuna Moolelo Hawaii. *Ka Nupepa Kuokoa*, Jan. 2, 1869–May 28, 1870.

    1995 [1959]. *Fragments of Hawaiian History*. Trans. Mary Kawena Pukui, ed. Dorothy B. Barrère, Honolulu: Bishop Museum Press.

Joesting, Edward.
    1986.   Review of *Islands of History*, by Marshall Sahlins. *The Hawaiian Journal of History* 20:220–222.

Johnson, Rubellite Kinney.
    1976.   *Kukini ʻAhaʻilono: Carry on the News*. Honolulu: Topgallant Publishing.

    1975.   *Ka Nupepa Kuʻokoʻa: A Chronicle of Entries, October 1861–September 1862*. Honolulu: Topgallant Publishing.

Jones, Stella M.
    1931a.   Letter to Mary Low of April 14. MS SC Kamakau, Box 11.3. Bishop Museum Archives, Bernice Pauahi Bishop Museum, Honolulu, HI.

    1931b.   Letter to Ralph S. Kuykendall of June 25. MS SC Kamakau, Box 11.3. Bishop Museum Archives, Bernice Pauahi Bishop Museum, Honolulu, HI.

Judd, Bernice, Janet E. Bell, and Clare G. Murdoch.
    1978.   *Hawaiian Language Imprints, 1822–1899*. Honolulu: University of Hawaiʻi Press.

Judd, Laura Fish.
    1928 [1880]. *Honolulu, Sketches of Life: Social, Political and Religious in the Hawaiian Islands from 1828–1861*. Honolulu: Honolulu Star-Bulletin.

Ka Elele Hawaii.
    1848. [no title]. Jun. 8.
    1848. Palapala Kuai. July 3.

Ka Hae Hawaii.
    1857. Na Nupepa ma na Aina E. Dec. 16.
    1858. Moolelo Hawaii. Apr. 7.
    1860a. Hoomanakii. Apr. 25.
    1860b. "Palapala pinepine mai ka poe lawe Hae..." Jul. 25.
    1861. "I ka malama o Maraki 1856..." Nov. 6.

Ka Hoku Loa.
    1859a. No ka Lapaau ana o na Kahuna Hawaii. Jul. 2.
    1859b. No ke Ano Hoomana Kii. Dec., Buke 1, Helu 6, 1.

Ka Hoku o ke Kai.
    1883. E Nalowale ana paha ka Olelo Hawaii? Jun., 133.

Kalaaukumuole, S. Z. E.
    1866. Hoomana i ka Ia. *Ka Nupepa Kuokoa*, Nov. 24.

Kalākaua, David.
    1870. He Manao Akea. *Ka Manawa*, Nov. 7.
    1888. *The Legends and Myths of Hawaii*. New York: C. L. Webster and Co.

Ka Lama Hawaii.
    1834a. O KA LAMA HAWAII. Feb. 14.
    1834b. No ka hiki ana mai o ka malamalama i Hawaii nei. May 9.

Kalama, S. P.
    1858–1859. Ka Oihana Lapaau Kahiko. *Ka Hae Hawaii*, Nov. 24, 1858–Jan. 5, 1859.

Kalanikuihonoikamoku, B. V.
    1865. I kuu mau makamaka e kakau mai ana i ka hopunipuni o na kahuna Hawaii. *Ke Au Okoa*.

Kaleilehua, L. P.
    1862. No na Kaao a me na Moolelo. *Ka Hoku o ka Pakipika*, Jan. 16.

Kamakau, Samuel Mānaiakalani (S. M. K.).
    1842a. Ke kuauhau no na Kupuna kahiko loa mai o Hawaii nei, a hiki mai ia Wakea. Mai ia Wakea mai a hiki mai i keia manawa a kakou e noho nei, i mea e maopopo ai i keia hanauna; a ia hanauna aku ia hanauna aku. *Ka Nonanona*, Oct. 25.
    1842b. "Lahaina, Okatoba 31, 1842..." *Ka Nonanona*, Nov. 8.
    1843. "Lahainaluna, Dek. 2, 1842..." *Ka Nonanona*, Feb. 14.

1845. "Lahainaluna, Iulai 22, 1845..." *Ka Elele*, Aug. 12.

1855. No Ka Make Ana A Me Ka Moolelo O A. Paki. *Ka Elele*, Sept. 15.

1865a. No ke Kaapuni Makaikai i na wahi Kaulana a me na Kupua, a me na 'Lii Kahiko mai Hawaii a Niihau (Ka Moolelo o Hawaii). *Ka Nupepa Kuokoa*, Jun. 15–Oct. 7.

1865b. Hooheihei ka Nukahalale, ka Nukahalale, onou ka leo o ka pahu o Opuku, Haalokuloku ka ua mai ka lani, ka eeke-eeke-eeke, e kii eeka-ka ka pakapakapuku o ka ua lohi maka. *Ke Au Okoa*, Oct. 16.

1865c. Kumumanao. *Ka Nupepa Kuokoa*, Oct. 28.

1865d. Letter to L. H. Gulick and Pareka of Oct. 18. H.E.A. Archives, Kamakau, Samuel Manaiakalani. Mission Houses Museum Library, Honolulu, HI.

1865e. No ka hoakea ana a me ka hoomolaelae ana, e pau ai ka pohohihi o ka Mooolelo Hawaii. *Ke Au Okoa*, Nov. 6.

1866a. "Kolikowailehua, Manua." *Ka Nupepa Kuokoa*, Aug. 25.

1866b. Ka Moolelo o Kamehameha I/Ka Moolelo o na Kamehameha (Helu 1–8 [9]). *Ka Nupepa Kuokoa*, Oct. 20–Dec. 29.

1867a. Ka Moolelo o Kamehameha I/Ka Moolelo o na Kamehameha (Helu 9 [10]–53 [57]). *Ka Nupepa Kuokoa*, Jan. 5–Dec. 28.

1867b. Sila! Sila! Sila! *Ka Nupepa Kuokoa*, Nov. 30, 4.

1868a. Ka Moolelo o Kamehameha/Ka Moolelo o na Kamehameha (Helu 54 [58]–96 [101]). *Ka Nupepa Kuokoa*, Jan. 4–Dec. 26.

1868b. Letter to W. Chamberlain of Mar. 5. H.E.A. Archives, Kamakau, Samuel Manaiakalani. Mission Houses Museum Library, Honolulu, HI.

1868c. Palapala Maia S. M. Kamakau Mai. *Ka Nupepa Kuokoa*, Sept. 12.

1868d. Kamakau Archived Material: MS 996.9 K127. Hawaiian Historical Society, Honolulu, HI.

1869a. Ka Moolelo Hawaii (Helu 97 [102]). *Ka Nupepa Kuokoa*, Jan. 2.

1869b. Ka Moolelo Hawaii (Helu 94 [103]). *Ke Au Okoa*, Jan 7.

1869c. Ka Moolelo Hawaii (Helu 98 [104]). *Ka Nupepa Kuokoa*, Jan. 9.

1869d. Ka Moolelo Hawaii (Helu 99 [105]–133 [139]). *Ke Au Okoa*, Jan. 14–Oct. 14

1869e. Ka Moolelo Hawaii (Helu 1–11 [12]). *Ke Au Okoa*, Oct. 14–Dec. 30.

1870. Ka Moolelo Hawaii (Helu 12 [13]–55). *Ke Au Okoa*, Jan. 13–Dec. 29.

1871. Ka Moolelo Hawaii (Helu 56–60). *Ke Au Okoa*, Jan. 5–Feb. 2.

1873. Ke kulana o ke Aupuni Hawaii i ke Au ia Kamehameha I. *Ka Nupepa Kuokoa*, Mar. 1.

1992 [1961]. *Ruling Chiefs of Hawaii* (Revised Edition). Trans. Mary Kawena Pukui, Thomas G. Thrum, Lahilahi Webb, Emma Davidson Taylor, and John Wise. Honolulu: Kamehameha Schools Press.

1964. *Ka Poʻe Kahiko: The People of Old.* Trans. Mary Kawena Pukui, ed. Dorothy B. Barrère. Honolulu: Bishop Museum Press.

1987 [1976]. *The Works of the People of Old: Na Hana a ka Poʻe Kahiko.* Trans. Mary Kawena Pukui, ed. Dorothy B. Barrère. Honolulu: Bishop Museum Press.

1991. *Tales and Traditions of the People of Old: Na Moʻolelo a ka Poʻe Kahiko.* Trans. Mary Kawena Pukui, ed. Dorothy B. Barrère. Honolulu: Bishop Museum Press.

1996. *Ke Kumu Aupuni.* Ed. M. Puakea Nogelmeier. Honolulu: Ke Kumu Lama.

2001. *Ke Aupuni Mōʻī.* Ed. M. Puakea Nogelmeier. Honolulu: Kamehameha Schools Press.

Kameʻeleihiwa, Lilikalā K.
  1992. Introduction. In *Ruling Chiefs of Hawaii* (Revised Edition), Samuel Mānaiakalani Kamakau, trans. Mary Kawena Pukui, et al., iii–v. Honolulu: Kamehameha Schools Press.

  1996. *A Legendary Tradition of Kamapuaʻa, the Hawaiian Pig-God.* Honolulu: Bishop Museum Press.

Kamehameha Schools Press.
  2002. *Ka Hoʻoilina: The Legacy* 1(1).

Ka Naʼi Aupuni.
  1905. Ka Ipu Alabata. Dec. 22.

  1906. Mai Haalele i Kau Olelo Makuahine. Jan. 4.

Kanepuu, J. H.
  1856. E Malama i ka nupepa. *Ka Hae Hawaii*, Oct. 1.

  1862. Ka poe kakau moolelo, a kaao paha. *Ka Hoku o ka Pakipika*, Oct. 30.

  1864. He mau Leta Kahiko. *Ka Nupepa Kuokoa*, Jan. 9.

Ka Nonanona.
  1845. Ka make o ka Nonanona. Mar. 18.

Ka Nuhou Hawaii.
  1873. Ua Ai Ke "Kuokoa" I Kona Luai. Nov. 25.

Ka Nupepa Kuokoa.
  1862. "He Kamakamailio." Apr. 19.

  1862. "O kapaia mai auanei makou he poe hookano..." Sept. 6.

  1864. [no title]. Jan. 30, 1.

    1867. O ua Hale pai nei. Aug. 24.

    1870. Ka Make ana o ka Mea Hanohano Ioane Ii. May 7.

    1919. E Hoopauia ke Kula Olelo Kepani! Nov. 14.

Ka Nupepa Kuokoa me Ke Au Okoa i Huipuia.
    1877. No ke Kula o Lahainaluna. Apr. 28.

Ka Puuhonua o na Hawaii.
    1917. Olelo Hawaii. Jan. 26.

Kāretu, Timoti.
    2002. Maori Print Culture: The Newspapers. In *Rere Atu, Taku Manu! Discovering History, Language & Politics in the Maori-Language Newspapers*, eds. Jenifer Curnow, Ngapare Hopa, and Jane McRae, 1–16. Auckland: Auckland University Press.

Kaulainamoku, S. M. B.
    1865. Olelo pane ia A. Lauwili, me A. P. Kuawili, me J. K. Kumukula. *Ke Au Okoa*, Nov. 27.

Kauwahi, J. W. H.
    1857. *He kuhikuhi o ke kanaka Hawaii, oia ka mea e ao mai ai i ke kanaka i ka ike i ke kakau ana i na palapala ae like, palapala hoopaa, palapala kuai a moraki no ka waiwai lewa, palapala hoolilo a moraki no ka waiwai paa, palapala hoolilo waiwai loaa, palapala hui waiwai, palapala hoolilo hope, palapala hookuu, a haalele kuleana, palapala haalele waiwai o ka wahine iloko o ka waiwai o kana kane, palapala kauoha a ka mea make, palapala hoopii, na kanawai e pili ana i kekahi mau pono nui o ke kanaka Hawaii, a me ke ano o ke kakau ana i ka puke kakau waiwai, a pela aku*. Honolulu: H. M. Whitney.

Keahiakawelo, J. B.
    1861. Kalaihi ka lani, Ku pilikii ka honua; *Ka Hoku o ka Pakipika*, Buke 1, Helu 1; 26 Kepakemapa, 2.

Kealakai, W. E.
    1861. Kahuna Lapaau Hoopunipuni. *Ka Hae Hawaii*, Mar. 27.

Ke Au Okoa.
    1865a. He olelo ao i ka poe e kakau mai ana e pai ia ma ka Nupepa. Apr. 24.

Keesing, Roger M.
    1989. Creating the Past: Custom and Identity in the Contemporary Pacific. *The Contemporary Pacific* 1(1 & 2):19–42.

    1991. Reply to Trask. *The Contemporary Pacific* 3(1):168–171.

Keiki o Kukuimalu.
    1865. Ia B. L. Koko. *Ke Au Okoa*, Nov. 13.

Kekela, James.
    1865. Letter to Dr. Gulick. The Marquesas Collection, Folder #25. Hawaiian Mission Children's Society Archives, Mission Houses Museum, Honolulu, HI.

Ke Kumu Hawaii.
    1837. [no title]. Mar. 15, 83.

Kent, Harold.
    1961. Acknowledgment. In *Ruling Chiefs of Hawaii*, Samuel M. Kamakau, trans. Mary Kawena Pukui, et al., ix. Honolulu: Kamehameha Schools Press.

Kepelino, Zepherin (Kahoaliʻikūmaiʻeiwakamoku Keauokalani).
    2007 [1978, 1932]. *Kepelino's Traditions of Hawaii*. Ed. Martha Warren Beckwith. Bernice P. Bishop Museum Bulletin 95. Honolulu: Bishop Museum Press.

    1978 [1932]. *Kepelino's Traditions of Hawaii*. Trans. Martha Warren Beckwith. Milwood, NY: Kraus Reprint Co.

    1858. *Hoiliili Havaii*. Honolulu: Pai-palapala Katolika.

Kepookulou (Kaawaloa).
    1835. No na Alii o ka Moku o Hawaii. *Ke Kumu Hawaii*, Aug. 19.

Kimura, Larry.
    1983. Native Hawaiian Culture. In *Report on the Culture, Needs and Concerns of Native Hawaiians, Vol. 1*, Native Hawaiian Study Commission, 173–224. Washington D.C.: The Commission.

Kirkpatrick, J.
    1986. Review of *Kingship and Sacrifice: Ritual and Society in Ancient Hawaiʻi*, by Valerio Valeri and Marshall Sahlins. *Choice* 23(6): 900.

Kirtley, Basil F., and Esther Mookini.
    1977. Kepelino's "Hawaiian Collection": His "Hooiliili Hawaii" Pepa I, 1858. *Hawaiian Journal of History* 11:39–68.

Kittelson, David J.
    1985. *The Hawaiians: An Annotated Bibliography*. Honolulu: Social Science Research Institute, University of Hawaiʻi.

Knauft, Bruce M.
    1996. *Genealogies for the Present in Cultural Anthropology*. New York: Routledge Press.

Koko, B. L.
    1865. He Moolelo no Lonoikamakahiki. *Ke Au Okoa*, Sept. 4–Oct. 23.

K. U.
    1878. He Mau Leho Hou: Kaehukai o Puaena [seaspray of Puaʻena]. *Ko Hawaii Pae Aina*, Aug. 31.

Kuaana.
    1866. Pau makemake i ka Nupepa "Au Okoa." *Ka Nupepa Kuokoa*, May 26.

Kuapuu.
    1861. No ka Hoku Pakipika. *Ka Hoku o ka Pakipika*, Oct. 3.

L., A.
    1868. Ka Moolelo a S. M. Kamakau. *Ke Au Okoa*, Oct. 8.

Lightner, Richard.
    2004. *Hawaiian History: An Annotated Bibliography*. Westport, CT: Praeger Pub.

Liliʻuokalani.
    1988 [1964]. *Hawaii's Story by Hawaii's Queen*. Rutland, VT: Charles E. Tuttle Company.

Linnekin, Jocelyn.
    1983. Defining Tradition: Variations on the Hawaiian Identity. *American Ethnologist* 10:241–252.

    1986. Review of *Kingship and Sacrifice: Ritual and Society in Ancient Hawaiʻi*, by Valerio Valeri and Marshall Sahlins. *The Hawaiian Journal of History* 20:217–220.

    1991. Text Bites and the R-Word: The Politics of Representing Scholarship. *The Contemporary Pacific* 3(1):172–177.

Low, Mary E.
    1931a. Letter to [Stella] Maud Jones of May 14. MS SC Kamakau, Box 11.3. Bishop Museum Archives, Bernice Pauahi Bishop Museum, Honolulu, HI.

    1931b. Letter to [Stella] Maud Jones of May 26. MS SC Kamakau, Box 11.3. Bishop Museum Archives, Bernice Pauahi Bishop Museum, Honolulu, HI.

Lowe, Lisa.
    1991. *Critical Terrains: French and British Orientalisms*. Ithaca, NY: Cornell University Press.

Lucas, Paul F. Nahoa.
    2000. E Ola Mākou I Ka ʻŌlelo Makuahine: Hawaiian Language Policy and the Courts. *The Hawaiian Journal of History* 34:1–28.

Luna Auhau.
    1867. No ke Kuokoa. *Ka Nupepa Kuokoa*, Feb. 16.

Luomala, Katherine.
    1966. Review of *Ka Poeʻe Kahiko: The People of Old*, by Samuel M. Kamakau. *Journal of American Folklore* 7(313):501–502.

M.
    1860. [no title]. *Ka Hae Hawaii*, Mar. 7, p. 193(4).

Mahoe, J. K. N.
    N.d. Mookuauhau o J.K.N. Mahoe mai a Paao mai, ke kupuna mua i Hawaii a me Kekumuhonua (w) pae ma Kumukahi Hawaii. Unpublished MS, private collection.

Malo, David.
    1971 [1903/1951]. *Hawaiian Antiquities (Moolelo Hawaii)*. Trans. Nathaniel B. Emerson, ed. Eloise Christian. Honolulu: Bishop Museum Press.

    1987. *Ka Moʻolelo Hawaii*. Trans. Malcolm Naea Chun. Honolulu: The Folk Press.

Manu, Moses.
    2002. *Keaomelemele: He Moolelo Kaao no Keaomelemele*. Trans. Mary Kawena Pukui, ed. M. Puakea Nogelmeier. Honolulu: Bishop Museum Press.

Masterman, Sylvia.
    1980. *An Outline of Samoan History*. Apia, Western Samoa: Commercial Printers Limited.

McGuire, James W. L.
    1995 [1938]. *He Moolelo Pokole o ka Huakai Hele a ka Moiwahine Kapiolani i Enelani i ka Makahiki 1887 i ka Iubile o ka Moiwahine Vitoria o Beretania Nui*. Reprint with foreword by M. Puakea Nogelmeier. Honolulu: Ke Kumu Lama.

McRae, Jane.
    2002. 'E manu, tena koe!' 'O bird, greetings to you': The Oral Tradition in Newspaper Writing. In *Rere Atu, Taku Manu! Discovering History, Language & Politics in the Maori-Language Newspapers*, eds. Jenifer Curnow, Ngapare Hopa, and Jane McRae, 42–59. Auckland: Auckland University Press.

Meyer, Manulani Aluli.
    1998. Native Hawaiian Epistemology: Contemporary Narratives. Thesis (D.Ed), Harvard University.

    2001. Our Own Liberation: Reflections on Hawaiian Epistemology. *The Contemporary Pacific* 13(1):124–148.

Michaelsen, Scott.
    1999. *The Limits of Multiculturalism: Interrogating the Origins of American Anthropology*. Minneapolis: University of Minnesota Press.

Michelson, Miriam.
    1897. Strangling Hands Upon a Nation's Throat. *The San Francisco Call*, Sept. 30.

Mitchell, Donald D. Kilolani.
    1982. *Resource Units in Hawaiian Culture*. Honolulu: Kamehameha Schools Press.

Moʻokini, Esther K.
    1974. *The Hawaiian Newspapers*. Honolulu: Topgallant Publishing.

Morris, Robert.
    1992. Review of *Native Lands and Foreign Desires: Pehea lā e Pono Ai?*, by Lilikalā K. Kameʻeleihiwa. *Journal of Homosexuality* 29(1):124–135.

    2003. Controlling Hawaiian Texts On (Same-) Sexuality Through Deliberate Mistranslation. Unpublished MS.

Musick, John R.
    1898. *Hawaii, Our New Possessions: An Account of Travels and Adventure, With Sketches of the Scenery, Customs and Manners, Mythology and History of Hawaii to the Present, and An Appendix Containing the Treaty of Annexation to the United States.* New York: Funk & Wagnalls.

Nailiili, Sebena W.
    1865. Makemake e loaa ona Palapala kahuna lapaau Hawaii. *Ke Au Okoa*, Oct. 9.

Nakanaela, Thomas K.
    1999 [1890]. *Ka Buke Moʻolelo o Hon. Robert William Wilikoki.* Reprint with foreword by Duane Wenzel. Honolulu: Bishop Museum Press.

Nākoa, Sarah Keliʻilolena.
    1993 [1979]. *Lei Momi o ʻEwa.* Ed. M. Puakea Nogelmeier. Honolulu: Ke Kumu Lama.

Nākoʻokoʻo, J.
    1870. E Hoakea ia na Kahuna-Lapaau Hawaii. *Ka Nupepa Kuokoa*, Jun. 11.

New Zealand Digital Library.
    http://www.nzdl.org/cgi-bin/library.

Newbury, Colin.
    1980. *Tahiti Nui: Change and Survival in French Polynesia, 1767–1945.* Honolulu: University of Hawaiʻi Press.

Nicole, Robert.
    2001. *The Word, the Pen, and the Pistol: Literature and Power in Tahiti.* New York: State University of New York Press.

Nida, Eugene.
    2004. Principles of Correspondence. *The Translation Studies Reader, Second Edition*, ed. Lawrence Venuti, 153–167. NY: Routledge.

Niranjana, Tejaswini.
    1992. *Siting Translation: History, Post-Structuralism, and the Colonial Conquest.* Berkeley: University of California Press.

Nogelmeier, M. Puakea.
    2001. *He Lei no ʻEmalani: Chants for Queen Emma Kaleleonālani.* Trans. Mary Kawena Pukui, Theodore Kelsey and M. Puakea Nogelmeier, ed. M. Puakea Nogelmeier. Honolulu: Bishop Museum Press.

Nowaki, Junko.
    2001. *The Hawaii Island Newspaper Index*. Hilo: Mookini Library.

O'Carroll, John.
    1994. Approaches to the Text. Unpublished course reader. Suva: 290. Quoted in Robert Nicole, *The Word, the Pen, and the Pistol* (New York: State University of New York Press, 2001), 2.

Obeyesekere, Gananath.
    1992. *The Apotheosis of Captain Cook: European Mythmaking in the Pacific*. Princeton: Princeton University Press.

Ong, Walter J.
    1991 [1982]. *Orality and Literacy: The Technologizing of the World*. London: Routledge.

    1995. Hermeneutic Forever: Voice, Text, Digitization, and the 'I'. *Oral Tradition* 10:1–10.

Osorio, Jonathan K. Kamakawiwoʻole.
    1994. Review of *Native Lands and Foreign Desires: Pehea lā e Pono Ai?*, by Lilikalā K. Kameʻeleihiwa. *The Contemporary Pacific* 6(1):233–236.

    1996. Determining Self: Identity, Nationhood and Constitutional Government in Hawaiʻi 1842–1887. Ph.D. dissertation, Department of History, University of Hawaiʻi.

    2001. Review of *Colonizing Hawaiʻi: The Cultural Power of Law*, by Sally Engle Merry. *The Contemporary Pacific* 13(2):574–577.

Pacific Commercial Advertiser.
    1859. Close of Vol. III. Jun. 10.

    1868. History of Kamehameha. Sept. 19.

Perkins, Roland F.
    1980. Kou Haole: The Image of Chief and Foreigner in the Lahainaluna Moʻolelo Hawaiʻi. *The Hawaiian Journal of History* 14:58–79.

Perreira, Hiapo.
    2002. Ke Kālailai Moʻomeheu ʻana i ka Moʻomeheu ʻana i ka Moʻolelo Hiwahiwa o Kawelo, ka Hiapaʻiʻole a ka Ikaika, ka Mea Nāna i Hoʻohaʻahaʻa ke ʻOʻoleʻa o Kauahoa, "Ka Uʻi o Hanalei." MA thesis, Department of Hawaiian Studies, Univesity of Hawaiʻi at Hilo.

Plews, John H. R.
    1969. Review of *An Account of the Polynesian Race: Its Origins and Migrations, and the Ancient History of the Hawaiian People to the Times of Kamehameha I*, by Abraham Fornander. *The Hawaiian Journal of History* 3:157–158.

Poepoe, J. M.
- 1906a. Ka Moolelo O Kamehameha I: Ka Na-i Aupuni o Hawaii. *Ka Nai Aupuni*, Jan. 30.
- 1906b. Ka Ipu Alabata. *Ka Na'i Aupuni*, Dec. 22.

Pogue, J. F.
- 1858. *Ka Mooolelo Hawaii*. Honolulu: Hale Paipalapala Aupuni.

Poli, Z., et al.
- 1865. Ka Hoomana Kahiko. *Ka Nupepa Kuokoa*, Jan. 5–Dec. 30.
- 1868. "I ka Makamaka Hawaii," a i ole ia, "I ka Enemi paha o ka Oiaio." *Ka Nupepa Kuokoa*, Apr. 11.

Pukui, Mary Kawena.
- 1937. Old Hawaiian Newspapers. Paper presented before the Anthropological Society of Hawaii, Dec. 1.

Pukui, Mary Kawena, and Samuel H. Elbert.
- 1986. *Hawaiian Dictionary, Revised and Enlarged Edition*. Honolulu: University of Hawai'i Press.

Pukui, Mary Kawena, Samuel H. Elbert, and Esther T. Mookini
- 1981 [1966]. *Place Names of Hawaii*. Honolulu: University of Hawai'i Press.

Ralston, Caroline.
- 1984. Hawaii 1778–1854: Some Aspects of Maka'ainana Response to Rapid Cultural Change. *The Journal of Pacific History* 11(1-2):21–40.

Reinecke, John E.
- 1969. *Language and Dialect in Hawaii: A Sociolinguistic History to 1935*. Honolulu: University of Hawai'i Press.

Remy, Jules.
- 1862. *Ka Mooolelo Hawaii, Histoire de l'Archipel Havaiien*. Paris: J. Claye.

Richards, William.
- 1828a. Letter to unknown addressee of Apr. 14. ABCFM Papers. Houghton Library, Harvard University, Cambridge, MA.
- 1828b. Letter to Jeremiah Evarts of Oct. 7. ABCFM Papers. Houghton Library, Harvard University, Cambridge, MA.

Rodgers, Charles T.
- 1898. *Education in the Hawaiian Islands: A brief statement of the Present Condition of the Public and Private Schools of the Republic*. Honolulu: Department of Public Instruction.

Rumford, James.
- 1993. *A Short, Elementary Grammar of the Owhihe Language*. Honolulu: Mānoa Press.

Sahlins, Marshall.
    1985. *Islands of History*. Chicago: University of Chicago Press.

    1995. *How "Natives" Think: About Captain Cook, For Example*. Chicago: University of Chicago Press.

Sahlins, Marshall, and Patrick V. Kirch
    1992. *Anahulu: The Anthropology of History in the Kingdom of Hawaii, Volume 1*. Chicago: University of Chicago Press.

Said, Edward W.
    1979 [1978]. *Orientalism*. New York: Vintage Books.

    1993. *Culture and Imperialism*. New York: Alfred A. Knopf.

Schmitt, Robert C.
    1977. *Historical Statistics of Hawaii*. Honolulu: University of Hawaiʻi Press.

    1989. Comment. In *Before the Horror: The Population of Hawaiʻi on the Eve of Western Contact*, David E. Stannard, 114–121. Honolulu: University of Hawaiʻi Press.

Schütz, Albert J.
    1994. *The Voices of Eden: A History of Hawaiian Language Studies*. Honolulu: University of Hawaiʻi Press.

Scobie, R. A.
    1961. Review of *Fragments of Hawaiian History*, by John Papa ʻĪʻī. *The Journal of the Polynesian Society* 70(2):253–254.

    1966. Review of *Ka Poʻe Kahiko*, by Samuel M. Kamakau. *The Journal of the Polynesian Society* 75(2):248–249.

Shapiro, Michael.
    1984. *Language and Politics*. New York: New York University Press.

Sheldon, John G. M. (Kahikina).
    1906. *Kaluaikoolau, ke Kaeaea o na Pali Koolau a me na Kaei O Ahi o Kamaile*. Honolulu: Keena Puuku o ka Teritore o Hawaii.

    1908. *Ka Buke Moolelo o Hon. Joseph K. Nawahi*. Honolulu: Honolulu Bulletin Publishing Co., Ltd.

    1987. The True Story of Kaluaikoʻolau the Leper. Trans. Frances N. Frazier. *The Hawaiian Journal of History* 21:1–41.

    1996. *Ka Puke Moʻolelo o Hon. Iosepa K. Nāwahī*. Trans. Lōkahi Antonio and R. Keao NeSmith. Hilo: Hale Kuamoʻo.

    2001. *The True Story of Kaluaikoolau as Told by His Wife, Piilani*. Trans. Frances N. Frazier. Līhuʻe: The Kauai Historical Society.

Silva, Kalena.
    2002. Introduction. *Ka Hoʻoilina: Puke Pai ʻŌlelo Hawaiʻi/The Journal of Hawaiian Language Sources* 1(1):Back Cover.

Silva, Noenoe K.
    1999. Ke Kūʻē Kūpaʻa Nei Mākou: Kanaka Maoli Resistance to Colonization. Ph.D. dissertation, Department of Political Science, University of Hawaiʻi.

    2004. *Aloha Betrayed: Native Hawaiian Resistance to American Colonialism.* Durham, NC: Duke University Press.

Smith, Linda Tuhiwai.
    1999. *Decolonizing Methodologies: Research and Indigenous Peoples.* London: Zed Books, Ltd.

Spencer, Thomas P.
    1895. *Buke Lapaau Hawai.* Ka Leo o ka Lahui, Dec. 2.

    2000. *Kaua Kūloko 1895.* Reprint with foreword by M. Puakea Nogelmeier. Honolulu: Bishop Museum Press.

Spoehr, Alexander.
    1961. Introduction. In *Ruling Chiefs of Hawaii*, Samuel Mānaiakalani Kamakau. Trans. Mary Kawena Pukui, et al. Honolulu: Kamehameha Schools Press.

Stannard, David E.
    1989. *Before the Horror: The Population of Hawaiʻi on the Eve of Western Contact.* Honolulu: University of Hawaiʻi Press.

    1991. Recounting the Fables of Savagery: Native Infanticide and the Functions of Political Myth. *Journal of American Studies* 25:381–418.

Stillman, Amy.
    2001. Re-membering the History of Hawaiian Hula. In *Cultural Memory: Reconfiguring History and Identity in the Postcolonial Pacific.* Ed. Jeannette Marie Mageo, 187–204. Honolulu: University of Hawaiʻi Press.

Stokes, John F. G.
    1931. *Origin of the Condemnation of Captain Cook in Hawaii.* Thirty-ninth Annual Report of the Hawaiian Historical Society for the Year 1930, 68–104.

    1932. New Bases for Hawaiian Chronology. Forty-first Annual Report of the Hawaiian Historical Society for the Year 1932, 23–65.

Takakura, Kikue (Esther K. Mookini).
    1967. A Brief Survey of the Hawaiian Language Newspapers. Unpublished MS. University of Hawaiʻi, Hamilton Library.

Testa, F. J., ed.
    2003. *Buke Mele Lahui: Book of National Songs.* Honolulu: Hawaiian Historical Society.

Thiongʻo, Ngũgĩ wa.
    1989. *Decolonising the Mind: The Politics of Language in African Literature.* London: J. Currey.

Thrum, Thomas G.
    1903. *Hawaiian Almanac and Annual for 1904.* Honolulu: Thos. G. Thrum.

    1912. *Hawaiian Almanac and Annual for 1913.* Honolulu: Thos. G. Thrum.

    1917. Brief Sketch of the Life and Labors of S. M. Kamakau, Hawaiian Historian. *Hawaiian Historical Society Annual Report for 1917,* 40–61.

    1919. *Hawaiian Almanac and Annual for 1920.* Honolulu: Thos. G. Thrum.

Tinker, Reuben.
    1839. Hawaiian History. *Hawaiian Spectator,* Jan. 1–Oct. 1.

    1840. Hawaiian History. *The Polynesian,* Jul. 28–Aug. 22.

Tobin, Jeffrey.
    1994. Cultural Construction and Native Nationalism: Report from the Hawaiian Front. *Boundary 2* 21:(1):111–133.

    1997. Savages, the Poor and the Discourse of Hawaiian Infanticide. *The Journal of the Polynesian Society* 106:(4[1]):65–92.

Tove, Skutnabb-Kangas.
    2000. *Linguistic Genocide in Education—or Worldwide Diversity and Human Rights?* New Jersey: Earlbaum Associates.

Trask, Haunani-Kay.
    1991. Natives and Anthropologists: The Colonial Struggle. *The Contemporary Pacific* 3(1):159–167.

U., K.
    1878. He Mau Leho Hou. *Ko Hawaii Pae Aina,* Aug. 31.

Unauna, A.
    1842. No Ke Kuauhau. *Ka Nonanona,* Nov. 8.

Unauna, John Koii.
    1865. Kanalua i ka Moolelo Hawaii. *Ke Au Okoa,* Oct. 9.

United States, Bureau of the Census.
    1975. *Historical Statistics of the United States: Colonial Times to 1970, Part 2.* Washington, D.C.: U.S. Government Printing Office.

Valeri, Valerio.
    1985. *Kingship and Sacrifice: Ritual and Society in Ancient Hawaii.* Trans. Paula Wissing. Chicago: University of Chicago Press.

Venuti, Lawrence.
    2004a. 1900s–1930s. In *The Translation Studies Reader, Second Edition*, ed. Lawrence Venuti, 70–74. New York: Routledge.

    2004b. 1900s. In *The Translation Studies Reader, Second Edition*, ed. Lawrence Venuti, 325–335. New York: Routledge.

    2004c. Translation, Community, Utopia. In *The Translation Studies Reader, Second Edition*, ed. Lawrence Venuti, 482–502. New York: Routledge.

Vinay, Jean-Paul, and Jean Darbelnet.
    2004. A Methodology for Translation. Trans. Juan C. Sager and M.-J. Hamel. In *The Translation Studies Reader, Second Edition*, ed. Lawrence Venuti, 128–137. New York: Routledge.

Waianuenue.
    1861. Pane Hope ia J. W. H. Kauwahi. *Ka Nupepa Kuokoa*, Nov. 16.

Waimanalo.
    1863. I ka Lehulehu. *Ka Nupepa Kuokoa*, Oct. 10.

Wells, Robert.
    1990. Review of *Before the Horror: The Population of Hawaii on the Eve of Western Contact*, by David E. Stannard. *The Journal of Interdisciplinary History* 21(1):159–160.

White, Geoffrey M.
    1991. *Identity Through History: Living Stories in a Solomon Islands Society.* Cambridge: Cambridge University Press.

White, Geoffrey M., and Ty Kāwika Tengan.
    2001. Disappearing Worlds: Anthropology and Cultural Studies in Hawai'i and the Pacific. *The Contemporary Pacific* 13(2):381–416.

Whitney, Henry M. (Wini, Heneri M.).
    1856. Na ka poe heluhelu i ka Hoku Loa. Ka Hoku Loa o Hawaii, Sept. 18.

    1861. *Ka Nupepa Kuokoa*, Buke 1, Helu 1, Oct. 1.

Wilkin, Peter.
    1999. Chomsky and Foucault on Human Nature and Politics: an Essential Difference? *Social Theory and Practice* 25 (2):177–210.

Wilson, Christie.
    2002. Census says 27% in Hawai'i speak English as 2nd language. *The Honolulu Advertiser*, Sept. 30: B1, B2.

Wilson, William H.
    1998. I ka 'Ōlelo Hawai'i ke Ola, 'Life is found in the Hawaiian Language.' *International Journal of the Sociology of Language* 132:123–137.

Wist, B. O.
    1940. *A Century of Public Education in Hawaii: 1840–1940*. Honolulu: Hawaii Educational Review.

Wood, Houston.
    1999. *Displacing Natives: The Rhetorical Production of Hawaii*. Lanham, MD: Rowman and Littlefield Publishers.

Young, George Terry Kanalu.
    1995. Moʻolelo Kaukau Aliʻi: The Dynamics of Chiefly Service and Identity in ʻŌiwi Society. Ph.D. dissertation, Department of History, University of Hawaiʻi.

Yzendoorn, Reginald.
    1931. Letter to Stella M. Jones of Sept. 9. MS SC Kamakau, Box 11.3. Bishop Museum Archives, Bernice Pauahi Bishop Museum, Honolulu, HI.